Dr. Jeffrey Donley's book *The Counterfeit Christmas* will surprise, captivate, and inspire readers who wish to learn the historical truth about the events surrounding the birth of Jesus. Jeffery's expertise in Biblical and ancient history, the topography of the ancient world, and the customs of the Jewish people are evident as he seamlessly blends history with his knowledge of human nature to create a compelling narrative. His expert use of dialogue draws the reader into the drama and conveys the feelings of Joseph and a teenage Mary when they learn of Mary's unique destiny to bear the Son of God. The book is both scholarly and extremely accessible at the same time. It is an ideal book to spark lively discussions at Bible Study groups or family conversations around the kitchen table. As an educator and scholar, Jeffery makes the past come alive in an interesting and exciting way.

Dr. Trudy McNair, attorney,
educator and author of the series
A History of Art and Civilization,
as well as numerous children's books.

Jeffery Donley's first person narrative is a penetrating and realistic account of the Biblical story of Jesus. The story opens the mind to dispel many of our modern misunderstandings of Jesus' birth. Not only does he present the true historical perspective in a first century AD context, but also he makes it real by bringing his readers' minds into the thoughts and actions of the main individuals – Joseph and Mary.

Though the Bible does not elaborate on the inner thoughts and feelings of Joseph and Mary, Jeffery in *The Counterfeit Christmas*, strategically pulls the reader into a deeper understanding of what might have occurred in the minds of the Virgin Mary and the man she was engaged to marry. This story helps Ministers, Bible Students, and Christians to truly experience the enormous self-sacrifice and faith of this Godly couple. I wholeheartedly recommend this book to be in the library of every home.

Jeffery, with his extensive background in historical Biblical studies is qualified to write this book. He is an astute Bible teacher who presents lessons with a wealth of background information leading to a deeper understanding of the message, which is evident by the volume of scriptural references presented. A man of the Word, Jeffery's love for sharing the Word of God resonates with this work.

After reading Donley's work, you will never look at the Biblical story of Jesus in the same elementary manner. Instead, you will find yourself eagerly reading each page with anticipation for the truth that's in the good news of Christ.

Trevor Williams, professional civil engineer, church servant, Deacon

In this eye-opening book, which I strongly encourage everyone to read, Dr. Donley talks about the incredible journey of the birth of Jesus using accurate facts straight from the Bible itself. This book is great for believers, but more so for nonbelievers who doubt the existence of Jesus. In a world like today where religion is dying as people become more immersed in self-happiness, this book will restore your faith in God as it did with me.

Paula Rueda, Emergency Medical Technician (EMT), college student, nursing

I have to say that this book challenges nearly every thought that I've always held regarding the birth of Christ and the truth of the Gospel accounts. To say that Jeffery's account is compelling is a gross understatement. His well-written and well-documented treatise is very powerful and logically presented. He meshes both the historical and Biblical perspective of the life of Christ and the prevailing culture and challenges faced by Mary and Joseph. He also gives some very pragmatic glimpses of some of their thought processes, as they had to deal with the realities and hardships that resulted from this monumental pre-marital pregnancy. I also enjoyed the preciseness that Jeffery engaged in presenting the various aspects of the miraculous birth, such as the actual birthing process, the explanation of the "Magi," and Herod's cruel involvement concerning the "King of Kings," just to name a few.

I believe that every Christian will benefit from this book from the perspective that it will delete all the myths and misnomers that we have come to believe about the birth of Christ and the incidents surrounding his early life, including his safekeeping to and exit from Egypt. These incidents are all presented with complimenting scriptural references to show their authenticity. Those who read this book will be forced to reconcile commonly held beliefs with the real truth as told from a deeper understanding of God's Word and historical accounts. I found the book to be very intriguing and an easy read and I couldn't wait to get to the next chapter.

The real special aspect of the book is that the seemingly minute details that are highlighted all serve to paint such a vivid picture that it impossible to miss the points. And if you're like me, you will come to the realization that there is so much more to the birth of Christ than the mere fact that he was born to be our Savior. You will come to appreciate such facts as how his birth was a glimpse into how and why he would die, and how his poor, lowly parents would be able to finance their journey to Egypt to escape the wrath of Herod. These are just a couple of the "aha" moments that the book affords.

Having met and befriended Jeffery Donley, I have really come to appreciate his desire to present the Bible in a dignified, scholarly, and common sense manner. I have sat through several of his Bible studies and heard him preach, and I can honestly say that his motivation is just to do his part to spread the gospel. He is unapologetic in his pursuit of the truth and in his insistence that we "get the story right." I appreciate his honest and sincere approach to take us back to Bethlehem and see life as it really was, and not the Hollywood version that most of us have come to believe. *The Counterfeit Christmas* is an inspiring account of these most important events that have had such a profound effect on mankind.

Victor Crumity, Director, CarePlus
Health Plan, Church leader, Elder

This book is so amazing! It clarified all of the unanswered questions I've had for years. *The Counterfeit Christmas* is written by one of the best teachers anywhere. He makes learning come alive. This book is very informative on the history of the birth of Jesus. I never knew there was so much history that dealt with the birth of Jesus until now. This is a must read. Destined to be a classic.

Alexia Greenwood,
university student,
Biomedical Sciences/Pediatrics

Dr. Donley is a master storyteller in his book *The Counterfeit Christmas* as he shows how the birth of Jesus really happened in our space-time universe. This book is very well written compared to other books about Christianity that I have read before. It gets to the point—it doesn't waste anytime with fluff. The style of writing flows like a story and Dr. Donley doesn't try to sound like a know-it-all. This book is honest and real and there's no sugarcoated nonsense. It gives you details and background information so that you are fully able to understand what you are learning. *The Counterfeit Christmas* is not boring at all and it is a completely different approach to the topic, which makes it refreshing.

Growing up as a Christian, I thought I was taught all there was to know. Now, I know the truth and all my questions have been answered. Other Christians should definitely read this book, for the reason that many of them, like myself, are not as educated in their faith as we should be. There are a lot of unanswered questions and gray areas that Christians may have. This book will finally clear up those questions.

The Counterfeit Christmas will open your eyes to the truth of Jesus' birth and provide you the reasons for what your Christian faith is based upon. This book really grabbed my attention and made me want to keep reading. Did the birth of Jesus really happen? Is it real? Is it true? You be the judge! If you read only one book—this is the one.

Hannah Miller,
college student, writer

I loved the book *The Counterfeit Christmas* because it explained in words and examples that I could truly understand about the real birth of Jesus the Christ and why things happened as they did.

Other Christians should read this book because it is very easy to understand and it points out facts that are not only interesting, but will leave you speechless. This book will make a difference in my life because now I know the whole truth and nothing but the truth.

Anyone reading this book will find it both factual and entertaining. It will leave you wishing for more. Jeffery did an outstanding job writing this book! I believe with the help of this book, I can win more souls for Christ.

James Benjamin, Jr., retired and
loving it! Church servant, Deacon

Jeffery Donley has written what I consider to be a spiritual masterpiece ... the insight and the information provided by this book will be helpful and useful to Christians on every level. I believe this book should be required reading for all those who preach the Word of God.

Wesley T Leonard, Minister of the Gospel

The Counterfeit Christmas pulls back the cover of warm fuzzies we've layered over the Biblical Christmas story. My favorite part—who the Wisemen were and how they rode into Jerusalem. Prepare to have your eyes opened and heartstrings tugged. You'll never look at another nativity scene the same way.

Bethany Jett, award-winning author of *The Cinderella Rule*

THE COUNTERFEIT CHRISTMAS

What the Gospels Really Teach About the Birth of Jesus

Jeffery Donley

WestBow Press books may be ordered through booksellers or by contacting:

WestBow Press
A Division of Thomas Nelson & Zondervan
1663 Liberty Drive
Bloomington, IN 47403
www.westbowpress.com
1 (866) 928-1240

ISBN: 978-1-5127-5637-1 (sc)
ISBN: 978-1-5127-5638-8 (hc)
ISBN: 978-1-5127-5636-4 (e)

Library of Congress Control Number: 2016915140

Print information available on the last page.

WestBow Press rev. date: 9/29/2016

For My Wife

Kathy

"I've fallen in love many times . . .

always with you."

~Author Unknown

CONTENTS

SPECIAL STUDIES

FOREWORD

Pack your bags and open your mind. You are about to go on a mental journey that has taken Dr. Jeffrey Donley a lifetime of rigorous study and critical thinking to develop. You will see Jesus as you have never seen him before – a treasure that is waiting for you to unwrap.

He begins with a question about the truth about a real person – the God-Man, Jesus. Each chapter is a new day filled with incredible facts about the most important man and the most important message of all time. Yet, as Dr. Donley opens your mind to the irrefutable truth about Jesus—he also opens his heart to share what this great man was and did as He entered into space and time to provide a physical and visible image of who God really is.

I am not a theologian, just a simple follower of Jesus. I have enjoyed over 50 years living with and enjoy the blessing of this personal God. However, Dr. Donley, with his wit and candor, opened my eyes afresh to the truth and reality of the God I serve, the Savior I love, and the Spirit who has the power to open my eyes to understand the true story of Christmas.

This book, *The Counterfeit Christmas*, is no mere collection of well-worn religious phrases, nor is it a tome of research and scholarly writings. Although this book contains a trove of scholarly research and is unashamedly based on a Christian worldview, it is simply the result of one man's lifetime effort to provide an answer to one of life's ultimate questions, "Jesus and Christianity. Are they real? Are they truth?"

Buckle-up! You are about to read one of the most exciting stories of all time – The historically true and real … Jesus. And yes, it **IS** Christmas every day.

Dr. Dan Blair
Dean, College of Business
Ohio Valley University
July 2016

For two decades, Dr. Blair dedicated his talents to the Hewlett-Packard Company, where he led several worldwide initiatives, including the development of HP's first worldwide training management system, under his directorship of the human performance technology and systems lab. He then made significant contributions to the training profession as American Society for Training and Development's Director of Research, where he created the Learning Executives' Network. Most recently he served the United States of America (DOD) as a senior advisor for career and organizational development. During the last three years, he co-developed and delivered an undergraduate course in career mastery and other business courses for Ohio Valley University (OVU). At OVU, he has established the Office of Institutional Effectiveness and currently serves as the Dean, College of Business. He holds Bachelor of Science and Master of Arts degrees, and a doctorate from the University of Southern California.

PREFACE, AKA WHY I CAN WRITE THIS BOOK

Let me introduce myself to you…call me Ishmael!

Just kidding, although I really like Herman Melville's masterwork *Moby Dick*—especially the 1956-movie rendition starring Gregory Peck. Did I just date myself?

I am a college professor, husband, a father of three, and a grandfather–which is amazing since I am only 37-years old. Okay, I'm a "little" bit older. I have been a senior minister, an associate minister, a youth minister in local churches, and a college professor. I've spoken at state, national, and international conferences on a host of topics and authored a few books. Over the years, I have spoken in numerous churches around the United States and overseas. I have been truly blessed but my start was difficult.

We have all heard that people talk about their life journeys. Sound familiar?

Instead of using the word journey, I want to use the word "race." The Bible states:

> "Do you not know that in a race all the runners run, but only one receives the prize? So run that you may obtain it" (1 Cor. 9:24, *New English Translation*).

> "Therefore, since we are surrounded by so great a cloud of witnesses, let us also lay aside every weight, and sin which

> clings so closely, and let us run with endurance the race that is set before us" (Heb. 12:1).

> "Brothers, I do not consider that I have made it my own. But one thing I do: forgetting what lies behind and straining forward to what lies ahead, I press on toward the goal for the prize of the upward call of God in Christ Jesus" (Phil. 3:13-14).

> "But I do not account my life of any value nor as precious to myself, if only I may finish my course and the ministry that I received from the Lord Jesus, to testify to the gospel of the grace of God" (Acts 20:24).

If you will permit me, let me briefly tell you about the race that I have been running.

Growing up in poverty in a small-town in Iowa, I was not raised in a Christian home. But, I still can remember being allowed to attend Vacation Bible School (VBS) at a very young age. I loved it! Spending all day, every day for a week in the summer, learning about Jesus! All the crafts! The mid-morning snack of cookies and Kool-Aid! Recess—where I played tetherball—I was the champion! Earning the prized blue stars for memorization of Scripture—oh, how I worked hard for those blue stars! Earning perfect attendance—you bet!

And lunch! Let me tell you about lunch at VBS. My mom would make me a boloney and butter sandwich—smashed—with potato chips and a piece of fruit. A feast for a Sultan! What a banquet!

Even with all of those wonderful things in Vacation Bible School, I still remember, as a young boy, asking my teachers if Christianity was true—"Is it real—is it true? How do we know?" My VBS teachers would say—"Yes it is!" But, they never really provided me with the evidence. Still, I always believed and never doubted.

I was isolated from friends since my high school was around

twenty miles away from my home. During the summers, I would work bailing hay so that I could buy some clothes and school supplies for the next school year. It was devastating hot work for a boy.

As a senior in high school, I loved classes in history—ancient history—and the American Revolution. In sports, I played football, basketball, and track and field. I won the state championship in the discus-throw, making the "All-State" team. My church youth group was quite small with only three of us—me, myself, and I.

My Sunday school teacher was one of the Elders at my church. I would go to his house often and his wife would make wonderful dinners! I can still remember asking my Elder about the truthfulness of Christianity, "Is it real—is it true? How do you know?" My Elder would assure me that "yes it is all true—it really happened!"

So, from a very young age, I wanted to know if what I was learning in the Bible about Jesus, His life, His miracles, and His physical resurrection from the dead were true and real—and not just fabricated stories.

Then my parents divorced, destroying my world. I can still remember standing in my back yard and praying to God, telling Him that I didn't know what to do. I had no money to attend the university. I was living in a small town with no jobs. I felt hopeless with no future.

Have you ever felt like that? Have you ever felt broken? Shattered into a million pieces? It's awful and terrible and lonely.

What I can tell you is that from my early days as a very young boy in Vacation Bible School (with those boloney and butter sandwiches) to this very day, I have never questioned God, never gotten mad at Him, never disbelieved in any teaching of the Bible, nor blamed Him for my low points in my life.

However, I am ashamed to admit that I have had many questions of "why"—just like Job did. And just like Job, I have never been given the answers to my many questions. But, that's okay. I have always believed that God is in control and that He wants the best for my life and me. Be assured—God wants the best for you and your life, too.

In my hopelessness, an Elder of my church knew a college president and asked him if I could attend—even though it was already three weeks into the fall semester. The college president agreed and this penniless nineteen year-old went to college.

Boy, was I scared! I didn't know if I could do college work. Where would I get a job so I could pay for my education? I was already three weeks behind. I didn't know anyone. But, I stayed and worked my heart out. I got some jobs working as a janitor and working at a funeral home—along with some weekend preaching ministries.

It was great!

For the first three years of college, I was the starting forward on the college basketball team. I stayed out of basketball for one year while I learned Greek. And, I was being equipped with the tools to see for myself the answers to the questions about the truthfulness of Christianity that I have been asking all of my life. Is it true? Is it real? How do you know? The "how do you know" questions were being answered in college.

I was quite content with how God was working in me and in my service ministries unto Him. But, being content with the *status quo* is not where God wanted me to be—or you, either.

When I was a junior in college, I heard a graduate school professor speak on the topic of grace at a lectureship sponsored by my college. What I heard changed my life. This scholar made the difficult so very easy to understand. He brought "color" to the Scriptures.

At that time, I made a decision to devote my life to studying God's Word in its original languages of Greek, Hebrew, and to learn Systematic Theology. But I had to really work hard at the languages. And, I would become an historian.

Did you ever have to work so very hard for something that you dearly wanted? If yes, then you know how I felt.

I earned my Bachelor of Arts degree and moved on to graduate school. There, I was provided even more tools to really check out the Scriptures to see if they spoke the truth.

As a result of that decision, God began to work in a deeper level in my heart. I worked extremely hard—even working two to three jobs to earn my Master of Arts and Master of Divinity Degrees—both in Systematic Theology. I studied Christianity and everything pertaining to it, not simply accepting what my professors said, but studying the Scriptures deeply myself.

The conviction that I felt through studying the Bible changed everything. Some serious Jeffery-Donley-paradigm-shattering happened in my life and consequently in my service and ministries. But, I kept asking the questions about Jesus and Christianity.

Is it true, is it real. How do you know?

I can remember that I earned an "A+" in my Advanced Hebrew course at graduate school. Yes, an "A+!"

Obviously, I was brilliant! Of course, I was going to be one of the greatest Hebrew scholars of all time! Yes, I was a genius!

Well … okay, I hear you loud and clear: "Jeffery, humility please—and give credit where credit is due!"

The truth is, I had a great and wonderful professor, one of the finest Hebrew scholars in the world! Thank you for your help! But thank you, first and foremost, to God.

I was motivated to be the best scholar, historian, and servant of God that I could be, but I must confess to you that part of my motivation in earning that "A+" in Advanced Hebrew wasn't to be the brightest or most-genius. No, it was much more than that. *I was hungry.* Part of that motivation was *food*!

You see, every day in class, my Advanced Hebrew professor would bring kosher corned beef sandwiches and potato pancakes to his graduate students who would ace their exams. For a young, poor, and yes, *hungry* graduate student, that was enough motivation for me. I ALWAYS had lunch provided for me in my Advanced Hebrew course, plus I always had that extra motivation to do the best that I could possibly do.

Come to think of it, food seems to have been a good motivating factor in my life from the boloney and butter sandwiches/cookies and Kool-Aid in Vacation Bible School to kosher corned beef sandwiches and potato pancakes in graduate school. Now, you know my innermost secrets!

Well, after three years of graduate school, I was hired by a college and became a full-time professor at the age of twenty-five.

I later earned my Master of Theology degree in New Testament studying and working with one of the leading scholars in the world on textual criticism and New Testament manuscripts. He inspired me to learn even more ancient languages—which I did.

I love Egyptian history so I learned Hieroglyphs along with learning Latin, Syriac, Coptic, and other Semitic languages. With that, I would be able to study the New Testament manuscripts and the non-canonical traditions of Jesus in their original languages.

By studying all of these ancient languages, I would never be at the mercy of someone else telling me what all of these ancient documents said, including the Bible. I would be able to read and translate them myself!

I immersed myself in the world of the first century BC through the first century AD, reading non-Christian Jewish and pagan texts from the Roman Empire and earlier. I tried to master everything written by those professing to be Christians from the first five hundred years of the church's existence, the Patristic Age.

I later earned a Master of Letters (MLitt) degree in Theology from a European university, did one year of a Doctor of Theology program (ThD) in history, and earned a PhD from the University of

Wales, United Kingdom. Altogether, I spent seventeen years after high school in my educational pursuits. Whew—I am tired just writing this.

Have you heard of the Dead Sea Scrolls?

Good!

I was invited to the University of Manchester, England, to translate one of the more famous of the Dead Sea Scrolls, the *Copper Scroll*. The *Copper Scroll* is the greatest buried treasure map hammered onto three copper sheets, a vast treasure of eight metric tons of gold and forty-eight metric tons of silver. This treasure was buried all over Israel. That was exciting!

I became a New Testament theologian and a historian of antiquity, and for thirty-four years now I have had a keen interest in doing research in these areas.

For the past twenty-five years, I have taught as a full professor (honors professor, too) in a secular college where my teaching about Christianity in my Greco-Roman and Introduction courses has been attacked by a number of college administrators and faculty members, hostile at my being a Christian and my teaching about Christianity.

Verbal and physical threats were par for the course. Twenty-five years in the lion's den! You know, God never promised that life would be free from persecution and trials. But, I never stopped teaching about Christianity. And, I persevered—only by the grace of God.

That was a short version of my race. What I can emphatically tell you is that it hasn't always been easy but God has given me **grace for my race**.

And guess what? He will do the same for you too!

Who am I? Of course, I'm not Ishmael!

May I get personal?

First and most importantly, I am a sinner saved by the cleansing blood of Jesus the Christ. I am undeserving of God's mercy in that He **does not give to me** what I do deserve (hell). And, I am undeserving of His grace in that God **gives to me** that which I do not deserve (salvation). I am so thankful for God's longsuffering and faithfulness unto me—a sinner.

Secondly, I am a servant of the Lord Jesus the Christ. Jesus is my Lord, God, Savior, and Master. It is to Him ALONE that I bend my knee.

What I want more that anything is to hear Jesus speak the following words to me one day:

> "Well done, good and faithful servant. You have been faithful over a few things; I will set you over many things. Enter into the joy of your Lord" (Matt. 25:21, 23).

Third, I am a teacher. I have taught in colleges and preached and taught in numerous churches around the United States and overseas. Being a teacher is the best!

And fourth, I am a historian who is dedicated to finding historical truth. I don't know about you, but I would never devote my life or give my money, time, and talent for all of these years to the Lord if I did not absolutely believe the evidence and proofs that substantiate that Christianity and Jesus are true and real.

So, after years of studying, I can tell you with great confidence that everything that I had previously been taught and thought about from my days of Vacation Bible School—the historical evidence of Jesus' virgin conception, His death on a Roman cross, His physical burial in a rich man's tomb, His physical resurrection from the dead, and His physical appearances to His enemies and disciples—are absolutely correct!

Did the virgin birth/conception happen? Yes!

Is it TRUE? Yes, it is!

Is it REAL? Yes, it is!

How do I KNOW? That is what I will briefly share with you in this book.

Until then, I can unquestionably assure you that the Bible alone is God's inspired, inerrant, therefore infallible, and authoritative Word. What the Bible teaches is historically accurate. The four Gospels are historical documents. The birth of Jesus, as told in Matthew and Luke, is a historically recorded, actual event.

If any questions or problems arise in the Biblical documents, those questions/problems are in our misunderstanding of that sacred text—and not in the Word itself.

In this book, I will provide you with what the Gospels really teach about the birth of Jesus. And, I will provide evidence to you of the great truths that God has revealed to mankind. The truth of the birth of Jesus is fascinating and life changing.

You see, Christmas, the birth of Jesus, is not to be observed only one day out of the calendar year. It is to be kept in our hearts, demonstrated in our life-styles, and is to serve as the basis of how we are to treat people—especially those in need EVERYDAY of the year. Why? Because the Jesus that was born many years ago is a real person of history—He is the Almighty Creator God and a perfect human male. He is the God-man!

Isn't Jesus more than wonderful? He has so many blessings for your life as you serve Him on this earth and in the eternal life to come in Heaven. Isn't that great?

IS BELIEF IN THE VIRGIN CONCEPTION NECESSARY TO GO TO HEAVEN

You ask, "Do I need to believe in the virgin conception/birth of Jesus who is God the Savior, to go to heaven?"

Yes, you do!

The virgin conception is evidence that Jesus is more than merely a good man and a wise teacher. It gives evidence of Jesus' divine origin, i.e., He is Almighty God.

THE ONLY MEDIATOR

The virgin conception also provides mankind with the only mediator between God the Father and mankind. In order for Jesus to be the Mediator between God the Father and man, He must have something in common with both parties. Jesus is God and a perfect human male.

The virgin conception allows Jesus to fully understand human beings. The Hebrew writer says:

> "For we do not have a high priest who is unable to sympathize with our weaknesses, but one who in every respect has been tempted as we are, yet without sin" (Heb. 4:15).

FROM THE APOSTLE JOHN

The Apostle John very clearly believed in the virgin conception. So, John stated very clearly that in order for a person to become a real Christian, he/she must believe in the virgin conception as a real event with real people of history.

Let's now go to one of John's Epistles—1 John. In 1 John 4:3, the Apostle John emphatically states:

> "By this you know the Spirit of God: every spirit that confesses that Jesus Christ has come in the flesh is from God, and every spirit that does not confess Jesus is not from God. This is the spirit of the antichrist, which you heard was coming and now is in the world already" (1 John 4:3).

What does this passage say? John clearly says that any person who does not confess/believe that Jesus Christ has come in the flesh (virgin conception) is not from God and is the spirit of the antichrist. Wow, very powerful isn't it! John believed that Christ has "come in the flesh," i.e., God became a human being. You see, according to

John a person cannot be a Christian ("from God") if he/she does not believe in the virgin birth/conception of Jesus. That unbeliever has the spirit of the antichrist.

Let's go to another scripture passage from John, from his second epistle. In 2 John 1:7, the Apostle John states:

> "For many deceivers have gone out into the world, those who do not confess the coming of Jesus Christ in the flesh. Such a one is the deceiver and the antichrist. (2 John 1:7).

Here John is even stronger in his affirmation of the virgin birth/conception in that if any person does not confess/believe "in the coming of Jesus Christ in the flesh," he is a deceiver and the antichrist. Those are not my words, but the Apostle John's.

So, John tells us that God became flesh, i.e., a human being. That's a very powerful testimony to the virgin birth/conception of Jesus.

And remember, without Jesus' historical virgin conception, there would be no death, burial, physical resurrection and physical appearances of Jesus, i.e., no Gospel (1 Cor. 15:1-8).

So, is the virgin conception of Jesus necessary to be believed in order to go to Heaven? Absolutely!

May you be blessed in the reading of this book and may all the glory be to God alone!

ACKNOWLEDGMENTS

My deepest thanks to:

Dr. Daniel Blair
Thank you for writing the foreword for this book.
It is more than I truly deserve.
Your accomplishments for the Kingdom are as the sands of the sea.
I am unworthy to loosen your sandal.

Wesley T. Leonard
I have heard hundreds of great Gospel preachers in my lifetime,
but you are the best!
You make the Bible come alive!
You have made me a better preacher!

Victor Crumity
You are the definition of a Biblical Elder—
and a singing Elder at that!
Your prayers are amazing and powerful!
You have taught me how to truly pray.

Dr. Trudy McNair
An attorney, an educator, and a writer of wonderful

Humanities textbooks and children's' stories,
and one of the finest teachers anywhere.

Bethany Jett
One of the top new authors, speakers, and editors.
On her way to becoming a #1 New York Times Bestseller!

Trevor Williams
An engineer by trade—but what a tireless servant of Jesus.
Your humility and selflessness are an example for me.
Your public reading of Scripture is the best!

James Benjamin, Jr.
You are an encourager like Barnabas—a rare kind of person.
Your positive attitude is infectious to those around you.

Alexia Greenwood, Hanna Miller, & Paula Rueda
You are top-notch students who will do well in life.
I pray God's blessing on you and your lives.

Dr. Walter C. Kaiser, Jr.
You are a highly respected, esteemed
and world-renown Biblical scholar.
I am truly humbled and grateful for your support
and endorsement of this work.

Dr. Kathy Donley
And most tenderly, thank you Kathy
for your love, your support, help, and your caring for me.

INTRODUCTION

Christmas— oh, boy! I love the Christmas season!

And just as an interesting fact, the word "Christmas" is derived from the Old English Cristes *Maesse* that was first recorded in 1038, which means "The Mass of Christ." *Cristes-messe* is also found being recorded in 1131. So actually, "Christ-mass" means the death of Jesus and not His birth. But, please bear with me. In this book the word Christmas means "the birth of Jesus."

Again, I love the Christmas season!

I love to see the beautiful Christmas trees sparkle with multi-colored lights and "a lot" of tinsel (My children call me the "tinsel king").

Christmas cards, candy canes, beautiful nativity scenes, stockings on the fireplace, drinking hot-chocolate, beautifully wrapped presents under the tree, family get-togethers, Christmas dinner—oh, the food, Hollywood movies about Christmas like *It's a Wonderful Life* (1946), *Miracle on 34th Street* (1947), *White Christmas* (1954), *Meet Me in St. Louis* (1944), *Holiday Inn* (1942), *Scrooge* (1951), another *Scrooge* (1970) and one of my favorites—*The Littlest Angel* (1969). Oh, I forgot to mention, I love watching the old Andy Williams Christmas television specials.

And, oh, yes, I love the animated and cartoon Christmas television specials.

My favorites are:

- *Rudolph the Red-nosed Reindeer* (1964)
- *Santa Claus is Coming to Town* (1970)

- *Mister Magoo's Christmas Carol* (1962)
- *Mickey's Christmas Carol* (1983)
- *Frosty the Snowman* (1969)
- *The Little Drummer Boy* (1968)
- *Dr. Seuss' How the Grinch Stole Christmas!* (1966)
- *'Twas the Night Before Christmas* (1974).

However, my all-time favorite is *A Charlie Brown Christmas* (1965). How about Linus talking about the birth of Jesus as he quoted the Gospel of Luke 2:8-14 in his "True Meaning of Christmas Speech" on national television! This wonderful show has aired every year since it made its debut in 1965—making it the longest running animated television cartoon special in history!

I love it!

But, with all of the shows just mentioned, there are three counterfeit Christmases that this book will deal with.

The first counterfeit Christmas is "The Gospel of Santa Claus." We will not spend much time on this one, but I did want to mention it.

The second one is a counterfeit Christmas created by a very tiny group of self-proclaimed scholars who teach and write that the birth of Jesus is nothing more than a fabricated story, i.e., it never happened.

And, the third counterfeit Christmas is the modern nativity scene that appears around the world.

COUNTERFEIT CHRISTMAS #1
THE GOSPEL OF SANTA CLAUS

I don't know about you but I have always watched the Macy's Thanksgiving Day Parade with Santa Claus coming at the end of the parade, heralding the official beginning of the Christmas season.

Have you seen it? It is definitely the greatest parade ever!

Every Thanksgiving, I always made my kids stop what they were doing the moment Santa came on screen, and to this day they'll text me when they watch Santa's appearance with their own kids. It's the "real" Santa—I say!

Did you ever wonder how we got our present-day Santa Claus?

The Americanization of Santa Claus began with John Pintard (1759-1844) who did woodcuts of Santa in 1804.[1] The Santa woodcuts portrayed a fireplace with hung stockings crammed full of toys. Sound familiar?

Then, in 1809, Washington Irving wrote a book titled *Knickerbocker's History of New York.* Have you read it? He portrayed Santa smoking a pipe, in a wagon flying over rooftops, giving presents to good children and switches to the bad ones. Getting more familiar?

> **Behold!** Did you know that Washington Irving also wrote stories titled, *Rip Van Winkle* and *The Legend of Sleepy Hollow*? Irving never intended that those classic literary works or his Santa Claus be considered real historical persons or events.

Then, in 1821, an anonymous writer wrote a poem titled, "The Children's Friend." This writer created a magical gift-giving Santa, dressed in fur and riding in a wagon pulled by one reindeer.

One reindeer? Where are the eight reindeers plus Rudolph? I tell you, I'm not happy without Rudolph!

In 1822, Clement Clarke Moore wrote a poem for his daughters titled "An Account of a Visit from St. Nicholas" also known as "The Night Before Christmas." Moore is responsible for recreating Santa Claus into the image that we are all familiar with today—a supernatural plump, jolly elf who flies from house to house in a miniature sled pulled by eight tiny reindeer, and who could miraculously ascend and descend chimneys with a nod of his head.

A political cartoonist, Thomas Nast, made a visual representation of Clement Moore's Santa image in a cartoon published in *Harper's Weekly* in 1881. Santa, with a white beard, was dressed in a red suit trimmed with white fur, carrying a sack of presents for good children. He worked with elves in a workshop at the North Pole and was married to Mrs. Claus.

Then Coca Cola published the Santa Claus image in the 1920 *Saturday Evening Post*. Later, Coca Cola commissioned an illustrator named Haddon Sundblom to create the iconic image of Santa that the world is familiar with today. This new Santa appeared in the *National Geographic, Ladies Home Journal,* and the *New Yorker* in 1931.

Yes, the gospel or good news of the supernatural Santa Claus delivering presents to children around the world is well known today by one and all.

BUT, WAIT A MINUTE!

At the beginning of this introduction, I said that I love the Christmas season. But, I was not talking about pop culture's commercialization of Jesus' birth. I'm sorry to tell you that we all know that Santa Claus "isn't real" although it's great fun for the grandkids.

He has no workshop at the North Pole where he makes toys with his helper elves. The eight reindeer led by Rudolph do not exist. Santa is not even married to Mrs. Claus—*whose name is Jessica by the way*!

I have never heard or seen a "First Church of Santa Claus" where people have given their lives to him along with their time, treasure (money in tithes and offerings), and talent.

Have you?

Why not create a new religion devoted to jolly Santa?

Why not?

The answer is that he isn't real! He's just a fabricated story. There is no historical, archeological, literary, or legal evidence for the modern Santa Claus. The modern Santa is the creation of the people that I mentioned above.

Let me ask you a question! Would you give *your life* to Santa Claus?

No one in their right mind would—would they? Of course not!

Anyone who actually believes in Santa and would give his or her life to him . . . is . . . well, let me give you the most scholarly and theological words for that—"less than mentally competent!"

The Santa Claus image is a counterfeit Christmas image.

Am I being too harsh? I don't think so.

COUNTERFEIT CHRISTMAS #2
SELF-PROCLAIMED ELITISTS

The second counterfeit Christmas is an extremely serious matter. There is a small group of men and women among skeptics, agnostics, atheists, and liberals, who self-promote themselves as elite scholars who have created a counterfeit Christmas. These men and women are the darlings and the toast of the secular news media, publishing companies, and many colleges/universities. These individuals are paid enormous amounts of money to teach their counterfeit Christmas on college and university campuses.

Hold on to your seat. Listen to what they teach:[2]

1) There is no God; He does not exist;
2) Miracles are impossible;
3) Mary was promiscuous and had sex with a Roman soldier making Jesus an illegitimate son;
4) Jesus was the illegitimate son of Mary with the story of His virgin birth being concocted as a cover-up of her adultery;
5) There was no special star of Bethlehem;
6) There were no Wisemen;
7) There was no plot by Herod to kill Jesus;
8) The nativity stories are parables not facts;

9) Jesus was born in Nazareth, not Bethlehem;
10) Joseph and Mary did not make a trip to Bethlehem;
11) The shepherds were fictional characters;
12) The Gospels of Matthew and Luke are made up stories—fiction;
13) There was no Roman Augustan census; and
14) Jesus is nothing more than a cross-cultural mystic and stand-up Jewish comedian who is "like a cowboy hero of the American West exemplified by Gary Cooper."[3]

If you have heard any of these claims, you have just heard "the" counterfeit Christmas.

Unbelievable, isn't it?

These men and women contend that Mary was a promiscuous and immoral woman who was having sex with many partners. They believe that Mary got pregnant by a Roman soldier while she was married to Joseph. These persons claim that Christians invented the Gospel narratives of the virgin birth as a cover-up for Mary being with child by a Roman soldier. These people also believe that the cover-up story of the birth of Jesus was stolen from pagan mythology.

Is this outrageous? You tell me!

These critics do not believe in God and His miracles. Therefore to them, there is no supernatural, no miracles, no Jesus being God, no star of Bethlehem, no angels, and nothing supernatural. They contend that all these details of history in the Gospels of Luke and Matthew were invented by a few people decades later and even over a century after the events.

Is this contemptible?

The critics believe that the Bible is nothing more than made-up stories called parables.

Is this nonsense?

To these critics, Jesus is not God; rather, he was a mystic who was a Jewish stand-up comedian and like the cowboy hero of the American West exemplified by the American actor Gary Cooper.

Is this blasphemous?

Additionally, these persons also teach that:[4]

1) There is no physical resurrection of Jesus;
2) All religions are equally valid;
3) Jesus never claimed to be God;
4) Jesus' substitutional atonement is a monstrous doctrine;
5) The Bible is a human cultural product of Israel and Christians and;
6) Jesus' dead crucified body was thrown into a shallow grave where it was dug up and eaten by wild dogs!

Don't get me started on what these individuals teach about the Christian Passover, which the world calls Easter.[5]

Rather, let me quote the Apostle Peter who predicted the coming of these men and women who have fabricated this counterfeit Christmas.

> "But false prophets also arose among the people, just as there will be false teachers among you, who will secretly bring in destructive heresies, *even denying the Master who bought them*, bringing upon themselves swift destruction. And many will follow their sensuality, and because of them the way of truth will be blasphemed. *And in their greed they will exploit you with false words.* Their condemnation from long ago is not idle, and their destruction is not asleep" (2 Pet. 2:1-3; *emphasis mine*).

Peter's judgment on these modern day people is clear. He says that they will exploit you, meaning to "make merchandise," of their fabricated stories about Jesus. That is exactly what has happened to these modern day critics—they make money on secular news shows, make money on publishing books, and make money lecturing at colleges/universities about their counterfeit Christmas. When you ask these critics, "Upon what evidence(s) do you base your conclusions?"

They respond, "Evidence? What evidence?" You see they have none. They have nothing to say. They have absolutely not one solitary logical fact to substantiate their bogus claims.

Where did these critics get such ideas?

These critics, with their counterfeit Christmas story of the birth of Jesus, are the product of the Enlightenment and what they call the "modern mind," i.e., miracles cannot happen, there is no supernatural, no God, therefore the Bible is a myth—a made-up collection of disjointed documents.

In their enlightened *naiveté*, these modern critics are taking for granted that miracles cannot happen in our space-time universe of matter and energy. So, there is no room in their so-called enlightened view for the supernatural, miracles, and the existence of God.

When they speak of the birth of Jesus, they are speaking of the birth of Jesus *within us*, i.e., it's a mystical feeling that the story generates in us—not that the birth of Jesus is real and historical.

I'm sorry, but this warm mystical feeling, as these critics proclaim, may just be indigestion and is not what would make me (or any sane person) give my life in service, give my money, or even lose my life over.

The best scholarly word that I have for this warm mystical feeling is stupidity!

These so-called "enlightened" critics also say that what happened in Mary, if anything at all, was a reproductive process known as parthenogenesis (virgin birth), i.e., asexual reproduction by unfertilized eggs such as in rotifers (microscopic organisms). Well, these critics do not know basic biology. Let me explain.

First, humans are not rotifers.

Second, it is a biological and scientific impossibility for parthenogenesis to occur in humans.

Even for the sake of argument, if Mary had conceived parthenogenically (which is impossible), she would have had a daughter, for a son would have been scientifically impossible. Geneticists have demonstrated that all mammalian females have two X chromosomes and all males have one X and one Y chromosome. Therefore, if an unfertilized egg could reproduce itself (and it can't), two female X chromosomes could only reproduce female X chromosomes resulting in a female.

Jesus was a male!

Enough said for unscientific and absurd speculation.

These critics would tell me that I am hung up on questions of factuality and that I need to get over the Gospels being historical documents. They would say that proving the Gospels historically with facts is fruitless and a distraction.

They want all Christians to just believe like they do—that the Gospels are nothing but made-up parabolic stories, i.e., myths. They believe that the divine miracle working Jesus is nothing but a fabricated story—a "souped-up" Santa Claus!

For me, I find meaning and purpose for giving my life, my time, my devotion and worship (with the possibility of persecution), and my money from real historical documents about real historical people, sayings, and events—not from fabricated made-up stories that are not real.

You see, many Christians have died for their Christian beliefs. It is sheer stupidity and insanity for any Christian to die for nice stories that are nothing more than products of someone's imagination—fabricated stories just like Santa Claus.

My language may sound a bit tough here, but remember what the Apostle Paul said in 2 Corinthians 10:4-5:

> "For the weapons of our warfare are not of the flesh but have divine power to destroy strongholds. We destroy arguments and every lofty opinion raised against the knowledge of God, and take every thought captive to obey Christ."

This book will provide answers to the critics' stronghold and arguments and every lofty opinion raised against the knowledge of God as it is historically recorded in the Bible. There will be no *ad hominem* arguments against the character of any critic in this book, but I will answer their arguments.

COUNTERFEIT CHRISTMAS #3
THE TRADITIONAL NATIVITY SCENE

There is a third Counterfeit Christmas and it is found in the millions of beautiful nativity scenes that are worldwide in front of church buildings, shopping malls, homes, and other venues.

What? Don't say it! Please do not touch our beloved nativity scenes!

Sorry, but I have to.

But, don't worry!

I am just going to correct the traditional nativity scene so that it is Biblical and historical.

THE FIRST NATIVITY SCENE

Have you ever wondered where the first nativity scene came from?

In 1223, a man named Francis of Assisi created the first nativity scene. The only account that we have is from a Franciscan monk's, Bonaventure (1274), work titled *The Life of St. Francis of Assisi.* Francis' first nativity was a "live" nativity scene on Christmas Eve night that included fresh hay, a donkey and an ox, in a cave in a small Italian town of Grecio.

As time went on, the practice of using nativity scenes continued with live animals and actors, but was later replaced with what are called "static nativities" made out of different materials. As nativities moved around the world, they adapted to local tastes and customs. The characters and items in the nativities became transformed from Biblical characters to look more like those of whatever town they lived in.

But, no matter where the nativities are located around the world, they all have the basic same characters.

Now, help me out. Get a pen and paper and make your list of who and what are typically included in every nativity scene around the world.

All right—begin making your list. Who and what are on our list?

- ✓ Yes, we would need Mary!
- ✓ Yes, Joseph! You are doing well!
- ✓ A manger crib of fresh straw!
- ✓ A warm fire!
- ✓ Animals (a donkey and ox)!
- ✓ Angels and shepherds!
- ✓ The star of Bethlehem!
- ✓ A mean innkeeper!
- ✓ And, three Wisemen who were kings.

You did great! But, we haven't included the most important person.

Yes, baby Jesus. We cannot forget Him!

And…and…what color is the blanket that baby Jesus is always wrapped in? You got it—blue or white!

You did well, but what we just described never happened!

Now, don't get me wrong—the birth of Jesus did happen in our historical space-time-universe. But the traditional nativity scene is wrong—a counterfeit of what truly happened.

There is only *one* story of the first Christmas. Did you note the use of the singular "one"? There is *one* historical narrative of the birth of Jesus. The Gospel of Matthew is the first Gospel written in AD 40-50 and while he doesn't provide the details of Jesus birth, he does speak of the virgin conception. Listen:

> "But as he considered these things, behold, an angel of the Lord appeared to him in a dream, saying, "Joseph, son of David, do not fear to take Mary as your wife, for that which is conceived in her is from the Holy Spirit" (Matt. 1:20).

Luke, who wrote his Gospel in AD 60, does provide the details of Jesus' birth. Matthew provides the announcement to Joseph, while Luke provides the grand announcement to Mary. The Gospels of Luke and Matthew are easily harmonized.

YOUR PURPOSE IN LIFE

If you search deep in your heart, you will find a longing for meaning and a quest for purpose in life. If you're like me, you are asking about Christianity—"Is it real? Is it true? How do I know?"

It gives me some comfort that I am not alone in asking these questions.

It is the historical birth of Jesus that powerfully speaks to our deepest yearnings. It tells us about God's promises and shows us His love toward mankind. The second person of the Godhead, God the Son, came to this earth and became a human being because He "so loved us." He did this for me and for you (John 3:16).

Read this book by yourself, with your family, or with a Bible study/Sunday School group and I pray that you will know that God's presence is with you as He gently touches your life.

There are three parts to this book. I have used the Christmas term of "unwrapping" to begin each part.

Part One – Unwrapping the Grand Announcement
Part Two – Unwrapping the Blessed Event
Part Three – Unwrapping the Search for the Historical Jesus

There are also five "**Special Studies"** that will provide you with additional information concerning the historical facts of Jesus' birth.

You will also notice some **"Behold**" synopses of interesting facts. The "**Do You Dig It**" synopses are archaeological discoveries.

And, at the end of this book is a "**Study Guide**" that will direct your teaching and learning of the material in each chapter.

I hope that as you read *The Counterfeit Christmas* you will do as Mary did when she found out about having been chosen to give birth to Jesus—have exceeding joy and SING praises unto the Lord!

I pray that you will react as Joseph did when God told him to take Mary to his home and to name her son Jesus—respond with an unquestionable obedience!

I pray that you will respond as the shepherds did, with great joy about Jesus' birth. They told everyone that they could about the birth of the Savior, Christ, and Lord.

I pray that you will bend your knee and worship Jesus just as the Wisemen did, not just as your King—but also as your Lord, God, and Savior.

The writings of this book seek to help you do these things.

Your faith will be strengthened not in a Jesus who did not exist, but with the real, living, Lord, God, and Savior whose name is—JESUS!

May He use these words to show you how!

PART 1

UNWRAPPING THE GRAND ANNOUNCEMENT

CHAPTER 1

JOSEPH SPEAKS TO MARY'S FATHER

A YOUNG WOMAN NAMED MARY

IT ALL BEGAN in 6-5 BC, during the mighty Roman Empire, with a Jewish young woman named Mary and a Jewish man named Joseph. We know nothing about Mary except for what is recorded in the Bible.

Names in the ancient world were very significant. Generally a person's name was connected with some circumstance of that person's birth. It could carry a spiritual significance, could play a part in the order of a birth, or could be from personal characteristics.

Do you know what Mary's name means?

Her name, Mary, means "excellence" (translated in Hebrew, it's Miriam). We are going to learn that her name was fitting because Mary was indeed a woman of excellence!

We know that Mary was a Jewess of the tribe of Judah, descended from King David. She grew up as a small-town girl from a small obscure and insignificant Galilean village of Nazareth. And, she was a poor, hardworking, and righteous young woman.

She was not royalty. She was not a princess. She was not rich. She had never been a mother. She possessed no family inheritance. She had no "claim to fame" nor was she part of the social elite.

Mary was just like many of us—an ordinary, hardworking, and Old Testament-believing person.

THE VIEW OF WOMEN IN THE ANCIENT WORLD

In the ancient world, women had very few rights if any at all. Back then, women were seen as "defective men" and were to keep their mouths shut, stay at home, and be used as breeding stock.

Listen to what some of the famous ancient writers thought about women.

> Euripides writes; "If only children could be got some other way without the female sex! If women didn't exist, human life would be rid of all its miseries."[1]

> Demosthenes said: "We keep hetaerae [prostitutes] for the sake of pleasure, female slaves for our daily care and wives to give us legitimate children and to be the guardians of our households."[2]

> Hipponax is quoted as saying: "There are two days on which a woman is most pleasing—when someone marries her and when he carries out her dead body."

> The Greek Philosopher Aristotle said, "The woman is simply an inferior sort of man."[3]

Likewise, the Jewish religious leaders did not have a high opinion of women.

What?

That's right! Listen to what they said:

> "But let not the testimony of women be admitted, on account of the levity and boldness of their sex, nor let servants be admitted to give testimony on account of the ignobility of their soul; since it is probable that they may not speak truth, either out of hope or gain, or fear of punishment."[4]

"Any evidence which a woman (gives) is not valid (to offer), also they are not valid to offer. This is equivalent to saying that one who is Rabbinically accounted a robber is qualified to give the same evidence as a woman."[5]

"Sooner let the words of the Law be burnt than delivered to women."[6]

"The world cannot exist without males and females—happy is he whose children are males, and woe to him whose children are females."[7]

In this kind of world, the Jewish religious leaders believed that God would never use a female to accomplish His purposes. But, God's ways were not their ways. This young woman named Mary was chosen for the most important role in human history.

AN HONORABLE AND CHASTE YOUNG WOMAN

Mary was pure, Godly, humble, obedient, and blessed. She was a person who knew her Hebrew Scriptures and lived and worshipped accordingly. She was a woman of faith who believed in and loved God.

God chose to do an unprecedented and miraculous work in this chaste and faithful young woman. She was a person that I need to be like as a Christian.

> **Behold!** Think about it! Mary was the only person to be with Jesus throughout his entire earthly life—from his birth until his ascension back into heaven. She gave birth to Jesus as her God and Savior, watched Him die as her God and Savior on a Roman cross (John 20:25-27), and was a part of the first Christians in the new church on the Day of Pentecost (Acts 1:14).

When we are introduced to Mary, the Bible tells us some very personal and intimate information about her. Mary was a "*parthenos.*" The word "*parthenos*" is used to tell us that she was a "virgin."

We all know what that means, don't we? It means the total absence of sexual contact, i.e., Mary was not a promiscuous woman. She was an honorable, chaste young woman who lacked any sexual experience.[8]

A TWELVE YEAR OLD WOMAN . . . WHAT

Perhaps the most startling thing about Mary is that when she was engaged or betrothed to a man named Joseph, she was 12 years old.[9] Yes, that's correct!

You see, girls in the ancient world could cook, sew, and take care of a household by the age of five. And girls physically became women at puberty, around ten years of age.

> **Behold!** Let me be delicate here. I raised two daughters. Menstruation (a period) is a major stage of puberty and usually begins around age twelve, but it can come as early as eight years of age. At that time, girls of antiquity were physically, emotionally, mentally, and spiritually women.

Now, it's true that in our modern twenty-first century, girls physically become women at puberty, at around 10-12 years old, but they are NOT emotionally, mentally, and spiritually women. Having raised two daughters, I would never have allowed them to marry at the age of twelve—or even dated for that matter!

But the ancient world was so much different than our present modern time. Under Jewish law, girls became women at twelve and could get engaged to a man at that time.

So, Mary got engaged to Joseph at the age of twelve.

Now, wait a minute! Again, to me a twelve-year-old girl is just that—a little pre-teen kid. But, my twenty-first century mindset does not belong in the context of the ancient world.

> **Behold!** On one occasion, the first Roman Emperor Caesar Augustus spoke against bachelorhood in an effort to stop fornication and adultery.[10] Instead of marrying girls of marriageable age, men were rebelling by marrying female babies. Augustus then decreed that the minimum age for a girl to be engagement/betrothed was ten years old.

A SPECIAL MAN NAMED JOSEPH

According to Matthew 1:18, we know that Mary was engaged/ betrothed to a man named Joseph. We know that Joseph was a righteous believer in the Hebrew God, a loving and compassionate man, and just an exceptional person. Ladies, Joseph is the kind of guy that you would want to bring home to your parents!

Joseph was a direct descendant of King David. He was a righteous man who kept the laws of Judaism. Like Mary, Joseph was from the small village of Nazareth.

JOSEPH THE STONEMASON

Joseph was a carpenter by trade. Now when you hear the word "carpenter," what do you think about?

When I hear the word *carpenter*, I think of someone working primarily with wood, building tables, chairs, etc. But, this is not what Joseph did. The Greek word used in the Bible in Matthew 13:55 to describe Joseph's occupation is "*tekton*."

A *tekton* was a "builder" and a "stonemason," i.e., a man who worked with heavy stone.

Yes, Joseph would have worked with wood and metal, but he primarily worked with stone. In order to be a stonemason, Joseph would have had to be a powerfully built and muscular man. Stone is quite heavy and if a man could not lift it, he needed to get a new job.

It was Joseph who taught Jesus the art and skill of a carpenter (stonemason).

> **Behold!** Isn't it interesting that the Hollywood movies about the life of Jesus always use actors who are thin and barely medium-sized to play the role of Jesus? Not so! As a carpenter (stonemason), Jesus would have been a powerfully built man. We must stop watching and listening to Hollywood!

It was this man, Joseph, whom God the Father chose to be the legal earthly father of Jesus. Joseph was entrusted by God to raise His Son (Jesus) in the Hebrew Scriptures and its spiritual observances.

> **Behold**! Would you entrust your only child or children to a person for the rest of their lives? That would be really hard—wouldn't it? But that is exactly what God the Father did. We will last meet Joseph in the New Testament when Jesus was twelve years old. Sometime after that, it appears that Joseph had died.

HOW OLD WAS JOSEPH

Now, how old was Joseph when he became engaged to Mary? We do not know for sure. But in the Roman world, boys became men at the age of thirty, when a person attained both physical and mental maturity and could therefore manage major responsibilities. It may be that Joseph was at least thirty years old though some sources teach that a Jewish male could marry at the age of 17-19. Also at age 20, Hebrew males were qualified for military service (Num. 1:1-3).

According to Jewish tradition, one could not enter into public ministry until the age of 30 since he was still considered a boy. No one would listen to a boy until he was thirty years of age. According to Jewish Law, a man who trained in Judaism for the priesthood could not enter into public ministry until the age of 30.[11] Number 8:24-26 says that males at the age of 25 could take part in the work at the tent of meeting, but 1 Chronicles 23:27 says that King David reduced the 25 age minimum to 20 years of age.

According to Genesis 41:46, the patriarch Joseph was thirty years old when Egypt's Pharaoh placed him in charge over all that he ruled. I Samuel 13:1 states that King Saul became king when he was 30. David, also, when he began to reign as king over Israel, was thirty years old.[12] Ezekiel 1:1 says that God called Ezekiel to be a prophet at age 30. This is why Jesus did not begin his public ministry until He was about thirty.[13]

IMAGINE WITH ME

Imagine with me seeing Mary through Joseph's eyes during their pre-engagement/courtship.

Ready! Here we go!

Joseph:

I've known her all of my life. She has the disposition and image of her lovely mother.

Did you know that she is an answer to prayer? Have I not been praying for years for a wife to love?

Mary's girlfriends said I was handsome, but Mary never seemed to even notice me. Her friends reproached her for being too earnest and way too religious. They said that no man would ever be captivated by her.

I remember telling Mary, "I've always thought you are the prettiest girl in Nazareth."

"Doesn't everyone," Mary teased.

"And the meekest."

"Well Joseph, I considered you just another man until that day when some of the other men were demeaning me for wanting to learn the sacred Scriptures. You came to my rescue. That was when I knew I would marry you."

"You did not!"

Mary acquiesced, "I did!"

"How did you know?"

Mary shrugged, "I just did."

You know—she never told me why she knew I was the one.

I can remember that Mary was always busy doing something. She could never just sit still.

Mary's father taught her about the Torah, the Prophets, and the Other Writings. Of course, it is his responsibility to do so. I have always accepted that Mary is the brightest person in Nazareth when it came to knowing her Scriptures.

Mary has always worn long ankle-length tunics. Her garments are woven at home from sheep and goat wool and hair. There is an old saying that "the poor wear sheep-colored clothes and the rich wear rainbow clothes."

She has the deepest black eyes that a man could get lost in. They are like large onyxes from the land of Havilah[14]—that are set off by the hint of olive in her skin. Her long black hair is always wrapped in a veil that had ends extending to the floor. Her hair streaks under her head veil and cascades down past her shoulders. The first time she will let her hair show in public will be on her wedding day—with me! Indeed, a woman's long hair is her glory unto the Lord and is only for her husband to enjoy.

Now Mary's mother is one of a kind. She taught Mary the Holy

Scriptures too, but it has been her mother that has taught Mary everything she needs to know how to be a good and loving wife and mother. Her mother is a great example to follow.

Boy, Mary can cook! She knows all of the dietary laws and keeps them. She makes the best bread ever—even better than my mother's. Of course I would never tell my mother that. At dinnertime Mary can easily whip up a thick porridge called a one-pot stew consisting of lentils, onions, leeks, herbs, and garlic—nothing better!

Mary knows about the special holidays and about the Sabbath. She knows all the meanings behind the events.

When Mary goes outside her home she has a veil covering her face. It is a symbol of modesty and is really two veils: a headband on the forehead with bands to the chin, and a hairnet with ribbons and knots. There have been times when we passed each other that she would lift her veil and smile or make a face at me.

Mary is gregarious and compassionate, with an unusual empathy that endears her to others. She laughs effortlessly and has a diverse clique of friends.

There's more, too. While God has blessed Mary with the most tender of hearts, in many ways she's stronger than I am.

We share the same morals and beliefs that are established by God and family; we view the world through a prism of black and white, right and wrong. I'm captivated with her homemaking abilities of weaving and spinning.

I've always known that Mary would make a good wife. But, there are a number of other men that she could have had picked, but she chose me!

THE TWO-PART JEWISH MARRIAGE

According to Jewish custom, a Jewish marriage was in two stages—a spiritual part and the physical stage.

IMAGINE WITH ME

Listen to Mary as she explains her engagement.

Mary:

The first stage of my marriage is called the *Kiddushin*en or *erusin*, i.e., the engagement/betrothal.

My engagement is an officially witnessed agreement to marry. For some time, Joseph's father has been conversing with my father about me becoming Joseph's wife. The agreement requires Joseph (the groom) and his father to come to my father's home. Joseph would then pay a *Mohar* or *bride price* to my father.

I recall when the day finally came.

I remember putting on my best tunic and using just enough make-up to impress Joseph that I was beautiful. My mother helped me get ready. She looked me up and down as if I was the rose of Sharon. Once I was ready, my father stood at our table awaiting Joseph and his father. Joseph was going to present the bride price to my father as proof of his love and willingness to provide for me.

"I'm ready," I replied breathlessly as I lowered myself into a chair at the table just outside the kitchen.

As time passed, I was fidgeting around on my chair not able to sit still. My father kept telling me to show no emotion that I would accept Joseph.

My heart laughed a bit at my father's squint.

One of my sisters came into the house in a rush to breathlessly say, "They're here!"

I didn't let myself dart to the door to look for him. I didn't allow myself a sprint to my mother's bronze mirror. I just sat there.

Despite myself, I giggled.

My father raised his eyebrows and peered from my mother to me and shrugged his shoulders and said, "I've never seen two women cut from the same piece of cloth."

I leaned back in my chair and tilted my head back to scan my mother's face. She dropped her head to conceal a smile.

"My daughter," Father said warningly at my posture.

"Yes, Father," I replied. I sat up straight and didn't move a muscle.

When Joseph and his father entered the house, my father welcomed them. He asked them to sit at our large table. I was already seated on the opposite side from where Joseph and his father would sit. My mother was not at the table, but was standing by the fireplace close to the kitchen area with the biggest grin on her face.

Joseph is a tall man around 6'0"—being a son of David who was also a tall man. I, on the other hand, am much shorter. He was older than I, which was what our Jewish custom and tradition required for a man to get engaged.

I can still see Joseph sitting there in front of me. He was serious and stern as my father spoke to his father. I would glance at him and then quickly turn my eyes away from him—only to repeat it again. Joseph's broad shoulders towered above the other men of Nazareth, with powerfully built arms befitting a stonemason. He had black eyes, silky short hair, and was considered the most attractive man by the unmarried women of Nazareth—and he wanted to marry me!

"And now to business," my father said to Joseph's father.

Joseph's father presented my father with the bride price of ten silver coins. I knew that this bride price was all that Joseph had and that he wanted my father (and more importantly, me) to know how much he was willing to pay for permission to marry me. He wanted my father to know how very valuable I was.

Then it came! The final verdict! Would my father and I accept the bride price from Joseph?

My father turned toward Joseph and said that he agreed for him to be my husband. In a loud voice Joseph said, "The price has been paid in full."

Father then turned to me as his countenance brightened at the sight of his daughter. I felt priceless!

The *Ketubah* or contract document was signed. This contract was the agreed upon terms of the engagement and Joseph's pledge to provide for me during our one-year engagement period of separation. Once the *Ketubah* was signed Joseph said, "It is finished!"

But, that was not the last word. I had to agree too. As if there were any doubts!

My heart and soul screamed "yes," and it was all I could do to not get up and run outside, singing to the world that I have a husband—Joseph! But, I stayed calm, cool, and poised.

My mother brought in a container of wine from the kitchen. She took a clean glass and held it up to the light and rotated it as if there was some defect. She offered the glass to Joseph who poured the wine into the glass and gave it to me. I gave a little giggle, and at once Joseph's face warmed. If I drank it—I'd accepted Joseph. If not, he'd still be a bachelor!

When Joseph handed me the glass of wine, his hand was trembling. Once I received the glass, I put both hands on it. I pressed the glass to my lips and looked at my father. He seemed sad somehow, but yet proud. I felt warm all over as I took a sip.

Yes! I was so happy and excited. I almost started singing!

My father then said in a loud voice, "You are now betrothed! You both are legally married."

Joseph then said to my father, "I came to your house for you to give me your daughter, Mary, to wife; she is my wife and I am her husband from this day and forever."

Then Joseph turned to me and said, "I have to go for I'm going to prepare the *Chuppah* (bridal chamber) in my father's house."

"Do not go my husband," I replied.

"It is better for you that I go, but I will come back," Joseph responded.

"When?" I asked.

"I do not know. Only my father knows the day or hour," Joseph said.

Joseph's father then presented Joseph the gifts (the *mattan*) that he had brought to give to me. These gifts showed his support for me during the one-year separation before we came together. Wow, one year of not seeing Joseph. But that was our Jewish way. I would be very busy sewing clothes and preparing a home for Joseph.

Joseph and I spent as much time together before the one-year period of separation began. When I went outside I wore a headband with the ten silver coins on it showing to everyone that I was engaged.

From time to time, Joseph would send his chaperon to check on how I was doing.

But, the gifts were really intended to remind me of Joseph.

As if I could forget him. No one else will be in my thoughts.

After the one-year engagement, there would be the coming together ceremony. But before that ceremony, I would immerse myself in water called the *Mikveh*, or cleansing bath. My past was now gone and I began a new life. I most certainly will remain clean.

Our one-year engagement began. I began sewing and making clothes for our future children and myself. I was preparing myself to become the woman of Proverbs 31:10-31, while Joseph was preparing our wedding chamber in his father's home for our honeymoon. Being a stonemason, he is building it right onto his father's house.

I was told that it is so beautiful—it is supposed to be. He's a pretty good stonemason if I say so myself. He is building a most beautiful wedding chamber for me—and my handsome Joseph.

While Joseph is building our wedding chamber, I am busy preparing for the second part of my marriage in the "taking" (*nissuin*) and our coming together celebration. I have saved every *mina* of money and bought cosmetics to make myself more attractive to Joseph. I want to be gorgeous!

Joseph's father will be the one to tell him when it is time for him to abduct and carry me off into the night. Joseph will get the opportunity when his father gives him the go ahead to "kidnap me" stealthily—like a thief in the night and he will take me to our wedding chamber in his father's home.

I don't know exactly when Joseph will come for me. My bridesmaid friends and I will continually be ready, having our lamps lit and clipped and all of my belongings ready to transfer into my new home. I understand that a bridegroom could come in the midpoint of the night—but what night?

Yes, Joseph will bring me home.

I anticipate the sound of the trumpet that will blow, the shofar or ram's horn, to let me know that he has arrived with his friends to take my bridesmaids and me to his father's home.

We will consummate our marriage in the wedding chamber while his best man lingers at the entrance of my wedding chamber. *How embarrassing.* He will proclaim to the wedding guests that the marriage has been consummated and a seven-day wedding celebration will begin.

After the seven days of festivities, Joseph will take me to our own home to begin our new life together.[15]

I cannot wait!

A LEGALLY BINDING CONTRACT

Marriage traditions were much different back then. Though Mary was not living with her husband Joseph, her engagement was a legally binding contract that was done before witnesses. The only thing that could terminate the marriage during the engagement period was physical death[16] or sexual infidelity.[17]

Sexual infidelity would result either in stoning the young woman or in a private divorce. The husband would make that decision.

MARY AND JOSEPH: A VERY UNIQUE COUPLE

Mary and Joseph were the ideal couple.

Joseph was a hard working stonemason who was ready to provide for his wife Mary. We are going to learn that Joseph truly loved Mary when he will be confronted with a heartbreaking situation concerning her. We will see that he will always do what God tells him without question or hesitation.

Mary was a pure and lovely young woman. We will also learn that she, too, will love her husband Joseph and be obedient to God without question or hesitation. We are also going to learn that she will be a wonderful mother to her first-born son—Jesus.

I really want to reemphasize my next point. One of the essential things that we will learn is that Jesus was not Joseph's physical son. Matthew 1:25a states:

> "And [he] knew her not till she had brought forth her first-born son."

Notice that Matthew said, "*her* first-born" and not "*their* first-born." Matthew 1:16 states:

> "And Jacob begat Joseph the husband of Mary, of whom was born Jesus, who is called Christ."

The Greek word "whom" is the genitive feminine singular relative pronoun "*hes*." Its grammatical antecedent can only be the female, Mary, not the male, Joseph. Jesus was only from Mary and not from Joseph.

But, will Joseph, being a remarkable man, legally adopt Jesus as his heir and as his own son?

Will both Mary and Joseph bring Jesus up as responsible parents?

Will a solid marriage with Joseph provide Mary's first-born son with a foundation of a loving home with loving parents?

Although they were poor Jewish people, God is about to use them in marvelous and wonderful ways that they could never imagine. They will become two of the most important people to ever live.

They are about to embark on one of the greatest journeys ever. Are you willing to join them?

Are you ready to learn more?

Good, then read on!

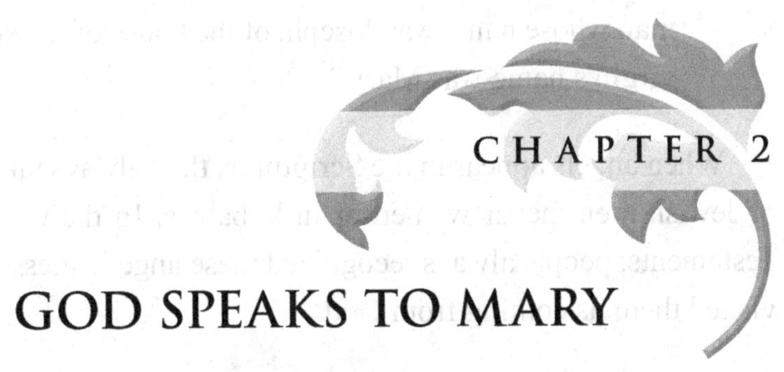

CHAPTER 2

GOD SPEAKS TO MARY

MARY THE CHOSEN ONE

ONE OF THE greatest announcements of all time was made to Mary while she was engaged to Joseph.

Luke tells us in his Gospel that the announcement was to Mary, not to Joseph. In a culture where women were treated as "less than animals," it would have been unthinkable for Luke, the Scripture writer, to tell the story with the greatest announcement ever being given privately to a woman, in the rural village of Nazareth. But, he did! It has the ring of truth.

The announcement was that God had chosen Mary to become the physical mother of the Messiah.

Wow!

How would you react if you had been Mary?

GABRIEL SPEAKS: MARY IS SPEECHLESS

In Luke 1:26-27, God sent His angelic messenger, Gabriel, from heaven to Mary with an astounding message:

> "In the sixth month the angel Gabriel was sent from God to a city of Galilee named Nazareth, to a virgin betrothed to a

> man whose name was Joseph, of the house of David. And the virgin's name was Mary."

When angels appear in the Scriptures, they always take the form of Jewish men, never women or little babies. In the Old and New Testaments, people always recognized these angelic messengers that visited them as coming from God.

> **Behold!** Do we see and recognize angelic messengers today in the twenty-first century? The answer is "yes" and "no." Yes, because Hebrews 1:14 states that angels are ministering spirits to Christians. But, no, because the book of Hebrews 13:2 says that we entertain angels *unaware*, which means that we would never know that someone is an angel. Have you ever met someone for a short time that helped you in some way with that person never being seen again from your interactions? *Perhaps* these helpers were angels.

I can just imagine how it could have been when Gabriel appeared to Mary.

Mary was alone, perhaps in her home busy tending to chores. When Mary saw the angel Gabriel, she must have been startled, dropping whatever she had in her hands. With big wide eyes, she crouched behind a table. Her heart was beating rapidly, her body was shaking, her knuckles were white, and she couldn't utter a sound.

Gabriel stood before Mary in brilliant splendor. He greeted her with a simple *hello*. Gabriel told Mary that she had found favor and grace with God and that the Lord was with her.[1]

Mary said nothing and didn't move. Tension and fear were thick. By Gabriel calling her "the favored one," Mary knew that she was a special person of God's grace and good pleasure, chosen for some special role. Yet she was still speechless and didn't know the reason why God had so favored her.[2]

> **Behold!** Mary is a prime example for Christians who freely receive God's special favor of grace in saving us. Grace is giving to us what we do not deserve, i.e., God does something special for us—salvation. Mary did not deserve to receive God's special favor, but she received it freely because of His purposes and His loving kindness.

I can just hear Mary thinking—"Me? I'm a poor woman with no status or social upbringing. Why does God favor me? How will He be with me?"

Even with the words of Gabriel, that God's presence was with her, Mary was still troubled and even fearful. Can you feel how tense Mary was—paralyzed and not moving or speaking?

But, even though she was afraid, Gabriel's words begin to reassure Mary of the fact that God was going to be with her, to help and to aid her with what was about to be told to her.

MARY IS PERPLEXED, CURIOUS, AND CONCERNED

Even with Gabriel's reassuring remarks, Mary was still very perplexed, curious, and concerned—and not moving from behind her table.[3] Mary was pondering or reflecting on Gabriel's greeting. A dozen different things were racing in Mary's thoughts. She was wondering what it meant for her to be "an object of God's favor" and what "God will be with you" meant.

What did God want to do with her?

Again, Gabriel sensed Mary's further concern and in order to ease her anxiety, he spoke in a voice of comfort calling her by her name—"Mary." She was told to not be afraid and that she didn't need to be concerned.[4]

This did the trick!

Again, I can just hear Mary's thoughts: "Yes, God is favoring me for some purpose of His. But, what special thing is God going to use me for?"

THE ANNOUNCEMENT OF ANNOUNCEMENTS

Gabriel then told Mary what that special use would be. Mary, a chaste young woman, would conceive and bear a son.[5]

Now that was a grand announcement!

Can you hear Mary's mixed emotions and thoughts as she was peering out from behind a table? "I'm a virgin! How can this be? Joseph and I have not yet consummated our marriage!"

And, at the same time, she was obedient to her God, "Oh, what joy it will be that I will bear a son—how wonderful! Me, a mother!"

Mary began to move from behind the table.

Gabriel also commanded Mary to name the child Jesus. You see, Jewish women were the ones who named their children much like today, but her son already had a name—Jesus, like Joshua of old.[6]

The angelic messenger Gabriel told Mary two things about the son that would be born to her.[7] But, what was about to be told to Mary must have left her stunned—completely speechless.

HE WILL BE GREAT AND CALLED "THE SON OF THE MOST HIGH"

Mary's son, Jesus, would be great and He would be called the Son of the Most High.

Wow! Mary's son, Jesus, would be great in His person and ministry. Mary definitely knew that the word "great" referred back to Micah 5:4, where the Messianic figure is depicted as "great from the ends of the earth."

But, more importantly, Mary knew that in the Old Testament, the use of the word "great" described Almighty God.[8] At this moment Mary knew that she was going to give birth to the Messiah. And this Messiah was God!

Mary's heart was racing as she heard Gabriel's words. Can you hear those rapid beats?

Breathlessly, Mary thought, "I'm going to give birth to the Messiah!"

But, Gabriel did not stop there.

Jesus, Mary's son, would be called the *Son of the Most High.* Again, Mary knew her Old Testament Scriptures. To Mary, the expression "Son of the Most High" meant that Jesus is the Son of God, i.e., God himself.

> **Behold!** The name "Son of the Most High" is another name for God Himself.[9] Only God is the "Most High" supreme authority. In the Bible when Jesus is called the "Son of God," it means "God the Son."[10]

Mary thought: "Okay, so far, I'm a virgin, but I am going to conceive a son who must be named Jesus. My son will be great and will be called 'Son of the Most High.' In other words, my son is God! Yes—my son!"

That is amazing!

MARY'S SON IS THE LAST OF THE DAVIDIC KINGS

Gabriel told Mary that the Lord God would give her son the throne of David. At this point, Mary's heart must have been singing: "My son is going to be King—regal and royal! Fulfillment of the Davidic covenant is in my son Jesus."[11]

Think about it! Mary's son was of the house of David through Joseph[12] and Mary.[13]

Gabriel continued by telling Mary that her son, Jesus, was not just going to be a king, but He was going to be the last of the Davidic Kings. Can you hear Mary's thoughts? "It is my son, Jesus, that is the end and fulfillment of all the line of Davidic kings."[14]

Why is this so important to Mary? Why does she care? Again, Mary's parents had taught her the Old Testament. As a woman, the rabbis would have neglected her, but her parents, especially her mother, taught her well! Mary knew that the last of the Davidic kings was the Messiah!

Mary exclaimed, "My son is the Jewish Messiah!"

HE WILL REIGN OVER THE HOUSE OF JACOB FOREVER

In fulfillment of Scripture, Gabriel told Mary that her son would reign over the house of Jacob forever with a kingdom that would not end.[15] So, though His father David's kingdom was temporary, Jesus' kingdom would be a majestic and everlasting rule.[16]

Mary must have been beaming with the prettiest smile you have ever seen. She knew that the "house of Jacob" referred to Israel.[17] Her son, Jesus, was to rule over the nation/people of Israel as its final and ultimate king. The words "forever" and "shall not end" clarify the everlasting duration of Jesus' rule. Nothing would overcome Jesus or bring a halt to His reign. The fact is the He, Jesus, would reign "forever."[18]

MARY ASKS A GREAT QUESTION

Mary had been silent and began to show herself from hiding behind a table all through Gabriel's presentation of God's grand announcement. But, then she totally came out from her hiding place and stood before the splendor and brilliance of the mighty angelic messenger Gabriel. She was no longer afraid.

As Mary was mulling over all that Gabriel had told her, she had one overwhelming question. She opened her mouth and quietly asked: "How? How can I give birth when I am a virgin?"[19]

Mary said, "I do not know a man," i.e., her current status was that she absolutely had no sexual experience.[20]

Mary hadn't forgotten that she was in the yearlong engagement with Joseph and had not even seen him in that time. Just like you and me, Mary understood simple biology. It was impossible for her to become pregnant.

Mary had been 100% faithful to Joseph and she didn't understand how it could be—but she trusted God.

GABRIEL GIVES A MIRACULOUS ANSWER

Now, it is vital to know that Mary did not doubt that she had been chosen to give birth to the God-man. She was simply puzzled! Most people in Mary's place would have asked Gabriel for some kind of sign to prove what he said. But, Mary did not.

Gabriel knew that Mary could not fully understand so he provided the answer that completely satisfied her. In Luke 1:35, Gabriel told Mary that God the Holy Spirit would come upon her and the power of the Most High would overshadow her.

This meant to Mary that the creative power of God, as the divine life-giving agent, would make this conception possible.

Mary knew full well that the Creator God had the power to create the universe from nothing, to create life on the earth, and to create human life from the dust of the earth. Surely, God had to power to make life at conception in a unique way, in Mary's womb, to begin God the Son's human existence.

Mary looked downward and folded her hands together and said, "I am to be overshadowed by God the Holy Spirit just like God's presence in the Shekinah cloud that rested on the tabernacle[21] and to God's presence in protecting Israel.[22] Yes, God's special presence is going to be with me to protect me."

God's presence with Mary was extremely comforting to her.[23]

When Mary heard these words from Gabriel she also understood that this would be a birth in the *near* future and not one that she would have after consummating her marriage with Joseph. This would be a miraculous conception and it was going to take place soon!

Think about it!

This creative power of God the Holy Spirit would use Mary's DNA in God the Son becoming a human being at the moment of conception. The miraculous conception would occur sometime before she met her relative Elizabeth.[24]

THE CHILD WILL BE CALLED HOLY—THE SON OF GOD

Mary's son would be much more than the Messianic deliverer. He will be the Davidic King of promise.[25] Gabriel also told Mary that her son would be holy and the Son of God, i.e., God Himself.

Mary's joy was spilling over. Her eyes were now full of tears as she whispered—"My son is God Himself."

A BONUS ANNOUNCEMENT

Gabriel then surprised Mary by telling her that her cousin, Elizabeth, was going to give birth to a son.[26] This would have brought extreme joy for Mary to know that her relative, who had been barren, was six months along in her pregnancy. We do not know why Elizabeth had not shared this with Mary, but the fact is that Mary did not know.

Before Mary could say anything else, Gabriel finished his grand announcement to her by saying: "Nothing is impossible for God."[27]

With those words, Mary would have immediately thought of Genesis 18:14 where the Angel of the Lord told Abraham that his very old and barren wife, Sarah, would have a son. "Is anything too hard for the Lord? At the appointed time I will return to you, about this time next year, and Sarah shall have a son."

LET'S REVIEW

What has Mary been told? Get a pen and paper and write them down. I will wait for you!

Are you back? You were fast!

Here is my list. Compare it with yours.

1. God has favored her;
2. God will be with her;
3. She, as a virgin, will conceive and give birth to a son;
4. This son will be great;
5. This son will be called the Son of the Most High;
6. This son will be given the throne of David;
7. This son will reign over the house of Jacob forever;
8. This son's kingdom will never end;
9. This son will be called holy; and
10. This son is the Son of God.

This is a bit overwhelming, isn't it? Mary was going to give birth to the God-man himself.

What would you have said in Mary's place? Would you have argued with Gabriel? Would you have refused? What would you have done and said?

MARY'S RESPONSE
"I AM THE SERVANT OF THE LORD"

Well, Mary's only response to Gabriel was:

> "And Mary said, "Behold, I am the servant of the Lord; let it be to me according to your word" (Luke 1:38).

Mary's response was nothing short of submitting herself totally to the Lord. This is the kind of submission that we Christians should have in our daily lives.

At those words from Mary, Gabriel, the angelic messenger of God, left her. Just as sudden as Gabriel appeared—he was suddenly gone!

Mary's eyes were darting from one part of the room to the other looking for Gabriel, but he was no longer there.

She only had one thought—visit Elizabeth! With haste, Mary made preparation for her journey to her cousin's home.

> **Behold!** At this point in time, the miraculous virgin conception had not taken place. What Gabriel told Mary is that it would take place in the near future.[28] Gabriel simply wanted to reassure Mary that God would always be with her.

MARY HURRIED TO SEE ELIZABETH

Now, what would do if you were Mary? Would you break the one-year engagement of separation from Joseph to tell him?

No, instead of finding Joseph, Mary immediately went to Elizabeth's side. She had been told of Elizabeth's condition and now traveled to see God's sign.[29] Her journey was made with haste into the Judean hill country, to a city south of Jerusalem. We are not told what city Elizabeth lived in, but the journey covered 80-100 miles and took four or five days. Can you believe that—a trip of 80-100 miles! Mary couldn't wait to see Elizabeth. Her departure reflected an instant response to God's leading.

ELIZABETH'S BABY LEAPED

Mary finally arrived and greeted Elizabeth. Perhaps Mary walked up to Elizabeth with a large smile and put her hands on Elizabeth's stomach after embracing her. What we do know is that Mary's greeting brought a leaping response from Elizabeth's baby in her womb.[30]

Elizabeth took the baby's response as a sign.[31] She told Mary that upon hearing the sound of her greeting—the baby in her womb leapt with joy. It is by God the Holy Spirit that Elizabeth perceived the person who was in Mary's womb.[32] By this time, the virgin conception had already occurred.

"BLESSED ARE YOU AMONG WOMEN"

Elizabeth blessed Mary. Mary was speechless because of the child that she would bear. Mary was a special vessel, chosen by God's grace.

"BLESSED IS THE FRUIT OF YOUR WOMB"

Elizabeth also blessed the child. The "fruit of the womb" is a Hebrew expression of speech. In the Old Testament, a fruitful womb was considered a blessing from God and was related to faithful obedience to God[33] or to God's sovereign provision.[34]

Elizabeth counted it an honor to be a part of these events.[35] She exclaimed, "How has this come upon me?" Her words expressed her humility. How was she worthy to share in Mary's visit and in these events?

MARY IS THE PHYSICAL MOTHER OF THE LORD

Elizabeth's description of Mary as "the mother of my Lord" meant that Mary was to be the physical mother of Jesus. Elizabeth's focus was not on Mary, but on her child. Elizabeth saw Mary's child as her superior, for Elizabeth said: "My Lord." This indicated that the virgin conception in Mary had taken place.

Elizabeth gave a final blessing to Mary for her faith. She addressed Mary as fortunate, happy, or blessed. It is the first beatitude in the Gospel of Luke.[36]

Mary was "the one who believes, because the fulfillment will come" and was a great example of faith.

Elizabeth used the word "completion or fulfillment" of what was spoken to her by the Lord.[37] God would complete His promises.

MARY'S SONG

Now, did you know that Mary sang? She was so happy that praise to the Lord burst forth from her soul. Mary offered praise to the

Lord in a hymn called the *Magnificant*, a name reflecting the Latin translation of the term "magnifies."[38] Amazing!

After Elizabeth finished speaking to Mary, Mary lifted up both of her arms and burst into a song of praise. Can you see the big smile on Mary's face? Imagine with me that you're a fly on the wall. The cousins haven't seen each other for some time, they're both pregnant, and after Elizabeth blessed Mary, she began to sing. I visualize it like a musical. An important scene happened and then the entire cast broke into song and danced to enforce the importance of what just occurred.

Now, I have a confession to make. In Mary's song, she references a great many Old Testament scripture passages. She did not have to go to the reference books and Old Testament commentaries to compose her song.

No, her song of praise was deep within her heart and immediately at her disposal. Remarkable!

This is quite humbling to me as a person who has six degrees including a PHD. This twelve-year-old young woman shames me—and rightly so! I am inspired by Mary to know my Old Testament better.

Doesn't Mary's overflowing of praise make you want to join her in song? It does me.

Now, those who know me are pleading for me not to sing now, but to go out into the wilderness away from civilization and torture the squirrels, chipmunks, and gophers with my singing.

Okay, I won't sing out loud, but I am singing praises silently in my heart—so there!

Mary ended her song—ten stanzas (verses)! Yes, ten! Elizabeth absorbed every lyric that Mary uttered. Mary must have been a wonderful singer with great vibrato and a silky timbre!

MARY RETURNS TO NAZARETH

Mary's visit with Elizabeth lasted three months, so Elizabeth's pregnancy was now at nine months.[39] What would they have been doing for the three-month visit? Perhaps Mary was helping Elizabeth sew, make baby clothes, and just helping her around the house until the time of delivery. After her three-month visit—Mary returned back to Nazareth.

Oh no, in our songfest of celebration we have forgotten Joseph! When Mary returned back home, she was three months pregnant. Joseph was certainly going to hear about this.

Remember that since Mary was legally married in this one-year period of engagement, she fully knew that this son that was about to be born to her would legally be her husband Joseph's son, under two conditions.

First, Joseph would have to accept Mary in her condition by taking her to his home, and second, he would have to name her son Jesus as Gabriel commanded.

All the way back to Nazareth Mary repeated to herself: "Will Joseph believe me? Will Joseph take me home as his wife? Will he believe me? Of course he will!"

As she neared Nazareth, Mary was resolute that Joseph would believe her.

"Yes, Joseph will believe me, Elizabeth did . . . !"

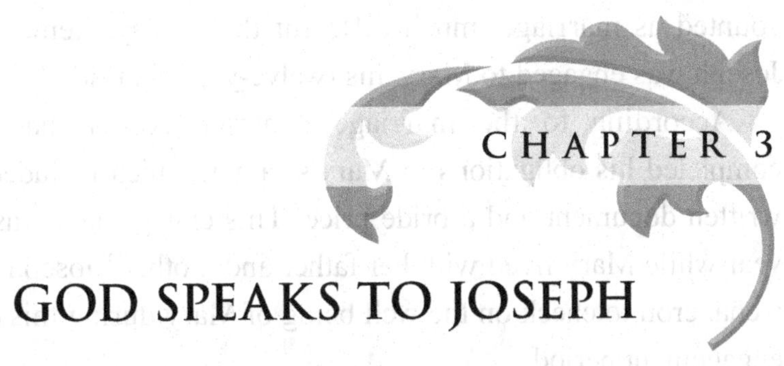

CHAPTER 3

GOD SPEAKS TO JOSEPH

A MAN NAMED JOSEPH

There's a lot of speculation regarding Mary's husband Joseph. We don't know a lot about him. But based on Joseph's reaction to Mary's pregnancy and his absolute obedience to God's instructions, we know that God also chose Mary because she had accepted a man worthy to be Jesus' legal and adopted father on earth.

Matthew 1:1 records the birth of the Messiah along with Jesus' Abrahamic and Davidic ancestry.[1] After the Bible writer carefully and firmly established Jesus in the setting of salvation history and genealogy, we are introduced to a Jewish man named Joseph.

The grand announcement from the angelic messenger Gabriel left Mary extremely joyful and happy that she had been chosen to give birth to the Messiah. After Gabriel left her, Mary hurriedly journeyed to her relative Elizabeth. After her three-month visit, Mary returned back home to Nazareth.

Once back in her hometown of Nazareth, Mary was three months pregnant—and Joseph finds out!

JOSEPH—MARY'S HUSBAND

Joseph was Mary's legal husband even though the "coming together" ceremony hadn't taken place. In Biblical times, the betrothal months counted as marriage, much different than today. Remember that Joseph was engaged to Mary, his twelve-year old bride.[2]

According to the marriage contract, Joseph had already completed his obligations to Mary's father, which included a legal written document and a bride price. This engagement was for one year while Mary lived with her father and mother.[3] Joseph did have a chaperon to check on the well being of Mary during this one-year engagement period.

Joseph, therefore, had legally binding authority over Mary during this one-year engagement. This was a binding contract conducted before witnesses. We already know that at this time, in Jewish culture, the role and value of women was viewed differently than in our modern Christian culture. Women were not held in high esteem; rather, they were viewed as property of the husband.

Once married, the only things that could end Mary and Joseph's marriage were physical death[4] or sexual unfaithfulness, i.e., adultery.[5] Unfaithfulness would result in either the guilty spouse being stoned to death for committing adultery or through official divorce proceedings.

Please don't forget that Mary is not living in Joseph's home—not yet!

During this one-year engagement, Joseph was busy building a wedding chamber in his father's home and a new home for Mary. Once Joseph was ready to accept Mary into his home and the one-year engagement was over, he would send word to Mary that he was ready for her to come to his house.

At that time, Mary, who would be around thirteen years old, would then go from her parents' home to the wedding chamber in Joseph's father's home and consummate the marriage in a public ceremony called "the coming together." Then Mary and Joseph would celebrate with family and friends in a one-week festive time of celebration.

Based on what we know, we can safely assume that Joseph had not even seen Mary during this engagement time and didn't know that God had sent the angelic messenger Gabriel to make the grand announcement to her. Joseph may or may not have known about Mary journeying to her relative Elizabeth and staying with her for three months.

JOSEPH FINDS OUT

Once Mary returned from her three-month visit with Elizabeth, the news of her pregnancy was out. Joseph must have been crushed!

Joseph loved Mary and wanted to spend the rest of his life with her. Joseph must have been thinking, "She's pregnant and we have not consummated our marriage yet. Whom has Mary been with?"

Remember, Joseph did not know that Mary's pregnancy was due to the creative power of God the Holy Spirit. The only thing that he could think about was that Mary had been unfaithful to him.

> **Behold!** He had to have felt like he'd been hit by a cement-truck, or in Joseph's situation—a horse-drawn chariot!

How would you feel if your spouse was unfaithful to you? What would you do? Your dreams of a new life with your spouse would be crushed. Your heart would be broken.

Yes, Mary was "found" to be with child, i.e., she was pregnant, but she was not an adulteress. This conception was done by the miraculous and creative act of God the Holy Spirit.

But, what about poor heartbroken Joseph? The only thing that Joseph knew for a fact was that he was not the father of Mary's child.

IMAGINE WITH ME

Imagine Joseph's reaction after talking with Mary but before God had spoken to him and shared the truth of her pregnancy. Poor Mary—how brokenhearted she would have been.

Mary:

A bodily cascade of numbness had washed over me just an hour before. Now it had given way to a depressing emptiness in the chasm of my soul. I stood just out-of-sight beyond Joseph's home in stillness for one hour. I felt inflexible as I stood like a Greek sculpture on the narrow path back to my home. I prayed that Joseph would come after me.

He didn't come.

A million things that I had intended to say, a thousand postures I'd planned to strike, vaporized as punctually as the Sea of Galilee froths once it slaps the seashore.

I elevated my chin and wiped away the tears from my cheek. I closed my eyes, intensely attuned to the night music. Dusk was setting in.

I felt an abrupt and desperate yearning for Mother.

I trod home.

As I approached my breath wedged in my throat when I saw her. She was waiting for me outside on a bench—her face was forlorn.

But, as always, Mother's timing was flawless.

She came and placed her hand in mine.

"Mother, can you see by my countenance that Joseph doesn't want your daughter?"

Her eyes brightened as she looked at me.

"Well," my mother asked nervously.

I put my forehead to her and lethargically whispered: "He said that he could not take me home with him—no coming together celebration."

"And," Mother probed with her head bowed.

I was fighting back the tears.

I wrapped my arms around myself and gulped down the sobs.

"Joseph was very sweet . . . to me. He's a righteous and good man. There will be no public trial . . . with me being stoned to death . . . as an adulteress. He's going . . . to divorce me quietly with a written document."

"Is he firm in his decision, my daughter?"

I nodded my head and the tears came, "Yes, Mother. There is no power on earth to convince him differently."

"My daughter, I think you will have him, if that is what God wants," she firmly but gently said. "You have been chosen by God for a momentous task, but you cannot do it by yourself."

"Do you believe that, my Mother?" I hopefully asked.

"More than life itself my child—more than life itself!"

She enveloped me and I sobbed as if I was her daughter of seven years old. She cuddled me and rocked me as if I was still her little girl. When I gazed up into her affectionate eyes, I observed tears on her cheeks.

She patted my arm, leading the way across the rock-strewn path to home. "Come inside," Mother pleaded.

I followed my mother single file through the door. As my mother and I came into our home, I felt the eyes of everyone in my family fasten upon me. No one said a word, but all—Father and my sisters— looked at me with compassion. I paused on my way to my bedchamber, placed my hand on my bedroom door, and turned to confront them. They looked downward, everyone but my mother, whose watery eyes fixed onto mine.

Tearfully I whispered to my family, "He doesn't believe me!"

I sluggishly tumbled into bed and sobbed inconsolably, cautious not to be overheard, concerned that the noise of my weeping would worry my parents and siblings. Rubbing the twinge of my neck, I slowly surveyed my room.

I brought the blanket high up beneath my chin, submerging my face in my pillow.

I couldn't get the image of Joseph out of my mind. I could still see him putting his hands over his face. His elbows rested on his knees and his head dropped. He was a defeated man with a broken heart.

I said out loud, "I was so sure that he would believe me!"

But as I trembled, night passed into morning. I was drained but would not fall into the mercy of sleep.

I felt that my heart could not be mended.

I could not remember feeling more alone.

I remained awake throughout the darkness, pondering how I could live without Joseph. But, then it came—my mind slowly drifted and my eyelids grew heavy as I felt myself letting go—bit by bit.

As my mind calmed, it drifted as helplessly as a piece of driftwood floating down the Jordan River.

When morning came, I pried ajar an eye to the dazzling sheen beaming in the open window. It took me an instant to place where I was. I chafed my eyes and waited. A knot materialized in my throat. "Oh Joseph," I cried.

The next few days were like the first, but I would wait.

My father asked me why I was not eating. One of my sisters shook her head in mocking sorrow.

My mother snapped one bright-eyed glance at me and said, "She is well. She will eat."

And then I waited.

I waited for another seven days and another seven nights—no message, no one.

And then, without warning, there was a knock on my door…

JOSEPH'S RIGHTEOUS DECISION

Poor Joseph!

We are told that Joseph was a righteous man. This means that he was devoted to obeying the Law of Moses.[6] In his life Joseph strived to obey God's laws. He is a model for Christians who strive to obey the Lord in their Christian lives.

But, Joseph was in a quandary. What should he do?

Husbands, what would you do?

A PUBLIC TRIAL AND STONING

Joseph's situation is plain. Mary was his legal wife, but the marriage had not yet been consummated with her. There were two options for Mary. The first was that since Joseph was her legal husband, he could pursue a public trial against Mary that would shame and disgrace her, resulting in her being stoned to death as an adulteress.[7]

Joseph was entirely in his right to have Mary stoned to death, according to the Old Testament Law. He was a righteous man who strived to follow God's laws and Mary's condition demanded legal action. But, remember that he loved Mary and his compassionate heart went out to her.

You see, even though Joseph believed (mistakenly) that Mary had wronged him, he could not bring himself to begin legal proceedings against her.

> **Behold!** According to Deuteronomy 22:23-2, Joseph could have addressed her suspected adultery, publically disgrace her, and have her put to death.

Unwilling to put her to shame through a public trial and execute her by stoning (Matt. 1:19), Joseph chose the second option and resolved to divorce her quietly.

Why?

The answer was simple. Though Joseph was heartbroken over his mistaken belief about Mary's condition—he still loved her!

> **Behold**! If a person was stoned to death, here was the process. A wooden platform standing around nine feet off the ground was where the adulterer stood. In this case, Mary would be stripped of all of her clothing. One of the two witnesses would take a large rock and crush it over her head. She would fall off the platform onto the ground where the second witness would take another large stone and crush it onto her chest. Then, the crowd would pick up stones and pass by Mary and throw their stones straight down on her.

DIVORCE HER QUIETLY

Even though he loved Mary, Joseph's conscience would not allow him to continue to be her husband and keep Mary as his wife. There was a second option that God's law provided. So, Joseph made the firm and final decision to divorce Mary "quietly" in a private (not public) divorce.[8]

This would be like a private annulment of the marriage contract. The only thing that Joseph had to do was to draft a written divorce statement and present it to Mary in the company of two or three witnesses as prescribed in Numbers 5:11-31 and Deuteronomy 24:1-4.[9]

> **Behold!** There were rules for divorce and adultery. There were laws for mandatory divorce when adultery was proven.[10] But Deuteronomy 22:25-28 states, however, that if the woman

was an unwilling partner, she was not to be harmed and only the man must be executed.

So Joseph had to make up his mind about what he was going to do about Mary. What other choice did he have? Joseph had to divorce her quietly because he didn't want Mary to be stoned to death. His plan was firmly set. But God's ways and plans were different from Joseph's plan and often from our plans as well. God was about to intervene.

GOD SPEAKS TO JOSEPH "IT ISN'T WHAT YOU THINK"

We don't know if Joseph confronted Mary or if when he found out about her pregnancy, he simply stayed away.

Picture this with me if you will.

Perhaps the very night that Joseph found out about Mary being pregnant—he was troubled, hurt, and having difficulty getting to sleep. He just lay there in his bed reflecting and reminiscing of what it might have been with Mary.[11] His dreams of spending the rest of his life with Mary were shattered.

Joseph was so weary, tired, and sick with stress. He rubbed his forehead in the silence in his room.

IMAGINE WITH ME

Joseph:

Mary, my betrothed, is with child—and the child is not mine. My heart is heavy with grief and pain.

I remember preparing the contract that would be a covenant for Mary and me. My father helped me write it. Once it was completed my father and I went to Mary's home and presented it to Mary and her father as proof of my love and willingness to provide for her.

No, I didn't even get the chance to go bring Mary home.

I didn't get the opportunity, upon arrival at Mary's home, to have the trumpet blown, the shofar or ram's horn, to let her know that I had arrived.

I didn't get the opportunity when my father gave me the go ahead, to kidnap Mary stealthily—like a thief in the night and bring her to our wedding chamber in my father's home.

I didn't get the opportunity to consummate our marriage in the wedding chamber while my friend lingered at the wedding chamber door. My friend would have proclaimed to the wedding guests that the marriage was consummated and a seven-day wedding celebration would have begun.

After the seven days of festivities I would have taken Mary to our own home to begin a new life together.

I didn't get the opportunity.

She didn't wait for me.

GOD COMFORTS JOSEPH

As Joseph's reminiscent thoughts made him toss and turn, God sent an angelic messenger to Joseph in a dream.[12] The angel addressed Joseph as "son of David," i.e., as a legal heir of King David.[13]

The angel told Joseph to:

> "not fear to take Mary as your wife, for that which is conceived in her is from the Holy Spirit. She will bear a son, and you shall call his name Jesus, for he will save his people from their sins" (Matt. 1:20-21).

Because Joseph was heartbroken and sick with worry, the angel commanded Joseph not to be afraid to take Mary as his wife. He told Joseph that the child that was conceived in her was from God the Holy Spirit.

> **Behold!** Joseph knew his Old Testament. He would have immediately remembered the address given to him by the angel since it was a normal birth announcement from the Old Testament.[14]

Even in Joseph's dream, you can imagine the instant relief that Joseph must have felt. His wife, Mary, was not unfaithful to him! She was totally innocent of any wrongdoing. God showed compassion on Joseph.

Mary's condition was the result of the creative act of God the Holy Spirit. That would have prompted Joseph to immediately think about God the Holy Spirit's role in creation of the physical and spiritual universe.[15] Joseph would also have thought about God's Spirit as the Creator and Giver of Life.[16]

TWO THINGS FOR JOSEPH TO DO

Joseph now had the true explanation for Mary's condition. Because Mary was innocent, the angelic messenger of God commanded Joseph to change his decision and to take two courses of immediate action.

TAKE MARY HOME AS YOUR WIFE

First, Joseph was commanded to welcome and take Mary home as his wife. Remember that this would be a public ceremony called "the coming together." Then Mary and Joseph would celebrate with family and friends in a one-week festive time of celebration.

For Joseph, he absolutely knew that if he took Mary to his home as his wife it would also include accepting her child as his own. So, this first course of action included the acceptance of Mary as his wife and her child as his own.

Perhaps Joseph was thinking that he might face possible ridicule in accepting Mary into his home and as his wife. Would the local rabbi take action against him? What would his parents think? Would his neighbors in Nazareth gossip about Mary? Would his steady customers not conduct business with him anymore? He didn't know for sure.

There was a great deal on the line here for Joseph.

NAME MARY'S SON

The angel told Joseph that Mary was going to have a son.[17] And, under divine direction, the second course of action that Joseph had to obey was to name Mary's son Jesus.

This doesn't sound like a big deal to us today. In fact, in America, the mother is the only person who is allowed to decide the baby's name for the birth certificate. When my oldest daughter had just delivered my first grandchild, the nurse came in to administer the birth certificate paperwork. When my son-in-law tried to answer the questions, the nurse looked at him stone-faced and said, "I need *only* the mother to answer these questions."

But there were different social norms at play here with Mary and Joseph. If Joseph named Mary's son, it meant that he was formally adopting Jesus as his own son, thereby making Jesus a legal heir as a "son of David."[18]

Do you remember that when God's angel began speaking with Joseph, he addressed him as "son of David?" The angel prefaced his message to Joseph as a gentle reminder that his ancestry was in the royal line of King David and if he named Jesus that would make Jesus a "son of David."

Joseph had to decide if he would name Mary's child or not—making Jesus a descendent of King David. Would he accept legal fatherhood of Jesus thus making Him an heir and son of David?

MARY'S SON WILL SAVE PEOPLE FROM THEIR SINS

Then, as if the angelic messenger of God had not already said enough, the angel proclaimed a cataclysmic announcement to Joseph. Mary's son would "save His people from their sins."

Why was this so important? It was more than important—it was galactic! In Joseph's mind, and in the mind of every Israelite, only God can save people from their sins.[19]

The magnitude of this announcement was also enormous because the Jewish people were looking for a political Messiah who would deliver them from Roman domination and then begin the restored Davidic kingdom on earth.

Joseph learned that Mary's son would deliver His people from a greater enemy than the Roman Empire—sin! Jesus would be a suffering-servant messiah and not a political deliverer.

> **Behold!** When Mary's son, Jesus, began His public ministry, He would NOT make a call for weapons, armor, espionage, and battle strategy against Rome, but He would call His people to repentance.[20] Jesus would also do what only Yahweh God can do, forgive sins,[21] shed His blood "for the forgiveness of sins,"[22] and die on a Roman cross "as a ransom for many."[23]

The words, "His people," implied the Biblical-remnant concept of a genuine Israel within national Israel. The Apostle Paul stated:

> "And Isaiah cries out concerning Israel, 'Though the number of the sons of Israel be as the sand of the sea, only a remnant of them will be saved, for the Lord will carry out his sentence upon the earth fully and without delay.'"[24]

Now, if you are a Bible Christian you are part of the faithful remnant of the saved. This remnant is not large in comparison to those who will go to hell.[25] We need to be thankful that we belong to the faithful remnant!

If you are not a Bible Christian then you still have the chance to be forgiven of all your sins and added to His Church.

MARY'S SON FULFILLS PROPHECY
MARY IS "THE" VIRGIN

Okay, back to Joseph.

The angel told Joseph that everything which had occurred, in reference to Mary and the son that she would deliver, fulfilled what the Lord spoke through the prophet Isaiah.[26] The Scripture of fulfillment concerning Mary's miraculous conception was Isaiah 7:14. It stated:

> "Therefore the Lord himself will give you a sign. Behold, the virgin shall conceive and bear a son, and shall call his name Immanuel" (Matt. 1:23).

Did you notice that Isaiah is very specific in that he didn't say "a virgin" will conceive, but THE ONE AND ONLY virgin will conceive and bear a son?

Isaiah's woman was a young woman who was at the marrying age of twelve, thus she lacked any sexual experience, i.e., she was a virgin.[27]

According to Matthew 1:23, Mary was the climatic fulfillment of the eighth century BC proclamation found in Isaiah 7:14 to David's house, the nation of Israel, and to all the Gentiles of the earth. And, those who Jesus saves will confess Him as Immanuel, which is translated "God is with us."

What did we just hear? More importantly, what did Joseph just hear?

Mary's son's name is "God is with us," i.e., this son was God himself. God the Son is now with us (mankind), in the womb of Mary, through the creative power of God the Holy Spirit.

Wow! Not only was Mary's son the Messiah, and a "son of David," He is Almighty God.

> **Behold!** Jesus was also named the Wonderful Counselor, Mighty God, Everlasting Father, Prince of Peace[28] and the "shoot from the stump of Jesse."[29]

Joseph was saying to himself, "Mary's son is God's Son and is also God with His people—affecting our deliverance. This is the ultimate manifestation of God's presence."

The importance of this statement was to ensure that we look for the fulfillment of Isaiah 7:14 not only in the virginal conception of Jesus, but in the whole complex series of events which "have come to pass" including conception, birth, and especially the naming of the child.

JOSEPH IMMEDIATELY OBEYS GOD

After God made his announcement, Joseph woke up, got up, and did exactly as he was told without hesitation or question.[30] Any questions that he may have had didn't exist anymore. This was a remarkable obedience and compared to Mary's humble obedience in Luke 1:38.

What did Joseph do? He rushed to Mary's home and lovingly took Mary to his house as his wife.

For Joseph to accept Mary as his wife required the public completion of the marriage by taking her to his own house ("the coming together" of Matt. 1:18), which would normally have been the point at which sexual relations began. But not in this case! We'll get to that in a minute!

Now, there was only one more course of action for Joseph to take. Would Joseph name Mary's son and officially accept him in a legal adoption as his legal son, heir, and as a "son of David?"

Yes, that was exactly what Joseph did. He named Mary's son "Jesus."

> **Behold!** The Greek name "Jesus" is the equivalent to the Hebrew name Joshua, i.e., "Yahweh saves." Jesus is Yahweh (God with us) who will save His people from their sins.

By accepting Mary as his wife and naming her son Jesus, Joseph completed the legal "adoption" of Jesus as his son and heir.

Are you impressed?

What really impresses me is Joseph's unquestionable obedience to God. What a model for me in my Christian life! What do you think about Joseph's obedience?

Let me reiterate! Joseph was obedient to God's command, first by taking Mary to his home as his wife and secondly, by giving her son the divinely appointed name, Jesus. Joseph's obedience demonstrated that he accepted Jesus as his own, thus legally adopting him into the Davidic line. As a son of David, Jesus came to liberate His people from the bondage of sin, and in doing so, He would mediate the divine presence as God's unique Son.

NO SEX UNTIL AFTER JESUS IS BORN

BUT, please make sure that you don't miss this next point.

The Bible very clearly states that once Joseph took Mary to his home he did NOT "know her," i.e., they did not have any sexual relations until AFTER her son, Jesus, was born.[31]

After Jesus was born, Joseph and Mary began normal husband and wife sexual relations. We know this to be true since Joseph and Mary had children after Jesus was born. These other children would have been Jesus' half-brothers and half-sisters.[32]

WHAT HAPPENED TO JOSEPH

What happened to Joseph?

Luke 2:41-52 states that Joseph and Mary were with the twelve-year-old Jesus in the temple. After this event, Joseph is not seen again.

Joseph treated Jesus as if He was his own son. He trained Jesus as a stonemason and they worked side-by-side. At some time in the future, Joseph died and Jesus, as the eldest son, would have taken over the family business.

John 6:42 is the last mention of Joseph in the New Testament. This passage states: "They said, "Is not this Jesus, the son of Joseph, whose father and mother we know?" Joseph is not mentioned again in the Scriptures.[33]

Whenever Joseph died, he was truly a remarkable man!

What do you think?

PART 2

UNWRAPPING THE BLESSED EVENT

CHAPTER 4

THE TRIP TO BETHLEHEM "NO DONKEY"

MARY:
And then I waited.

I waited for another seven days and another seven nights.

And then, without forewarning, there was a long-awaited knock on my father's door . . .

For a moment I felt faint, but my mother's hand was secure beneath my arm, and I steadied myself.

My father opened the door and there he was. *Joseph! It's Joseph!*

My father bid him come in, "Welcome, Joseph, to my home."

My mother stepped forward and welcomed Joseph, "Yes, you are welcome."

Joseph's eyes went past my mother to me, where I am standing alone. He was looking at me and I at him, and it was so peaceful that I could hear my heart briskly beating. How it sang!

For the first time Joseph smiled, a heartfelt glimmer that dispersed across his striking broad countenance.

With his smile I froze. Now, I couldn't hear my heart beating! However heart-stopping his grin and truthful his eyes, I was nervous. What would he say to me?

He took a step toward me, and then an additional one, until he had walked past my father and mother and I was face-to-face with him.

My heart beat wildly but I remained silent, listening and watching.

"Mary, I have come for you," Joseph said.

"The Lord spoke to me in a dream last night and told me about your child. I will name him Jesus, making him my legal heir and a son of David."

"Forgive me, Mary, for not believing you."

The tension was fierce and overpowering. Even though I wanted to, I didn't answer right away. I waited . . . waited . . . and waited.

"Well then?" he said with his virile but boyish grin.

I smiled up at him.

My eyes looked at my father for his permission. He nodded *yes* and smiled.

I eyed my giggling sisters in the corner of the room as they shared my delight.

I glanced over at Mother. She was rosy with blushes and her eyes were inundated with gleaming tears. With both arms she raised them and looked up into heaven and nodded her head as if to say, I told you so!

I beamed and nodded back.

I immediately remembered my words to my Mother that "no power on earth would get Joseph to change his decision." I was right—it was a divine heavenly power that did!

Then I finally spoke!

"Yes!" Oh Yes!"

My father asked, looking from my flushed teary face to Joseph, "Good—it is settled! My son, can we offer you some refreshment?"

Joseph turned from looking at my father and bent forward looking directly into my eyes and said:

"How about some of Mary's lentil stew!"

AN IMPERIAL INTERRUPTION

No sooner than Joseph had taken Mary to his home, an imperial decree from the Roman Emperor Caesar Augustus was announced that must be fulfilled.

In 8 BC, the Roman Emperor Caesar Augustus decreed that the Roman world should be enrolled/registered. He needed money to build a War Machine, a juggernaut to control his vast empire and to live in luxury himself.

Now roughly two years have passed since the Augustan Imperial Census was decreed and there was a delay because the Jewish people did not want to pay it. Order was finally brought to Israel and the census would be completed.

The word that is translated "taxed" is a form of the Greek *apographo*, which means, "to enter in a registry" and not taxation specifically. But, taxing the people was the common thing to also do. Everyone had to go back to his/her place of birth/origin, i.e., back to his/her ancestral home to be registered and taxed.

The administrative representative in the position to carry out the Augustan census in Israel was Quirinius. Although he was not the governor of Syria, he was exercising control over it.

This tax of Caesar Augustus was a census/head tax. Each person would pay a Roman silver denarius.[1] A denarius was a day's wage for a common worker and for a Roman soldier. Mary, along with all women, would also be accountable to go back to her place of origin.

If Joseph and Mary did not register and pay the tax, they would be charged with treason and revolutionary sentiment against Imperial Rome. The charge of treason meant death—death by Roman crucifixion.

So, in 6-5 BC, Joseph and the pregnant Mary, both being descendants of King David, had to go back to their ancestral home of origin—Bethlehem. Mary's pregnancy was at term and she could deliver her child at any moment. But, when the Emperor spoke and commanded—people listened and obeyed. Joseph and Mary were off to Bethlehem!

GOING "UP" TO BETHLEHEM

Mary and Joseph started their journey by "going up" from Nazareth of Galilee, in the northern part of Israel, down to Bethlehem of Judea.[2]

But how can this be? How can Mary and Joseph being in the northern part of Israel "go up" to Bethlehem when this town is south of Nazareth? There must be an error in the Bible—right?

Wrong! Perish the thought!

Here is the answer:

In topography, Bethlehem is at a higher elevation than the northern town of Nazareth. Therefore, for Joseph and Mary to travel from Nazareth of Galilee, going south to Bethlehem of Judea, they would travel "upward" to higher ground even though they were going from the north to the south.

Don't you love the easy answers?

"O LITTLE TOWN OF BETHLEHEM"

Bethlehem, a small town located in the fertile countryside five miles south of Jerusalem, was constructed in a 2,500-foot high grey limestone ridge. The ridge had a summit at each end and a valley like a saddle between the summits. Bethlehem looked like a town set in an amphitheater of hills. It was previously called Ephrath or Ephrathah. The name Bethlehem means the "House of Bread."

The little town of Bethlehem held historic significance. Rachel was buried there with a memorial pillar built by her tomb.[3] Rachel was the younger daughter of Laban, wife of Jacob, and the mother of Joseph and Benjamin, who became two of the twelve tribes of Israel.[4] Ruth also lived in Bethlehem when she married Boaz.[5]

> **Behold!** The little town of Bethlehem was the home and city of King David (1 Sam. 16:1; 17:12; 20:6), was later fortified by Rehoboam (2 Chron. 11:6), and was predicted to be the town where the Messiah would be born (Micah 5:2).

Now, Israel was divided into three districts: Galilee in the north, Samaria in the middle, and Judea in the south. If Joseph and Mary traveled straight from Nazareth in Galilee, through Samaria, to Bethlehem of Judea, it would be about a three-day journey on foot.

However, the Jewish people bypassed Samaria because they believed that the people living there, called the Samaritans, were the very worst race of people on planet earth.[6] Therefore, Samaria was off limits!

Because of Augustus' census decree, and their unwillingness to go through Samaria, Mary and Joseph most likely traveled southeast from Nazareth across the Plain of Esdraelon, down the Jordan River to Jericho, up to Jerusalem, and then on to Bethlehem.

WHY THE DETOUR

There are a few reasons why Joseph and Mary chose the long route instead of sneaking through Samaria. Who could blame them, with Mary ready to give birth at any moment, right? However, it was unthinkable.

To understand why, let's go back in time for a moment.

REASON #1: IDOL WORSHIP

When the ten tribes of Israel were conquered by the Assyrians and taken into captivity in 722 BC, the Assyrian king colonized Samaria with Assyrians from Cutha, Ava, Hamath, and Sepharvaim.[7]

The Assyrians (an extremely ungodly people) stayed in Samaria and intermarried with Jewish women, thus producing the offspring called the Samaritans.

At that time, the Samaritans adopted idol worship that was combined with the Jewish religion, i.e., a *syncretic* religion.[8]

Instead of worshipping in the temple in Jerusalem, the Samaritans built their own temple on Mount Gerizim and continued their idolatry. They rejected all of the thirty-nine books of the Old Testament except for the first five books of Moses, called the Torah or Pentateuch. This was absolutely unacceptable to the Jewish people.

REASON #2: CRIMINALS

We also know that criminals from Judea would flee to Samaria as a place of protection and refuge from Jewish justice.[9] Safety was a huge concern for travelers back then, as it is today, but at least our modern day vehicles offer protection from thugs hiding in the brush on the sides of the highways. This was not so in Joseph and Mary's day!

REASON #3: RACIAL DIVISION

As un-PC as this is, the truth of the matter is that the Jewish people considered the Samaritans "half-breeds" and had no associations with them.[10] Despite being God's people, the Jewish people hated and despised the Samaritans. Remember, it was Jesus who broke down the barriers between the Jews and the Samaritans by preaching the gospel of peace to the Samaritans,[11] and the apostles later followed His example.[12]

A DONKEY—WHAT DONKEY

Now, back to Mary and Joseph!

Their trip to Bethlehem was on the authoritarian decree of Caesar Augustus, but God used this census to get Mary to the city of David, Bethlehem, to fulfill the prophecy of Micah 5:1-2.

HOLLYWOOD IS WRONG AGAIN

Now, how did Joseph and, especially, Mary get to Bethlehem? Our twenty-first century counterfeit Christmas nativity scenes, Hollywood movies, and church pageants, have Mary riding a donkey.[13]

But where does the Bible tell us that Mary rode a donkey?

It doesn't.

In fact, I don't believe that she did.

JOSEPH AND MARY'S FINANCIAL SITUATION

Let's go forward to the time "after" Jesus birth (40 days later) when Joseph and Mary went to the temple to offer a sacrifice.

The sacrifice called for a lamb for the burnt offering and a turtledove as a sin offering.[14] However, if Jewish parents were too poor to buy a lamb, the law allowed for them to substitute two birds (turtledoves or pigeons), one for the burnt offering and the other for the sin offering.

LAMBS WERE EXPENSIVE

For example, for the Passover, the cost of a Paschal Lamb was not very affordable. A lamb cost three days' wages. Households would come together and share a lamb between them. You have to understand that a person worked from 6:00 am to 6:00 pm at night seven days a week. No weekends off! After each day of labor one would get paid for that day only.

That person would then buy food for his family for that night and the next morning and then begin the process over again the next day. If one did not get paid for a day's work, he and his family would likely not eat that day. So, three days' wages was an enormous sum of money for most people.

Joseph and Mary offered two birds for their sacrifice, which demonstrated that they were poor indeed.

With this in mind, if Joseph and Mary could not even afford a lamb to offer as a sacrifice, how could they possibly afford a donkey for Mary to ride to Bethlehem? The wealthy owned donkeys. A donkey would have cost considerably more than a lamb that they could not afford for their sacrifice.

So, please take Mary off that donkey! Our modern counterfeit Christmas nativity scenes need to remove the donkeys.

Now, I hope that I don't sound cruel. I really do hope that Mary rode a donkey to Bethlehem. But, the Biblical evidence does not support such a vehicle of transportation for her.

The pregnant Mary walked!

MARY'S ROAD—REALLY A PATH

The last time I was in Israel, I went to Nazareth during the hot summer months. I was told that the modern paved highway from

Nazareth to Bethlehem was built right by the ancient road that Mary and Joseph (and all other travelers) traveled those many years ago.

I had to see the road that the pregnant Mary walked all the way to Bethlehem.

When it was time for me to leave Nazareth, I was in an air-conditioned vehicle traveling on a nice paved highway to Bethlehem.

Now, I knew that the ancient road was to my right as I traveled. But, during the first few miles, I didn't see any kind of road. As I continued down the road for a number of miles, I still didn't see the road used by Mary and Joseph.

Getting perplexed as I saw nothing but rugged terrain to my right, it hit me like a bolt of lightning!

Foolish me, I was looking for a nice straight flat road. But, that kind of "modern" road did not exist in the time of Mary and Joseph.

The road, *if you can call it a road,* was basically a path that people (in caravans or individuals) would travel on. That terrain was extremely rugged.

That poor young woman walked that three-to-nine day journey on foot.

While women in the ancient world would work and travel right up to the time that labor pains began, the discomfort she must have gone through is unimaginable for me.

As Joseph and Mary set out for Bethlehem, Mary is doing pretty well. But a few miles down the road Mary is having some difficulty.

IMAGINE WITH ME

Joseph:

Mary stopped walking. "Joseph my back is hurting and my hips are sore. The baby is putting pressure on my lower back."

"Let's stop and rest," I replied. "I'll rub your back, hopefully you will feel better."

After some time had passed, we were back on the path.

I could see that Mary was growing increasingly tired to the point of exhaustion. My heart went out to her!

"My husband, I just don't have the energy to walk anymore."

"Here, eat this bread. It will give you a boost of energy. We have a little bit of cheese, pieces of fruit, and some vegetables. After you eat, try to sleep."

Mary replied, "I'm not sleeping well, I can't seem to get enough sleep."

"I know, try! I'll pray for you!" I said.

We continued our arduous trek to Bethlehem on the orders of the Roman Emperor, Caesar Augustus—but more importantly to fulfill God's prophetic will.

Finally, Mary and I stood together gazing toward Samaria. The day's light extinguished and the night grew dark and silent.

"My husband, can we journey through Samaria just this once?"

I replied, "No it is not safe for us."

"Yes, you are right."

Road weary, we passed vanishing trees and acres of farmland where sowers would sow their seed in just a few months.

As time and miles passed, it became nightfall again.

"My wife, let's stop for the night. I'll build a fire. You rest. Are you ankles swelling?"

"Yes, just a little bit."

"I have a rock for you to put your feet up on. Rest my wife while I get our camp ready and something for you to eat."

Mary tried to make herself as comfortable as she could.

"Mary, dinner is ready. I made some lentils and onions."

For a moment, Mary watched me as I stirred the pot.

After retrieving another spoon from a bag, she dipped the tip into the lentil stew and tasted it.

I could tell by the look on her face that this wasn't going well.

"This is … um, good," she commented, raising her eyebrows.

I wasn't quite sure how to respond, and I thought she saw this in my expression, for she laughed almost immediately.

"It's okay, my husband. Let's just say charred lentils and onions are an acquired taste!"

I smiled, knowing what she said may not be that true. My first experience as a cook had been less than an earth-shattering success.

As the night passed, I made sure that Mary was well guarded and protected.

As we settled down for sleep, I put Mary next to the fire. I took my outer garment and covered her. Then I used myself as a blanket to cover Mary in order to keep her warm.

"How's that? Are you warm?"

She drew a long breath, hiding the weariness in her tone. "Yes, Joseph, I am very warm and content with you."

At daybreak, our journey continued to our destination of Bethlehem.

It had been drizzling on and off all day—just teasing us. Looked like a good storm was rolling in from the Mediterranean.

"My wife, has the nausea left you?" I asked.

She nodded "yes" with a shaky smile.

The rainy weather persisted on and off through the next couple of days.

Mile after mile slipped into the past. Mary lowered her gaze, watching her endless steps as she walked on wobbly legs.

"Jericho is in sight," I said with excitement. "There we will rest."

After a well needed break we traveled to Jerusalem and then just five more miles to Bethlehem!

Even though the goal was in sight—those last five miles seemed like fifty.

It was getting late in the evening and it was dark.

"There's Bethlehem, my wife. We made it. The Lord has been good and merciful to us."

"Oh, my husband, the town is a most welcomed sight."

"I will immediately look to secure an upper guest room for us," I replied.

"Yes, for us—and for one more, Joseph. The time of His arrival is at hand. Please hurry."

"Mary, we can travel to Elizabeth's home if you are ready to deliver."

"No, she is too far from us. We don't have enough time. Bethlehem is the place where my son will be born—not by the decree of Caesar Augustus, but by the prophetic will of God."

We walked onward.

Suddenly, looking straight ahead, we saw a magnificent yet inhospitable sight—the outskirts of the little town of Bethlehem.

"Come my wife—we have arrived!"

NOW, please indulge me in that my heart goes out to Mary for her endurance during that arduous trip to Bethlehem. She was faithful and made the journey, fulfilling the most powerful man's edict to register. More importantly, she went to Bethlehem to fulfill the omnipotent Creator God's prophecy that the Messiah, the God-man, would be born in the city of David, Bethlehem.

MARY HAD NO CHOICE

Now, let's think about something together, okay?

It was mandatory for Mary to make this journey to Bethlehem. This tax of Caesar Augustus demanded all men and women to register—Mary had no choice.

Joseph was so loving and sweet to Mary.

The blessed event is about to happen.

But, where the birth took place will surprise you!

It did me.

CHAPTER 5

THE ARRIVAL IN BETHLEHEM "NO UPPER GUEST ROOM"

MARY AND JOSEPH ARRIVE IN BETHLEHEM
BUT . . .

AFTER THAT ARDUOUS journey from Nazareth to Bethlehem, Joseph and Mary finally arrived in Bethlehem to register for the Augustan census. After their arrival in Bethlehem, Luke 2:7 notes that there was no room for them in the inn.

We do not know how long Joseph and Mary had been in Bethlehem, but as I read the text of Luke 2:6, it seems to me that Mary and Joseph had not been in Bethlehem that long.

We are told that "while" they were there in Bethlehem, the days for her to give birth were fulfilled, i.e., it was time for Mary to give birth (Luke 2:6), in fulfillment of the prophecy of Micah 5:1-2.[1]

We are told that while Joseph and Mary were in Bethlehem, they could not secure a place for Mary to give birth, with modern translations saying "there was no room in the inn for them."[2] But, this sounds like there was no hotel available for Joseph and Mary.

Does it sound like a hotel to you, too?

Well, this is completely an inaccurate translation.

NO UPPER GUEST ROOM AVAILABLE

We all remember from "the counterfeit Christmas" that has been told that there was a bad innkeeper who refused Mary and Joseph. But, where does the Bible say this? It doesn't! The bad innkeeper is part of the counterfeit Christmas story of the birth of Jesus.

The idea of an "inn or hotel" is the creation of our western culture and did not exist in Bethlehem. What Luke actually says in Luke 2:7 is that there was no "upper guest room" available for Mary and Joseph.

The word "upper guest room" (*kataluma*) was NOT a hotel in any sense of the word.

The *kataluma* was a private "upper-room" called the "guest room." The upper level of a two-story home was where a family lived. Each Jewish family had their guest room in that upper level available for family, friends, and strangers.

THE TYPICAL TWO-STORY JEWISH HOME

What would a home in Bethlehem look like?

Let's find out!

Because the houses were built on the slopes of the limestone ridge, the people of Bethlehem often hollowed a cave-like stable out of the limestone rock below the upper second floor of their homes.

So, the typical peasant Jewish home had two stories. Again, when the town of Bethlehem was built, it was cut right into a high rock area. The family lived in the upper quarters and their animals were stabled on the ground floor. There were no separate stables from one's dwelling place in the ancient world.

THE UPPER GUEST ROOM

The upper guest room was located in the second floor of a two-story Jewish home. This upper floor had an outlet for a chimney with a fire to provide cooked daily meals and warmth for the family.

Luke used the definite article "the," i.e., it was THE guest room in the upper floor of a home that was not provided for Mary.

Luke used the very same word for "upper room" in Luke 22:11-12.[3] In this scripture passage Jesus said to his disciples:

> "and tell the master of the house, 'The Teacher says to you, Where is the guest room, where I may eat the Passover with my disciples?' And he will show you a *large upper room* (*kataluma*) furnished; prepare it there" (*emphasis mine*).[4]
>
> **Behold!** When Doctor Luke tells us about the tax collector Zacchaeus who brought Jesus home for table-fellowship, i.e., to share a meal, Luke says that Jesus went "to be the guest" [*kataluo*] at Zacchaeus' house.[5]

So, Luke used the noun *kataluma* for an upper guest room in a family's upper story of their two-story house. Luke also used the verb *kataluo* to refer to a guest, Jesus, who would stay in the upper guest room of Zacchaeus' home.

NOT A COMMERCIAL INN

Luke even used a different word than *kataluma* in the parable of the Good Samaritan in Luke 10:34, 36. He used the word *pandokheion*, which was the word for a lodging place, i.e., a commercial inn. The Good Samaritan took the injured man, put him on his animal, and brought him to an inn (*pandokheion*).

This inn (*pandokheion*) was not what you and I think of when we hear the word "inn." This ancient inn was an outdoor raised terrace (on the ground) where a traveler would pay for a space to sleep on that terrace floor. One's animals were also kept right there with all of the lodgers. So, even in a commercial inn, there were no rooms, but only spaces on the floor to pay for. It was a far cry from our Embassy Suites and Comfort Inns.

> **Behold!** An inn (*pandokheion*) was an absolutely unsuitable place for a woman to give birth. To pay for a space with men all around her was unthinkable. These inns were located on major roads outside of larger towns. Because Bethlehem was a small town, it had no inn (*pandokheion*).

To reiterate, Bethlehem didn't have any hotels. The Greek word *kataluma* is the furnished upper guest room on the second story of a two-story home, and that's what Mary and Joseph were asking for when they arrived in Bethlehem.

A COLD, DAMP, STINKING, URINE/FECES FILLED FIRST FLOOR OF SOMEONE'S HOME

Again, when Luke wrote that there was no room in the inn, he meant that no one was willing to give Mary an upper guest room in their two-story home. The only option for Mary and Joseph was a cold, damp, smelly and urine/feces filled ground floor of someone's two-story home where animals were kept. Someone finally gave in and allowed them to stay there. Thus, Jesus was born in a first-floor of a Jewish peasant home.

This first-floor had no outlet for a chimney to make a fire and animal droppings and urine would have been all over the rock floor.

Stabling the animals within the house protected them from the weather, predators, and from theft. Some of the animals provided milk and cheese for the family's daily meals. The dung was used for fuel and fertilizer. Tools and agricultural produce were also stored in the rock first-floor.

If a large number of people were traveling for this Augustan census, it is possible that all upper guest rooms were taken. But, I believe there were other motives in play in Bethlehem that night.

Mary had to settle for a cold, damp, stinking, urine/feces-filled first floor of someone's two-story home where animals were kept safe and locked up at night time.

HOSPITALITY
NONE FOR JOSEPH AND MARY

In those days, births always took place in the warmth of the second floor of a Jewish home and nowhere else. The soon-to-be-mothers were always provided special help but this was not the case for Mary.

It was customary for Jewish people to allow strangers to stay in the upper-guest rooms of their homes so that they would not have to stay at an inn—if their town had one. This was the famous "Jewish hospitality" that the Law of Moses prescribed.[6]

We find this special Jewish hospitality demonstrated by Lot in Genesis 19:1-4, the man in Gibeah in Judges 19:19-21, and by the Shunamite woman, who built a "guest room" for the Prophet Elisha in 2 Kings 4:10.

If Joseph and Mary had been welcomed in a Jewish home, even with the upper-room full, that host or master of the house would NEVER have turned a pregnant Mary away from having her child in that upper-room. It would have been unthinkable to send her to a cold, damp, stinking, urine/feces filled first floor of someone's home with the animals. The host or master would have made arrangements for the expectant Mary. But, this is not what happened.

THE RETURNING SON

Let's go back to Joseph for a moment. He is a "son of David" and has just returned to his ancestral home of Bethlehem. It is logical that Joseph had relatives living in Bethlehem. Remember that special Jewish hospitality is a must, being commanded by the Law of Moses.

And, a "returning son," like Joseph, coming back home, would have been royally treated. A host or master of a house would have given his own family room for Mary and Joseph.

But, this is not the case.

A "returning son" would have insulted his family and friends if he had gone to stay at a commercial inn. So, Joseph would not have done so.

Here's the point!

No one, no friend, stranger, or relative of Joseph provided Mary an upper guest room for her to give birth in. This was the *ultimate* insult for Jewish people. It begs the question, why was Joseph treated this way?

Perhaps Joseph's family in Bethlehem rejected him because they had heard of Mary's "early" pregnancy and they might have believed that she was unfaithful to him. We do not know.

What we do know for certain is that "no-one" would rent/provide a proper place for Mary to give birth.

NO PALACE FOR A KING

Do you get the sense of this?

The second person of the Godhead—God the Son, who is the Creator of the universe, who holds it together, who is the King of Kings—was not going to be born in a palace fit for royalty. Nor would he be born in the comfort that all Jewish newborns were entitled to.

In fact, Jesus was not even born in a warm manger of fresh straw with a crackling fire in a sweet-smelling barn like our modern day nativity scenes display.

No, our modern day nativity scenes are wrong. They are counterfeit Christmases!

Now, journey back with me to that time when Joseph and Mary arrived in Bethlehem.

IMAGINE WITH ME

Mary:

Joseph and I entered into the neighborhood of Bethlehem; a moment later, we walked to the first home that we came into contact with and I roused myself with a weary smile.

"Sorry about being so quiet. I guess I'm sort of tired," I whispered.

Joseph grabbed my hand and said, "It's okay. It's been a long journey. There's a home here. Mary, stay here and I will secure an upper guest room for us."

"Hurry Joseph," I replied.

After some time passed, Joseph did not return

I continued to wait for Joseph—but no Joseph.

Finally, Joseph came running back to me.

He said, "No one is willing to rent us an upper guest room, but I did manage to acquire a room for us."

I smiled. "Good," I said softly.

Joseph then took me to a nice home. I stared toward the house in thanksgiving and praise. Silhouetted against the other homes, it was a welcomed image; the upper second floor looked like a palace and was just the place that I needed. Oh, to be warm again! My hopes rose.

Joseph said, "Here's where we will spend the night."

"My husband, can we afford this?" I said in exhaustion.

Joseph did not reply.

But Joseph escorted me, not up into the upper guest room where it was warm and cozy, but into the animals' housing—the first floor of that nice home. My eyes widened. For just a moment, I was frozen, unable to speak.

As we entered the first floor, I stood at the entrance, staring into the animal living quarters. I walked in. It took my eyes a moment to focus—resting first on Joseph, then to the animals in the room, then back on Joseph. I blinked as if awakening from a dream.

I glanced up at the rock ceiling and seemed to be steadying myself before turning my gaze on Joseph. There was no warm fire. I turned slowly from side to side.

Looking at Joseph, I met his eyes. They seemed to be sparkling with unshed tears.

I blinked my eyes rapidly and gave a small sniff.

Yes, that aroma was fresh animal urine and feces.

"Joseph . . . it's . . . here?" I asked.

Joseph took my hand. He too could smell the exotic perfume of the animals all over the rock floor.

"This was all that was available. There was no upper guest room available," Joseph apologetically replied. "This was the best that I could find."

Joseph looked at me and I am sure that my expression was full of questions as I faced him.

But I didn't say a word. I waited . . . and . . . waited . . . and waited.

I looked around and knew that my choice was either this or delivering my baby outside.

"I couldn't have dreamed of anything better. It's better than a palace!" I said.

I laughed, and feeling the tension break, I put my hand on his and squeezed it.

"Yes, a palace!"

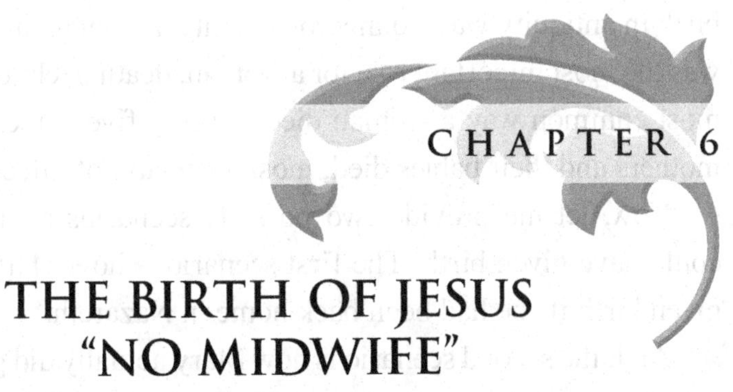

CHAPTER 6

THE BIRTH OF JESUS "NO MIDWIFE"

MARY'S FIRSTBORN SON

MARY'S TIME HAD come; she was in a cold, damp, stinking, urine/feces-filled first floor of someone's two-story home. And then it happened!

Mary gave birth to her firstborn son.[1]

The word "firstborn" indicates that she later had other children with her husband, Joseph. Since Jesus had no earthly father, these children would have been His half-brothers and half-sisters.

The word "firstborn" is also significant in that Jesus was Joseph's legal heir and was the one who had the right to Joseph's inheritance. This is why Joseph naming Jesus (that we discussed in a previous chapter) was so important.

THE BIRTHING PROCESS

Have you ever wondered "how" Mary gave birth without a bed, boiling water, and a doctor to help? In our modern twenty-first century world, most women lie down or recline to deliver their babies, but no woman in the ancient world knew how to lie down to give birth.

In that cave-like stable of a two-story peasant home, Mary settled amidst the animals and gave birth to her firstborn—Jesus. Giving birth in antiquity was a dangerous reality. Although having children was the most important role for a woman, death in childbirth was the most common way a woman died. Twenty-five percent of birthing mothers and their babies died, mostly because of infection.[2]

Now, let me provide two possible scenarios about how Mary could have given birth. The first scenario is how Mary would have given birth if she had been back home in Nazareth.[3]

And, the second scenario is how Mary actually did give birth in a cold, damp, stinking, urine/feces filled first floor of someone's home.

CHILDBIRTH
IF MARY HAD BEEN AT HOME IN NAZARETH

First, if Mary had been at home in Nazareth, how would she have delivered her child? Have you ever thought about that?

A MIDWIFE AND TWO ASSISTANTS

If Mary had been at home in Nazareth, a midwife, not a physician, would have been assigned to her. Physicians did not deliver babies unless there was some kind of complication. The job of delivering babies belonged to the midwives. Mary's assigned midwife would have been in charge of the entire process of giving birth.[4]

Mary's midwife would have had two female assistants who were in training to become midwives. They would have assisted for the entire time of labor and delivery.

ALL THE WOMEN WERE PRESENT

We know that Mary's mother, mother-in-law, grandmothers, sisters, cousins, female friends from Nazareth, and all of the little girls of the village would have been present at Mary's delivery. This would have created a tremendous support system for Mary. Recent research has shown how important emotional support is while giving birth.[5]

Why would little girls from the village of Nazareth be present to watch the birthing process?

Remember that girls around the age of five could already cook, sew, and take care of a household. In just a few years, around age twelve, these girls will be viewed as women and would be looking to get engaged and possibly have their first child within the next year.

These little girls must know how to give birth so they would have been present at Mary's delivery—"if" Mary had been at Nazareth.

WHAT ABOUT MEN

What about husbands—the men? Would men have been present when babies were born? Great questions!

Well, men did not participate in the delivery of babies because it was seen as women's work. Only women were involved in the birthing process in the ancient world. Men never helped with childbirth because it was the work of women. It wasn't until a few decades ago in our time that men were even allowed into the hospital birthing rooms with their wives.

WALKING AND THE BIRTHING CHAIR

Fortunately for a young woman like Mary, she was taught how to "self-deliver" and how to take care of the newborn child herself. But, where would Mary have lain down to give birth?

She wouldn't have! No woman would have lain down to give birth. Women would have sat on a stone chair called a "birthing chair/stool." Some midwives would have had their own birthing chairs or stools, but every Jewish town had a number of "birthing chairs" which were chiseled out of stone.[6]

But when a woman began to go into labor, the two assistants of the midwife would have positioned themselves on both sides of the mother and held onto her as they walked with her—outside!

It didn't matter if it was inclement weather or not. If labor came—you walked! The assistants would have walked the mother to get the baby to drop into position for delivery and to get her water to break. Labor might have lasted for hours, depending on the individual woman, just like it does today.

Why were there two female assistants?

If hours passed in the process of labor the mother would become too tired to continue to walk, the two assistants would hold up the mother and drag her on her feet, if need be, until the baby dropped and her water broke.

Once the expectant mother's water had broken, she would have been taken into a house where the midwife was waiting for her.

The midwife would have been sitting on the birthing chair, waiting for the expectant mother. The pregnant woman would have sat on the midwife's lap and a cloth would have been placed between her legs.

Yes, you heard me right!

Mary, along with every woman in the ancient world, would have sat up when delivering babies. And she would have sat on the lap of the midwife who was sitting on the birthing chair itself.

> **Behold!** In Old Testament times women gave birth sitting on another person's knees (like a chair). We are told that Rachel's maid gave birth to a child, "upon my [Rachel's] knees" (Gen. 30:1-3). And: ". . . the children also of Machir . . . were born upon Joseph's knees" (Gen. 50:23). Exodus 1:16 states that after the Exodus in 1446 BC, Hebrew women sat on a "birthing stool (chair)" while giving birth.[7]

The midwife would have then put her arms around the expectant mother and would have begun pushing on her in a downward motion.

In this situation, the two female assistants would have been on both sides of Mary. They, too, would each have pushed downward on Mary's sides. Plus, Mary would have been doing her part too!

As the baby was born, the assistants would have caught the baby. They, along with Mary, would have begun to clean the baby and wash it.

The umbilical cord would have been tied and cut around two minutes after birth. The midwife would have allowed the placenta to separate itself from the uterine wall and then would have had Mary push to expel it. Once the placenta was delivered, it would have been wrapped in a cloth to be thrown away.

There would have been great joy and a festive time of celebration for Mary, her family, friends, and neighbors—"if" Mary had been back home in Nazareth.

Unfortunately for Mary, she was a long way away from home in Nazareth, her mother, mother-in-law, her sisters, cousins, friends, and neighbors. She was alone in Bethlehem. And, remember that no one had provided her a suitable place, "an upper guest room," to give birth.

But, was Mary really alone? Who was with Mary?

You are correct!

Her loving husband Joseph!

CHILDBIRTH IN BETHLEHEM WHAT REALLY HAPPENED

So, how did Mary really give birth to her firstborn son, the child who would be named Jesus? There was no midwife assigned to Mary and no two assistants to walk with Mary once her labor began. And there was no "birthing chair" for Mary to sit upon as her son was being born.

Mary did not have her support system of relatives and friends. She only had one person—Joseph, who was completely untrained for delivering a baby. But Joseph, being an exceptional man, would have assisted Mary in any way that he could. Little did Joseph know that he was in for a once-in-a-lifetime experience!

THE SONG "SILENT NIGHT"

What about the modern song "Silent Night?" Was Jesus' birth really silent?

Good question.

Joseph Mohr, an Austrian Catholic priest, wrote the lyrics to "Silent Night" in 1816. Later, in 1818, a schoolmaster and organist named Franz Xaver Gruber composed the carol or song "Silent Night." This song was later published in English, in the form that we are today all familiar with, by an Episcopal priest named John Freeman Young in 1859.

The song speaks of the birth of Jesus being silent and calm.

Well, no!

Mothers, you will back me up on this one!

Now, I do believe that through all the trauma of giving birth, the cries of baby Jesus were a sweet melodious symphony in the night for Joseph and especially for Mary.

LABOR PAINS BEGIN IN BETHLEHEM

When the labor pains began, Mary would have started walking. With no midwife and her two assistants to aid Mary, she would have asked Joseph to grab her and hold her and escort her outside.

We don't know how cold it was, but I believe that it was in the wintertime.

We don't know how long Mary was in labor, but Joseph would have walked Mary around and around and back and forth, helping speed her delivery until her water broke. Remember, Mary had already walked 80-100 miles to get to Bethlehem!

When the time of her delivery came, Mary only knew that she must sit on a birthing chair/stool or on the lap of a midwife who was sitting on a birthing chair to deliver her baby. No birthing chair! No midwife!

Friends, we've got a problem in Bethlehem!

There was really nothing for Mary to sit on. It was just a rock area where animals, tools, feed, etc., were kept for safety. But—Joseph could stand in the place of the midwife! Mary could sit on his lap, but there was no birthing chair for Joseph to sit on.

As Mary thought about it, she knew that there was only one thing that Joseph could sit on for him to become a chair.

Think about it … this is a hard one!

Yes, you got it—the stone feed trough!

The only thing that Joseph could possibly sit on was the hollowed-out feed trough that was used to feed the animals. It would be about two feet off the rock floor.

Joseph would have taken his place sitting on the feed trough. Mary would then have sat on Joseph's lap.

A cloth would have been placed on the stone floor under Mary to prevent her baby from coming into contact with the dirt, urine, and animal droppings.

Mary would have had to tell Joseph to put his arms around her and start pressing on her from the top of her abdomen, pushing in a downward motion, just like a midwife would have done. By bracing against Joseph's body, Mary would have pushed. Mary would have begun to press on both of her sides with every contraction, just like the two assistants would have done.

With only Joseph and the animals as witnesses, Mary self-delivered, subjecting herself to the forces squeezing her body and to gravity.

Once Mary's baby was born, she would have caught and held her baby.

CUTTING THE UMBILICAL CORD

Mary would have started to clean and wash baby Jesus. She would then have tied off the umbilical cord and cut it around two minutes after giving birth. Now, you need to sit down to hear the next part. Mary would have cut the umbilical cord with a—A PIECE OF BREAD!

That's right!

Soranus, the Greek gynecologist, tells us that if a woman was too poor to afford a new knife, she would use a piece of old hard bread.[8]

No one sterilized medical instruments until our modern time. I believe Mary cut the cord with a piece of bread. Now, the bread was not like the bread that we buy in supermarkets or grocery stores. This bread would have hardened and could be used to saw through the cord.

There was no sterilization of knives or anything else in Mary's time to prevent infection. Even a new knife would not have been sterilized and would have cost a tidy sum of money. Mary would have used a hard piece of bread to cut the umbilical cord.

How crazy is that!

Mary would then have wiped baby Jesus, cleansed His skin with salt and oil, and swaddled Him in the only extra cloth she had.

IMAGINE WITH ME

Mary:

"Joseph, my husband, I'm in labor. You have to hold on to me and walk with me—outside."

"Walk? Mary, we have just walked one hundred miles," Joseph replied.

"Yes, walk with me."

Joseph held on to me and we went outside in the dark and started to walk me back and forth. How long? I don't know!

Joseph told me, "Here, put on my outer garment. How are you doing, my wife? Your hands are cold. Let me rub them as we walk."

"I will let you know when it's time to go inside."

It seemed like days of walking.

Once my water broke, I told Joseph to take me back inside.

Once inside, Joseph left me and said, "Let me move these animals to the back. I have a cloth that I will soak up the urine and I will gather the animal droppings and throw them outside. Just wait for me—I will not be long."

"Hurry Joseph!"

After a few minutes, Joseph returned.

"I'm here now. How can I help you?"

I looked around the dark rock room. There was no place to sit. Only Joseph was present and he didn't know what to do.

But, I knew.

There wasn't a birthing chair or stool. I had no lap of a midwife to sit upon and there wasn't really anything for Joseph to sit on. Then I spotted it—the animal feed trough from where animals ate!

"Joseph, you're going to become a chair," I exclaimed. "Sit on the feed trough and place a cloth in front of you. Let me sit on your lap. Okay, now put your arms around me and press on my stomach in a downward motion."

"Like this," Joseph asked?

"Yes, that's right."

With only Joseph and the animals as witnesses, I self-delivered, subjecting myself to the forces squeezing my body and to gravity.

Once my baby was born, I caught and held my son.

Immediately I started to wipe baby Jesus. "Joseph, hand me that piece of bread," I said. I then tied off the umbilical cord and cut it around two minutes after giving birth.

My placenta was delivered and Joseph wrapped it in the cloth and took it outside to be discarded.

I wiped baby Jesus, cleansed His skin with salt and oil, and Joseph and I swaddled Him in the only extra cloth we had, and fed him.

"Now my little lamb, have a nice long sleep," I whispered moments later, looking down into the face of my son.

Isn't God good in His mercies!

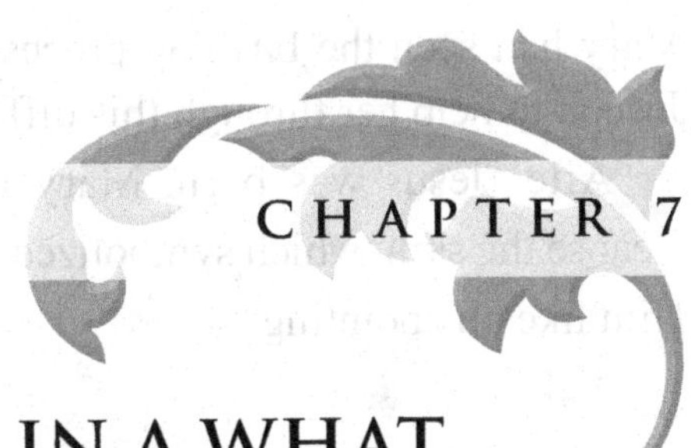

CHAPTER 7

WRAPPED IN A WHAT "NO BLUE OR WHITE BLANKET"

ONE BIRTH NARRATIVE

JESUS HAS BEEN born!

Halleluiah!

Glory to God in the highest!

Now, it is mistakenly believed that there are two narratives of Jesus' birth: Matthew 1:18-2:23 and Luke 2:1-20. But, in fact, Luke 2:1-20 is the *one* and only narrative account of Jesus' birth (Luke 2:1-20). Now, it is true that Matthew just mentions the birth when he said:

> "When Joseph woke from sleep, he did as the angel of the Lord commanded him: he took his wife, but knew her not until she had given birth to a son. And he called his name Jesus" (Matt. 1:24).

Matthew does not give any details on Jesus' birth. Only Luke provides the details in Luke 2:1-20.

MARY WASHES BABY JESUS

Yes, Jesus was born in extremely undesirable conditions—in a cold, damp, stinking, urine/feces filled first floor of someone's home. There was no birthing chair, no midwife, and no assistants. Though

Mary had seen the birthing process numerous times, she only had Joseph to help her through this difficult time.

After Jesus was born, Mary washed baby Jesus with salt to cleanse the skin, which symbolized truth and honesty. She then oiled Him like an anointing.

MARY AND JOSEPH SWADDLE BABY JESUS

After baby Jesus was cleansed, Mary and Joseph swaddled (snugly wrapped) baby Jesus to keep Him warm and to help keep His limbs straight.

> **Behold!** "Swath" (*sparganoo*) means "to clothe in strips of cloth." That is exactly what Mary and Joseph did with her newborn son. She wrapped Him in strips of cloth, with enough room at the bottom of the cloths so that baby Jesus could bend and stretch His legs up and out from His body, exactly how many mothers swaddle their babies today.

Interestingly, once a baby was swaddled, the baby feels comforted and soothed. Mary and Joseph tightly wrapped Jesus' body to comfort the child, provide a proper posture, and protect the baby's tiny limbs. The swaddling would make the newborn child feel protected like it was in his mother's womb. Swaddling also helped the baby to sleep and helped the baby's nervous system to develop. It was the belief at the time that a swaddled baby would grow up to be tall and righteous.

NO BLUE OR WHITE BLANKET

Remember those counterfeit Christmas nativity scenes that you see at Christmas time? Most of them have baby Jesus wrapped in either a blue or white blanket. He looks so pleasant, warm, and regally draped with blankets of color. But, the truth is that there were no blue or white blankets for baby Jesus!

Sorry!

You see, the colors of blue and, especially, white would have cost a small fortune to own. They were the colors of royalty. They were colors that the first Roman Emperor, Caesar Augustus, could afford but were not the colors that two poor Israelites from Nazareth could afford.

During the time of Mary and Joseph, white was the color of wealthy politicians from the Roman Senate. White was extremely difficult to manufacture and to keep clean. It was very expensive.

So, Joseph and Mary, who could not afford a donkey for Mary to ride upon to Bethlehem and who were not even able to afford a lamb to sacrifice when they took Jesus to the temple,[1] did not possess expensive white or blue blankets.

SHEPHERDS SWADDLED PERFECT LAMBS

In his Gospel, Luke tells us that on the night Jesus was born there were shepherds tending their flocks near Bethlehem. Luke states:

> "And in the same region there were shepherds out in the field, keeping watch over their flock by night" (Luke 2:8).

We know that this was the time of lambing season in Israel. Once the little lambs were born, shepherds would swaddle these newborn lambs to keep them from injury. These lambs were bred for later use, to be sacrificed as atonement for the people's sins in the Jewish temple during Passover.

FIRSTBORN LAMBS WITHOUT BLEMISH

These special young lambs had to be "firstborn" and "without spot or blemish." Jesus likewise was firstborn and was without spot or blemish, i.e., as a human being, Jesus never sinned, not even one time. Yes, Jesus is God, but He is also a perfect sinless man.[2]

If the temple lambs were injured in any way, they would be disqualified for sacrifice so swaddling was the normal course of action. Once a lamb was swaddled, it would be placed in an animal's feed trough. Later, after the lamb calmed down, it would be "unswaddled" and given back to its mother for nursing.

> **Behold!** There was a place just outside of Bethlehem, but still within the region commonly known as Bethlehem, where specially trained shepherds kept Passover lambs. These lambs were born in the "tower of the flock" known as Migdal Eder.
>
> Born under the watchful eyes of the shepherds, the lambs would be inspected and either certified for use as sacrifices in the temple or designated to be released for common use. The new lambs would be wrapped in special swaddling cloths once certified.

MARY KNOWS WHO JESUS IS

Mary knew the identity of her little baby. Now, this does not mean that she knew everything—she didn't—but Mary knew that her son is the Messiah, the God-man. She also knew her Old Testament Scriptures. She was very familiar with the prophecies from Isaiah 53:4-12 and Psalm 22:14, 18.

The angelic messenger Gabriel had already told Mary that:

1. God has favored her;
2. God will be with her;
3. She, as a virgin, will conceive and give birth to a son;
4. This son will be great;
5. This son will be called the Son of the Most High;
6. This son will be given the throne of David;
7. This son will reign over the house of Jacob forever;
8. This son's kingdom will never end;
9. This son will be called holy; and
10. This son is the Son of God.

Mary knew that Jeremiah 11:19 and Isaiah 53:7 spoke of the coming Messiah being brought "like a lamb led to the slaughter"[3] and whose sufferings and sacrifice would provide redemption for Israel.

As Mary and Joseph swaddled baby Jesus, Mary's wonderment and awe burst forth from her.

> **Behold!** There is a beautiful 1991 song titled "Mary Did You Know." Mark Lowry wrote the lyrics of this lovely song with the music written by Buddy Greene. The lyrics of the song ask if Mary really knows the true identity of her newborn son. The answer is, yes! Mary knows!

SWADDLED IN A WHAT

So, Mary and Joseph swaddled baby Jesus just like any good Jewish parents would have done. But when they wrapped their perfect little lamb, they swaddled Him just like the shepherds did to the perfect newborn lambs that would later be sacrificed in the Jewish Temple.

What did Mary and Joseph wrap baby Jesus in? That's a great question. Thanks for asking!

Mary and Joseph needed strips of cloth 4-6 inches in width and

15-20 feet long to properly swaddle baby Jesus. Where did they get them?

The only available cloth long enough to swaddle baby Jesus would have been the linen burial garments that Mary and Joseph wore around their waists.

"Now wait a minute! Are you telling us that Mary and Joseph wrapped up baby Jesus in a burial garment like a little dead person?"

Yes, I am!

Here's the explanation.

In the ancient world when people journeyed long distances away from home, they wrapped a gauzelike cloth around their waists. If a person died while traveling away from home, he had to be buried where he died.

Jewish custom insisted on prompt burial as a matter of respect for the dead, a consideration of particular relevance in hot climates.

> **Behold!** Deuteronomy 21:23 refers to hanged criminals being buried the day they died. But, because the climate was so hot in Israel, the body would rapidly decay and smell. To allow a body to decay was disrespectful. Remember that the Israelites did not cremate like the Romans nor mummify like the Egyptians.

As Joseph unwound his burial garment and tore it into strips, Mary prepared baby Jesus to be wrapped. Joseph and Mary would gently wrap baby Jesus in a burial garment.

Interesting isn't it!

In his Gospel, Luke parallels Jesus' birth and His death:

> Luke 2:7: "wrapped him in swaddling cloths and laid him in a manger."

> Luke 23:53: "Then he took the body down from the cross and wrapped it in a long sheet of linen cloth and laid it in a new tomb that had been carved out of rock."

LAID BABY JESUS IN A WHAT

Mary had just given birth to the King of the Universe, its very Creator God. She and Joseph swaddled baby Jesus from strips of a burial garment. The symbolism of Jesus being "born to die" is strong. Then, Mary did another astounding thing to baby Jesus. She laid him in an animal-feed trough.

Yes, you heard me! An animal-feed trough!

The Greek word translated "manger" is derived from a verb meaning "to eat" and literally means a "feeding-place." A manger was a hewn stone trough from which domestic animals ate or drank.

The traditional counterfeit Christmas nativity scenes show baby Jesus lying in a fresh bed of straw in a beautiful manger with a warm fire close by. No! This is the counterfeit Christmas!

Remember, that Mary and Joseph are in a cold, damp, stinking, urine/feces filled, rock first floor of someone's home.

The only place for Mary to lay her swaddled, newborn baby lamb was in an animal feed trough.

Yes, I can hear your thoughts! The shepherds swaddled their perfect newborn lambs and placed them in feed troughs after they were swaddled. But, why would this loving wonderful mother, Mary, and Joseph, lay baby Jesus in a feed trough?

AN ANIMAL FEED TROUGH WAS A MINIATURE TOMB

Well, we know that Mary knew who Jesus was. She knew that her son, the Messiah, had been born to die for the sins of the world.

Mary and Joseph swaddled Jesus in a burial garment like a little dead person and placed him in a miniature tomb.

What? A tomb?

Yes, a tomb! Feed troughs were proportional in size to a rock tomb that would have been used for a person's burial at that time.

> **Do You Dig It**! Archaeologists discovered animal eating troughs in the region of Bethlehem that were cut out of limestone. They measured approximately three feet long, eighteen inches wide, and two feet deep. In Mark 15:46 we are told that Joseph of Arimathea laid Jesus' dead body in his new sepulcher, which was hewn out of solid rock. The stone slab in the tomb was approximately twice as long as it was wide, a similar ratio to a feed trough.
>
> Interestingly, at Jesus' birth, He was laid in a miniature tomb, the stone animal feed trough; on the day of His death, He was laid in Joseph of Arimathea's stone tomb.

Now, you see that the feed trough that Mary would have used for a bed for her swaddled perfect little Lamb of God, already wrapped for burial, was like a miniature tomb for Him.

IMAGINE WITH ME

Muffled voices are getting louder. Can you hear them? They are coming from a cold, damp, stinking, urine/feces filled first floor of someone's home. Let's listen!

Mary:

"Joseph, my husband, please give me the cloth so I can wipe Him off. Isn't He beautiful?"

"Yes, my wife, I agree. Here is the salt and oil to cleanse His skin. Truth will be in every word He speaks."

As I cleansed the skin of my son, a multitude of thoughts danced through my mind.

"Yes, He will speak as no man has ever spoken before." I swaddled baby Jesus tightly. "He will grow tall and He will be righteous in all ways."

"Yes, Mary, He will rise above all men, for He is in the line of the Kings of Israel who are head and shoulders above all men."

I then took care of myself. I cleaned myself up as Joseph held my son in his arms. Through labor and delivery, I was perspiring and it felt like ice was caked all over me. I quickly put on my outer garment and rubbed my arms to get warm.

Once I was dressed, Joseph gave me my son.

"Joseph, we know *who* this little lamb is. Think about it? He is the Creator God! He is before all things and in Him all things hold together."

"Yes, Mary, it is astounding to think such things. But, they are true. God Himself has come to this world. Your son is 'Immanuel!'"

I agreed, saying, "Yes, my son is Immanuel and the Messiah, now a perfect little lamb that will be sacrificed in the future. *We* know who you are little lamb! We *know* who you are!"

I cradled my son in my arms and sang a lullaby to Him.

Oh, what a night of nights
I will sing a song to you,
Hush, hush, my son.
Hush, hush.
Hush, hush, my little lamb,
Hush, hush.

Oh, what a night of nights
I will sing a song to you,
Hush, hush, beautiful child,
Hush, hush, free from trouble and hurt,
Hush, hush, free from trouble and hurt.

Oh, what a night of nights
I will sing a song to you,
Silence over Bethlehem,
Hush dear child,
We will guard you.

Oh, what a night of nights
I will sing a song to you,
Tell me little boy,
Where do you come from,
From Heaven you say,
Sleep Immanuel sleep.

As I sang unto my Lord, I could not help thinking about the Prophet's words.

I looked at Joseph and said:

"How appropriate, my husband, for the Prophet has said that He will be like a lamb that is led to the slaughter and cut off out of the land of the living. And they will make His grave with the wicked and with a rich man in His death because He will pour out His soul to death and be numbered with transgressors. Yes, He alone will bear the sins of many and make intercession for the transgressors."

Joseph looked tenderly into my large onyx eyes and said: "Yes, God's angelic messenger told me that He will save us from our sins. He was truly born to die—Amen!"

Without a fire in our animal living room, I was shivering.

Joseph noticed and huddled around the miniature tomb keeping both my son and I as warm as best he could, while we both experienced the joy of Immanuel finally coming to the earth.

Joseph said, "Mary, are you getting any warmer? Is our little lamb warm, too?"

"I am cold but getting a little warmer, my husband. I am so content. My son is snug and warm. Thank you for being such a wonderful man of God and loving husband."

My thoughts immediately reflected back to my mother when she said that I could not do this alone. She was so right!

The three of us, Joseph, myself, and my son, drifted off into sleep, forgetting that we were in the lowest of places. We were a family.

Amazing and powerful, isn't it?

PART 3

UNWRAPPING THE SEARCH FOR THE HISTORICAL JESUS

CHAPTER 8

SHEPHERDS SEARCH FOR JESUS

WHILE MARY, JESUS, and Joseph, were trying to keep warm in a cold, damp, stinking, urine/feces filled first floor of someone's home, a stupendous announcement was being proclaimed to shepherds who were keeping guard over their flock close to the town of Bethlehem![1]

TO PEOPLE JUST LIKE US

If you were going to make the announcement that the God-man had been born, to whom would you first make that proclamation?

Would you get the word to the Roman Emperor Caesar Augustus?

Would it be to the Jewish religious leaders? Or even to Herod the Great, King of Judea?

Perhaps.

But, God made the first announcement not to Caesar Augustus, not to the Jewish religious leaders, and not to Herod the Great, but to common folk like us—to shepherds.[2]

SACRIFICIAL LAMBS

These shepherds were living and guarding their flocks in the fields that are now called "Shepherd's Field," which is about two miles from

Bethlehem. These were no ordinary sheep. They were *sacrificial* lambs.[3] In the early spring they would be slaughtered at the Passover. Interestingly, on the night that THE sacrificial Lamb of God who takes away the sin of the world was born, the announcement was made to shepherds tending to sacrificial lambs.

Was Jesus born in December? The timing of the shepherds and their flocks gives us this answer!

> **Behold!** The Jewish *Mishnah* tells us that sheep were not fed in their pens but grazed year-round in the fields and valleys (hot days and during the rainy season) near Bethlehem and then were sacrificed at the Temple in Jerusalem.[4]

Throughout Israel, sheep were brought, from the wilderness, closer to the towns and villages during the cold winter months.

COLD WINTER MONTHS

Now, I can hear your thoughts! "Winter! Are you saying that Jesus was born during the winter months?" Yes, that is what I am saying. Great minds think alike!

Here is why!

One of the leading authorities on sheep and the lambing season in Israel is Professor H. Epstein, Professor Emeritus of Animal Breeding at the Hebrew University of Jerusalem, Israel. Professor Epstein has very clearly stated that the lambing season of the main breed of sheep in Israel, the Awassi sheep, takes place in December-January.[5]

Plus, the winter months in Israel are not what you and I think of when we say cold winter months, i.e., twenty below zero! This is not the case in the wintertime in Israel. The winter is mild with temperatures in the 47 to 60 degrees Fahrenheit range with an average temperature of 55 degrees Fahrenheit.

Before the end of December in Bethlehem, rains would have produced grass on the hills for sheep to graze with the rainfall decreasing toward the end of December.

This is exactly what the gospel writer Luke tells us. Luke writes:

> "And in the same region there were shepherds out in the field, keeping watch over their flock by night."[6]

Now, please don't forget!

Yes, I believe that Jesus was born in December or January, but that does not mean that I believe that Jesus was born on December 25. Here's the bottom line. Jesus was born during the winter, probably in December or January, but the Bible does not say Jesus was born specifically on December 25. That is where I stand.

SHEPHERDS DESPISED IN EGYPT

History tells us that shepherds were a despised group in Egypt at this time. Remember Moses fell from being a potential Pharaoh to becoming a lowly shepherd. It was Moses, as a shepherd, who commanded Pharaoh Amenhotep II to let God's people go in the Exodus of 1446 BC.[7]

But, what did the Jewish religious leaders think of shepherds/herdsman?

> **Behold!** A rabbinic teaching stated: "A man should not teach his son to be an ass-driver or a camel-driver or a barber or a sailor, or a herdsman or a shopkeeper, for their craft is the craft of robbers ..."[8]

Shepherds were considered outcasts, so removed from society that they weren't even allowed to give testimony in court.

SHEPHERDS IN THE BIBLE

But, let me present another picture here of the shepherds as being humble and lowly people who listened to and responded to God's Word.[9]

In both the Old and New Testaments, God portrays shepherds as the opposite of outcasts. Do you recall that Abraham, Moses, and King David were shepherds? Even Jesus is called the Good Shepherd.[10]

It is striking that God, through one of His angels, made an announcement of Jesus' birth to lowly shepherds instead of to the Roman Emperor, Herod the Great, or to the Jewish religious leaders. God always exalts the lowly and shames the strong. God's ways are not our ways!

SPECTACULAR APPEARANCE TO SHEPHERDS

It is nighttime when God's angel made his sudden appearance, standing right beside the shepherds.[11]

With the glory of the Lord shining around them, the angel appeared to the shepherds. The glory of the Lord was the bright Shekinah Glory of God, which means "His majestic presence."[12]

This appearance must have been spectacular in the nighttime darkness, but yet fearful!

Accordingly, the shepherds were filled with exceedingly great fear.

I would be right there with them in fear. This appearance would startle, shock, and alarm me. How about you?

ANGELS SHARE THE GOOD NEWS

Having just suddenly appeared in the stillness and darkness of the night, God's angel first calmed the shepherds' fear. The angel told the shepherds not to be afraid.[13]

The angel announced the good news to the shepherds, news that would cause great joy to all the people of Israel.[14]

TODAY IS THE DAY

So, what was this good news that brought joy to the shepherds?

The good news proclaimed to the shepherds was that "TODAY, the Messianic Savior is born in the city of David, Bethlehem, who is not only the Savior, but is the Christ and the Lord."[15]

Did you notice how personal the message was that the angel shared with the shepherds? The angel personalized the announcement to the shepherds, "to you," to common shepherds. The "all people" includes the lowly shepherds.[16]

It even includes me!

THE CHILD IS THE SAVIOR, CHRIST, AND LORD

The angel made the astounding announcement by saying that "today" in Bethlehem, the one true God, Savior, Christ, and Lord, had finally come to the earth. This was groundbreaking and monumental!

This Savior had come to deliver and rescue mankind not from the political domination and subjugation of the Roman Empire, but to deliver mankind from sin.

This Savior is the Christ (Messiah is the Semitic equivalent), the son of David, and is the Lord—Yahweh God.[17]

Now hear this!

Because the angel said "Lord," there is no other way that the shepherds would have understood what the angel told them except that this baby born in Bethlehem is God in the flesh! Astounding!

Jesus is the Lord![18] This is a way of saying that He is Yahweh—God Himself.

A BABY SCAVENGER HUNT

God's angel had made one of the greatest announcements in the history of the world to lowly shepherds, sharing that the Savior, who was the regal, Davidic Christ, and the Lord Yahweh, had been born. But, also, these lowly shepherds were commanded to find and visit this God-man.

But, how in the world would the shepherds find this baby, at nighttime, in the town of Bethlehem? God anticipated this question and had His angel give the shepherds a "sign" of identification.

The angel used the familiar Old Testament phrase, "this will be a sign," to let the shepherds know that this sign would be Biblical and from God Himself.[19]

GOD'S TWO-PART SIGN

What kind of sign would you provide to these shepherds in order to find this child?

God's momentous sign had two parts to it.

First, the shepherds would find this babe who is the Savior, Christ, and Lord, already swaddled. Now, the shepherds would immediately think of how they swaddled the newly firstborn lambs that were without spot and blemish.

The second part of the sign would be that this swaddled babe would be lying in an animal feed trough. Again, the shepherds would immediately have been reminded how they put their swaddled lambs in feed troughs to calm the lambs down. Plus, these shepherds would have known where feed troughs were located—in cold, damp, stinking, urine/feces filled first floors of people's homes.

So, these two parts of the sign were just perfect for the shepherds. They most definitely had two understandable frames of reference that they could use in their search for the newborn babe.

The shepherds knew that they were to look for a newly born, swaddled child lying in an animal feed trough.[20] The word "baby" refers to a newly born child,[21] though it can refer to the unborn baby[22] or to a young child.[23]

The shepherds must have been astounded that the Savior, Christ, and Lord, had not been born in a palace with regal garments on. They must have known, like Mary, about the prophecy of the suffering servant Messiah in Isaiah 53. Jesus was born to die for all people, shepherds, those who are humble, those who are hungry, and the poor.[24]

THE SINGING ANGELIC ARMY

After the angel provided the two-part sign for the shepherds, suddenly there appeared with that angel a multitude of the heavenly army praising God[25] and appearing to the shepherds.[26]

This multitude of the heavenly army of angels was not all of God's elect angels, but no doubt they were the best angelic singers of the heavenly choir.

We know that God has an army of angels, but did you ever think about an angelic army that sings? That's mind-blowing!

THREE-PART HARMONY

The heavenly choir sang, "Glory to God in the highest, and on earth peace among those with whom he is pleased!"[27]

Did you notice the angels' "triple pairs?"

The first of the three "pairs" used by the angels was "glory and peace."

The second was "heaven and earth."

And, the third was "God and men."

Great three-part harmony—don't you think?

REAL PEACE

Peace is what we have when our sins are forgiven and we are no longer enemies of God. We then have peace with God.[28]

> **Behold!** This "peace" was not what the Roman Emperor Caesar Augustus brought to the world in his *Pax Romana* (Roman Peace). The Roman Peace was from 27 BC to AD 180, virtually a 200 year time period of unprecedented peace, economic stability, and cultural achievement, in which the Roman Empire reached a population of 70 million people. This time period was also the time of the great Romanization of the western world. Augustus laid the foundation for the *Pax Romana* that subsequent emperors maintained up through Emperor Marcus Aurelius in AD 180. Rome maintained the "peace" by means of its relentless and unstoppable Roman War Machine that crushed any and all rebellions against Imperial Rome.

This peace between God and man exists because this babe will provide a means by which sins can be forgiven. This peace is provided to all "men of goodwill," which means God's elect people.

> **Behold!** The New Testament says that the birth of Jesus Christ was not planned by God to establish political-social peace on the earth. Jesus said in Matthew 10:34, "Do not think that I have come to bring peace on the earth: I have not come to bring peace, but a sword."

The Apostle Paul said that the peace that Jesus provided for the world was a peace with God the Father that could only be gained by faith in Him. In Romans 5:1, Paul states:

> "Therefore, being justified by faith, we have peace with God through our Lord Jesus Christ."

This babe, swaddled in a burial garment and laid in an animal feed trough, will die for mankind's sins, but the only people to actually benefit are those who are "people of goodwill."

Are you a person of God's goodwill?

I hope so!

THE SHEPHERDS SEARCH FOR THE CHILD

Once all of the heavenly stanzas were completed, the mighty angelic heavenly choir left the shepherds and went back into heaven. Luke 2:15 states:

> "When the angels went away from them into heaven, the shepherds said to one another, 'Let us go over to Bethlehem and see this thing that has happened, which the Lord has made known to us.'"[29]

There was urgency in the shepherds' search for this child. In their search they finally found the family together—Mary, Joseph, and the swaddled babe. This swaddled babe was lying in an animal feed trough just as God's angelic messenger had told them.[30]

> **Behold!** The Greek word "found" means "to find after a search." It took some time before the shepherds found the child. They worshipped Jesus and reported the news to others, "glorifying and praising God."[31]

Now think about it. How did these shepherds go about searching all of the cold, damp, stinking, urine/feces filled first floors of peoples' homes? How many masters of the homes that they searched were upset and unhappy with shepherds waking them up, asking if a newborn child was swaddled and lying in their animal feed trough? I wonder how many people thought these shepherds were crazy.

SHEPHERDS REPORT THAT THE BABE IS GOD

We don't know how long the shepherds searched, but the shepherds finally found the babe and then testified to others about everything that God's angelic messenger had told them.[32]

Everyone that heard these shepherds marveled concerning the things spoken by the shepherds to them.[33] They were totally surprised at what they had heard and had seen.

Question? What did the shepherds say? Answer—just what they had been told to say.

"This child is the Savior, Christ, and Lord,[34] i.e., this babe is God!"

There was great celebration from the audience that heard the eyewitness testimony of the shepherds.

MARY PONDERED THESE THINIGS IN HER HEART

We are told that Mary was keeping all these things, pondering them in her heart.[35] In an ongoing way and in order to better understand all that had happened, Mary reflected and meditated on all the events of the night.

Mary was putting all the pieces of what was transpiring together into a coherent whole.[36]

After the shepherds shared the good news with others, they returned home, back to the fields where their flocks were located. As they went, they were glorifying and praising God in all the things that they had heard and had seen as it had been spoken to them.[37]

The shepherds' praise was like the angelic heavenly choir's praise recorded in Luke 2:13-14.

Wait a minute!

Are you asking yourself if I forgot to talk about the three Wisemen? The kings who were at the birth of Jesus?

Thanks for asking!

I did not leave out the Wisemen. In fact, the Wisemen were NOT at the birth of Jesus.

The counterfeit Christmas nativity scenes have the Wisemen there at the birth, but they were not there!

How about you and I doing a little investigation about the Wisemen?

But before we do this inquiry, just take a break and get a soft drink, a cup of hot chocolate, or a cup of coffee—okay?

See you after the break!

CHAPTER 9

THE WISEMEN SEARCH FOR JESUS PART 1

I'M BACK FROM having a glass of cold unsweetened almond milk! Nothing better!

Alright! Let's get down to the business of our investigation.

NOW, fast-forward about two years into the future from Jesus' birth! Yes, about two years!

We last left Mary, Joseph, and baby Jesus in a cold, damp, stinking, urine/feces filled first floor of someone's home in the city of David, Bethlehem. They were in Bethlehem because the Roman Emperor Caesar Augustus decreed that everyone in the Roman world be enrolled/registered in a census. The date was 6-5 BC.

Jesus was circumcised eight days after His birth. Then thirty-two days later, Mary undertook the purification ceremony, which was forty days after giving birth.[1]

As Mary and Joseph were coming to the temple for Mary's purification, both a prophet named Simeon and a pious elderly woman named Anna testified about the babe Jesus.[2]

After this, Joseph, Mary, and baby Jesus moved to a two-story home in Bethlehem. It was in Bethlehem that Joseph worked as a stonemason (carpenter). Mary was a good and loving mother and "Jesus progressed in wisdom, physical stature, and moral growth before God and men."[3]

NO WISEMEN AT JESUS' BIRTH

I know what you are thinking. "What about the Wisemen? You forgot to mention the Wisemen at the birth of Jesus. Every nativity scene in the world has the Wisemen there with baby Jesus."

No, I did not forget about the Wisemen. It's just that the Wisemen were not at the birth of Jesus. Yes, that's right!

And yes, all nativity scenes include the Wisemen. But all of those beautiful nativity scenes are all counterfeit Christmases.

Now, don't worry, I am not going to do away with the nativity scene. But, I will correct it and make it historical and Biblical—okay?

Now, do we know anything about the Wisemen? Do we know who they were?

The answer to both questions is—yes! In order to understand the identity of the Wisemen and where they came from, permit me to take you back to the Roman Empire's rival super power—Parthia.

Now, please, let me give you a little background on the Parthian Empire. This information is vital to understanding Herod the Great's reaction to the arrival of the Wisemen in Jerusalem.

THE SUPER POWER IN THE EAST
THE PARTHIAN EMPIRE

The Roman military war machine was the greatest military power in the West. But, there was a super power in the East who rivaled Rome for supremacy—the Parthian Empire.

The Parthian Empire ruled over the Middle East and Southwest Asia from 247 BC to AD 228 in ancient Persia. In about 150 BC, the Parthian King Mithradates I (ca. 195-138 BC) conquered Media, i.e., the Medo-Persian Empire.[4] It is here in Parthia that we meet one of the most powerful assemblies of men in world history—the Parthian Wisemen called the *Megistanes*. More on them later!

So, at the time of Jesus' birth there were two adversarial superpowers—Rome in the West and Parthia in the East. The boundary line between the two adversaries was the Euphrates River. Neither enemy dared cross the boundary.

THE POWERFUL *MEGISTANES*

In the Parthian Empire, the most powerful assembly of men was called the *Megistanes*, i.e., the Wisemen. They were a privileged group that had a dual priestly and political office. They wielded enormous power in the ancient world. The *Megistanes* advised, controlled, and could even use force to depose a Parthian king.

The Parthian *Megistanes* was a feared and venerated bicameral council composed of the Arsacid Royal family and the "Magi," the "Nobles," or "Great Men."[5]

Did you know that our English word "magistrates" is derived from the name *Megistanes*?

Who were the Wisemen called the *Megistanes*?

THE *MEGISTANES* WERE KING-MAKERS

Have you ever wondered how kings were selected in the ancient world? In the Parthian Empire, a most unusual way of selection was done.

Now get this!

No one became a Parthian king unless the *Megistanes* said so. They were the "king-makers" of the ancient world. No, they were NOT kings—but king-makers!

Though our traditional nativity scenes, church pageants, plays, and Hollywood movies always have the Wisemen as three kings, it is not so. Sorry—the Wisemen were not kings and there were not three of them!

HOW MANY *MEGISTANES*

Three Wisemen? There are three Wisemen in every counterfeit Christmas nativity scene around the world. Were there really three Wisemen? No! This, too, is not true!

Some time ago, around Christmas time, I had just finished an evening dinner with friends and I was pulling out of their driveway to go home. Once in the middle of the road, I glanced across the street and looked at the nativity scene in someone's front yard. After a glance, I did a double take and focused on that nativity scene.

Low and behold, guess what I saw?

A fourth Wiseman! That's right—four kings!

I got out of my car and left it in the middle of the street and walked right up into someone's yard—at nighttime! I wasn't concerned about the police being called because I was prowling around in someone's front yard. No, my only intent was just to get a closer look and see this great sight—a fourth Wiseman! But when I drew near to that fourth Wiseman, I saw that it was Elmo of Sesame Street dressed up like a king.

I could not believe it! Now, it was bad enough that the Wisemen, three kings, were part of that nativity scene, but Elmo as the fourth Wiseman? Please!

I almost grabbed King Elmo and put him into my car to take him for a little ride in the country. Inconspicuously drop him off—and leave him!

I didn't, but oh, how I was tempted!

There were no Wisemen at Jesus' birth. The Wisemen were not kings and they were not three in number.

So, where does the number "three" come from? Where does the Bible tell us that there were "three" Wisemen?

Well, it doesn't! Are you shocked?

> **Behold!** The counterfeit Christmas of three Wisemen all began in the third century AD, with the heretic Origen (AD 185-254) who said three kings worshipped Jesus because the Gospel of Matthew mentions three gifts.[6]

Origen was absolutely wrong! Three gifts do not necessarily equate to three Wisemen.

PROTOCOL GIFTS

In the ancient world, gifts of gold, frankincense, and myrrh were "protocol gifts" that were presented to newborn kings in all countries. The number of gifts had nothing to do with the number of Wisemen.

Please do not forget that the Wisemen are the Parthian *Megistanes*—okay?

Even if 100 *Megistanes* Wisemen had traveled to worship Jesus, they would have only brought the three protocol gifts—gifts worthy of a newborn king.

The only thing that we know about the number of *Megistanes* is that the Bible uses the plural form of the word "Wisemen" (*Magoi*). So, we know that there was more than one Wiseman (*Megistanes*) who brought gifts and worshipped Jesus—at least two!

HOW MANY *MEGISTANES* IN PARTHIA

Here is a great question!

Do we know how many *Megistanes* Wisemen lived in Parthia?

Yes, we do.

You'd better sit down for this—okay?

"Their numbers ... are reckoned at eighty thousand."[7]

Amazing—80,000 Wisemen?

Now, please don't get me wrong. I am not saying that all 80,000 Wisemen made the journey to seek out He who was born King of the Jews—Jesus. The most we can say is that the historical Biblical evidence indicates that at least two of the powerful Parthian *Megistanes* traveled from Parthia to worship Jesus.

Because the journey was seen as such an important mission, there were probably more than two Wisemen on the quest.

So, all we can say is that at least TWO Wisemen (*Megistanes*) came to worship Jesus, but I think it was many more.

What else do we know about the Parthian *Megistanes*?

THE WISEMEN WERE NATURAL PHILOSOPHERS

The *Megistanes* were a powerful council of politicians who were the king-makers of the superpower Parthian Empire. And the *Megistanes* were 80,000 strong! Is there anything else that we know about them? Yes, there is!

Philo Judeaus (about 25 BC - AD 50), the Jewish philosopher and contemporary of Jesus, from Alexandria, Egypt, wrote in praise of a particularly prestigious Persian (Parthian) school of Magi and their great learning and understanding of the natural world. He commended them for their research of nature. Philo said:

> "And in the land of the barbarians . . . there are very numerous companies of virtuous and honorable men celebrated. Among the Persians there exists a group, the Magi, who investigating the works of nature for the purpose of becoming acquainted with the truth. . . initiate others in the divine virtues, by very clear explanations."[8]

The Parthian (Persian) *Megistanes* were esteemed as honorable and virtuous natural philosophers. Today, we call the ancient natural philosophers "scientists." They were the teachers of all the various disciplines, i.e., they were the scholars of Parthia. They also taught the sons of the existing king and trained them in scholarship, military prowess, bravery, and what it meant to be a king.

These Parthian *Megistanes* were the Wisemen of Matthew's Gospel, men of vast political power, scholarship, and scientific inquiry who visited and worshiped Jesus.

THE WISEMEN (*MEGISTANES*) WERE NOT SORCERERS

There is an erroneous tendency to associate these Parthian *Megistanes* with sorcery. Now, it is true that elsewhere in the New Testament *magi* are viewed quite unfavorably.[9] They were men who studied the stars. In pagan Greek, too, *Magos* (Magi) was sometimes used to mean a "charlatan."[10]

But, the celebrated Macedonian philosopher Aristotle of Stagira (384-322 BC) has told us that the Persian Magi (the *Megistanes*) had nothing to do with sorcery. The Wisemen who visited Jesus were the powerful Parthian *Megistanes*, the king-makers of the ancient world—not charlatans, magicians, or false prophets.

THE WISEMEN (*MEGISTANES*) WERE NOT KINGS

We all know that most, if not all, counterfeit Christmas nativity scenes worldwide, Christian plays, pageants, and Hollywood movies portray the Wisemen as kings. Again, where in the Bible are they called kings? They are not!

The Christian Bible never identifies the Wisemen as kings. The first historical reference to the Wisemen as kings comes from

Tertullian (AD 155-220), who lived in the third century AD. He referred to the Wisemen as *fere regis*, which means "almost kings."[11]

Now, what does "almost kings" mean? It means nothing.

Tertullian had no evidence that they were "kings" or "almost kings." From what we know of these Wisemen, they were the "king-makers" of the mighty Parthian Empire. They were the Parthian *Megistanes* who were educated men who welded tremendous power and influence in political decisions at the time.

WHO CAME WITH THE *MEGISTANES*

Wait a minute! What do you mean—"who" came with the *Megistanes*? I thought they came alone on camels.

Please do not forget that these Parthian *Megistanes* were some of the most powerful men in the world. They were powerful politicians, scholars, king-makers, and scientists. Because of their status, they would not travel alone or unprotected just as the President of the United States requires a security contingent at all times when traveling.

> **Behold!** We know that in 91 BC, ambassadors from China were escorted to Parthia by a 20,000-man cavalry. The Jewish historian Josephus writes that treasure convoys transported costly gifts to Jerusalem, from Jews residing in Parthian country, with "as many as ten thousand men" as escorts.[12]

In his work titled *Crassus, 21*, the Greek historian and biographer Plutarch (AD 45-120) records that a single member of the *Megistanes*, Surenas, who was also a Parthian military commander, was accompanied by a caravan of cavalry, servants, and attendants the size of "a barrage train of 1,000 camels … at least ten thousand men" when he was traveling on a routine business trip. Here is a record of just one man, a *Megistanes* military commander, who was escorted by ten thousand soldiers!

A TWENTY THOUSAND MAN CAVALRY

So, the Parthian *Megistanes,* who came looking for He who was born King of the Jews, would not have traveled unescorted. Armed cavalrymen, too, would have protected them. Therefore, if one *Megistanes* was protected and escorted by 10,000 men on horseback, we are safe to say that there would have been at least two *Megistanes* who came looking for the new king, accompanied, escorted, and protected by at least a 20,000 cavalry-men.

Now think about it! If a 20,000-man cavalry was required to escort Chinese ambassadors and 10,000 soldiers escorted just ONE *Megistanes* military commander, how many soldiers would escort the most powerful and important Parthian *Megistanes* on a journey to find He who was born King of the Jews?

Surely, the Parthian *Megistanes* were escorted with a larger military contingent than foreign ambassadors or just one *Megistanes* military commander. Based on the evidence that we have and the importance of the *Megistanes*, the Wisemen (at least two) who visited and worshipped Jesus may have been escorted by at least 20,000 soldiers – and probably a great many more!

A CARAVAN OF IMMENSE SIZE

Additionally, it is important to remember that, in ancient times, traveling with expensive items required a large army to protect those items. From Parthia, the *Megistanes'* journeyed to seek He who was born King of the Jews would have been a trip of 1000 to 1200 miles.

Undoubtedly, the Parthian *Megistanes* spent weeks preparing for the trip. They probably traveled in an enormous caravan with their costly treasures of gold, frankincense, and myrrh. Because of the wealth and the importance of the *Megistanes*, Parthian soldiers surely escorted them. Their staff for such an arduous trip incorporated personal servants, servants to care and tend to the animals, and chefs. The caravan that traveled with the *Megistanes* would have been daunting to anyone who would have seen it.

WHO WAS HEROD THE GREAT

Are you with me? Great, let's proceed.

Now that we know that the Wisemen were the mighty Parthian *Megistanes* who came from the country of Parthia, let's learn about Herod the Great (73-4 BC), King of Judea.

We all know, at least, that Herod was the king who tried to murder Jesus by killing male children in Bethlehem who were two years of age and younger.

Okay, why was Herod called "the Great?"

Believe me, Herod the Great was not "great" because of his moral character or life style. He was "great" because he was known as one of the greatest builders in the ancient world. For example, he rebuilt Solomon's temple. It took 10,000 men ten years just to build the retaining walls around the Temple Mount.

THE POWERFUL JEWISH HASMONEAN DYNASTY

Was there a ruling class of men in Judea? Yes, there was.

The ruling class or family in Judea was the Hasmonean dynasty. But, Herod was not of this dynasty and was seen as an "outsider." Herod's father, Antipaer, was Idumean and his mother, Capros, was an Arabian princess from Petra in Nabatea.[13]

Herod's father, Antipater, was the chief minister of Judea. In 47 AD, he appointed Herod to be governor of Galilee when Herod was around twenty-six years old.

Though Herod claimed to be Jewish, he was not "fully" Jewish.[14] So, even though Herod believed himself to be Jewish, he was in reality a wealthy Arab-Edomite.

HEROD'S RIVAL TO THE THRONE

It was Herod the Idumean, not the Israelite, who was the one who would become King of Judea. But, Herod had a rival to the throne of Judea—his name was Antigonus II.

Antigonus II, of the Hasmonean dynasty, was the last of the Maccabees[15] and believed he was the rightful King of Judea. Remember that the ruling class or family in Judea was the Hasmonean dynasty. But, how could the Hasmonean Antigonus II ever think to replace the Idumean Herod?

It would take a strong army to conquer Judea and its capital city, Jerusalem. So, in order to rid Herod from the throne of Judea, guess who Antigonus II paid to help him ascend to the throne of Judea and bring Hasmonean rule back to Judea?

You got it—Rome's dreaded enemy—the Super Power in the East—the Parthians!

MURDER ATTEMPT ON HEROD'S LIFE

In 40 BC, the powerful Parthian army invaded Judea (which was Roman territory) and marched to Jerusalem, attempting an assassination attempt on Herod the Great. The powerful Parthians and Antigonus II were victorious over Herod and his forces. Herod escaped and fled to Masada, then to Petra, and finally to Rome where he sought the support of the formidable Roman politician and general Mark Antony. Meanwhile, Antigonus II became the Parthian puppet king in Israel.

> **Behold!** So, after receiving a hefty bribe, Mark Antony and the Roman Senate gave Herod the title of King of Judea. With Mark Antony sending part of his impressive military back with Herod, Herod finally defeated Antigonus II and the Parthians. The Parthians were pushed out of Israel and Antigonus was killed.

Herod became the King of Judea in 37 BC by the direct order and authority of Mark Antony and the Roman Senate.

Now, what does the history of the Parthians trying to assassinate Herod have to do with the Wisemen who came to worship Jesus? Well, the Wisemen came from the East to find He who was born King of the Jews. These Wisemen were the *Megistanes* from the Parthian Empire, the most feared and powerful group of Parthian king-makers. These noble Wisemen entered Jerusalem in the later days of the reign of Herod the Great while he was the ruler in Jerusalem.[16]

Now that we know the background of the Wisemen, the Parthian *Megistanes*, we are ready for the arrival of the Wisemen in Israel.

Are you ready for the *Megistanes'* arrival in Jerusalem?

Don't be looking for the Wisemen (*Megistanes*) to be riding slowly into Jerusalem on camels!

No, they road on . . . .

Just read on and you will see!

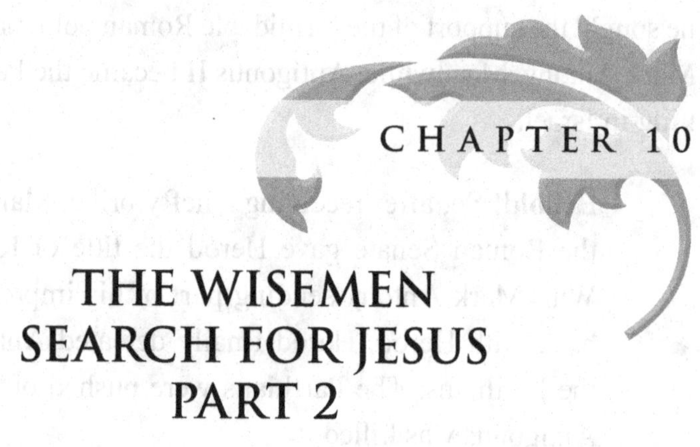

CHAPTER 10

THE WISEMEN SEARCH FOR JESUS PART 2

LET'S GO BACK to a time after Jesus was born in Bethlehem,[1] around two years AFTER the census was taken by Caesar Augustus in 6-5 BC, in the days of Herod the Great the King of Judea. It was then that Wisemen from the east arrived in Jerusalem.

In Matthew 2:1, the Apostle Matthew uses the word *after* to describe when the Wisemen came to worship Jesus. The word that is used, *after*, does not mean the next hour or day. A comparison of Matthew 2:1a with Matthew 2:7, 16 indicates that the Wisemen evidently arrived about two years after the birth of Jesus.

According to the Scriptures, "during the days of King Herod" is the time frame for what we are about to learn. For you see, it is important to identify an approximate date of Jesus' birth as before Herod's death, which was in the spring of 4 BC.

A NEW TROUBLING EVENT

We are told that it was in the days of Herod the Great that something new came onto the stage of world history. The word "behold" announces an alarming new incident that transpired during the days of Herod the Great.[2]

But, what new alarming event or, better yet, WHO would greatly terrify Herod the Great and all the people of Jerusalem?[3]

That troublesome new incident was that Wisemen, the Parthian *Megistanes,* who had been journeying from the east, have finally arrived in Jerusalem.[4] Please don't forget that the *Megistanes* came from the mighty Parthian Empire and inquired where to find He who was born King of the Jews because they had seen His star ("when it arose").

The Parthian *Megistanes* had been led by a star and finally arrived in Jerusalem, the capital city of Herod the Great.[5] The powerful *Megistanes,* along with a caravan, were now in Herod's capital city of Jerusalem. The caravan would have camped outside of the city.

Remember, the awe-inspiring *Megistanes* were the enemies of Rome and were now in Israel, which was Roman territory and Herod, as King of Judea, worked for Rome.

Please recall that when one *Megistanes* traveled, he was accompanied, escorted, and protected by 10,000 cavalrymen. I wonder what the arrival of the *Megistanes* (at least two) would have looked like with at least 20,000 thousand soldiers approaching the city of Jerusalem?

> **Behold!** Herod's kingship was merely a political office and he went to great lengths to guard against any potential rival. Jesus' kingship, like David's,[6] was genuine and legitimate, given to him by God at birth.[7] It was appropriate that the *Megistanes* arrived in Jerusalem, David's capital city, the city of the great king.[8]

WHERE IS HE WHO WAS BORN KING OF THE JEWS

Once in Jerusalem the formidable Parthian *Megistanes* made a fearless announcement to the people of Jerusalem. They asked:

> "Where is he who has been born king of the Jews? For we saw his star when it rose and have come to worship him" (Matt. 2:2).

Did you notice that the *Megistanes* did NOT ask Herod this question?

There is one word in what the *Megistanes* just said that was EXPLOSIVE! Did the word "born" jump out at you? It did to me, too!

This inquiry from the mighty *Megistanes* was an announcement to all the Jewish people in Jerusalem that their real king was He who was "born king" and they were looking for Him—and it was not Herod.

Did you hear the insult from the *Megistanes* to Herod? Boy, I did!

The intimidating *Megistanes* had just insulted King Herod the Great! We have already learned that Herod was not Jewish and had no such ancestral right to the throne. Herod was considered to be a "half-breed" because his father, Antipaer, was Idumean and his mother, Capros, was an Arabian princess from Petra in Nabatea.[9]

You've got it!

Herod was not "born" King of the Jews, but Jesus' royal lineage was due to His Davidic sonship. Interestingly, the title "King of the Jews" was the exact title that Rome gave to Herod.[10]

The *Megistanes* said they were looking for He who was "born" King of the Jews. They were not looking for Herod who received his kingship through political manipulation. The *Megistanes* knew exactly what they were doing!

With absolutely no fear, the Parthian *Megistanes* insulted Herod. Of course, Herod would have heard this.

THE STAR OF BETHLEHEM

We are told that a star led the *Megistanes* from the country of Parthia from the East to Israel—which was Roman territory.

Can we talk about this "star"—this "Star of Bethlehem?" Great! Let's do it!

The *Megistanes* said that they saw His star ("He who was born King of the Jews") in the east and came to worship Him.[11] Was this a literal star? Absolutely not! This "star" couldn't have been a literal star because we are told that it appeared, rose, went ahead of the *Megistanes*, disappeared, and then remarkably "the star" stayed stationary over the very house where Jesus lived.[12] Only the *Megistanes* saw it, because Herod had to ask the *Megistanes* when it appeared.

If this star was a literal star, it would have vaporized the house where Jesus was living; it would have vaporized Bethlehem, Israel, and the world.

And, the "Star of Bethlehem" was NOT an arrangement of planets in the sky, a supernova, or a comet. Have you heard these theories before? We all have.

> **Behold!** Now, because of the earth's rotation, the heavenly bodies usually move from east to west, yet this "Star of Bethlehem" led/guided the *Megistanes* in a southward direction from Jerusalem to Bethlehem. Again, this "star" appeared and went ahead of the *Megistanes* to lead and guide them until it was right ON TOP of the house that Jesus was in.

Please don't get me wrong. The Star of Bethlehem was real, but not a real star. There is no doubt that this star was a supernatural phenomenon that appeared "as" a star, i.e., it was shiny. Do we have any idea what this star was if not a literal star? I think so!

The "Star of Bethlehem" was the Shekinah Glory or dwelling of

God that led these *Megistanes.* Do you remember the leading of the Israelites that the Shekinah Glory accomplished as a pillar of fire and as a cloud?[13] The Shekinah Glory has led people to certain places and it appears and disappears to people.[14] How cool is that?

TIME OUT

When my first daughter was five months old, I wrapped her up and held her close to me as I went outside our home in a Nebraskan blizzard. I took my daughter out to look for the "Star of Bethlehem" that Christmas Eve.

We (really, just me) looked to the east and there was a star in the sky with a blue aura around it. Ever since that time, I have taken my three children and now my grandchildren out to search for the Star of Bethlehem on Christmas Eve.

Even when I do not get to spend Christmas with my children, we get on our cell phones and together we go out to search for the star. Every year, there is a star on Christmas Eve with a blue aura around it!

Do you believe me?

No?

Okay, I'm pulling out the big guns! Here's definitive proof!

In an animated Peanuts made-for-television-special, *I Want a Dog for Christmas, Charlie Brown,* first aired on ABC on December 9, 2003, the peanuts gang recited a script for a Christmas play at the end of the television special that says:

"We are here to tell you of a wondrous light,
A wondrous light that was a star.
The Wisemen saw the star and followed it from afar.
They found the stable in the night,
Beneath the star so big and bright.

The Wisemen left the presents there,
Gifts so precious and so rare.
Look up! Look up!
The star still stands seen by millions in the lands.
The star that shown at Bethlehem,
Still shines for us today."[15]

You see, the Star of Bethlehem appears every Christmas Eve. It must be true since the Peanuts characters said so!

Now, do you believe me?

Still "no?"

Okay, I know exactly what you are thinking about the Star of Bethlehem! Is it real? Is it true?

You are correct! What my family and I have been looking at every Christmas Eve is not the real original Star of Bethlehem.

Thank you for keeping me on the straight and narrow!

BACK TO THE *MEGISTANES*

What did the *Megistanes* come to do? To worship! They came to worship this new king who was "more" than a king—He was/is God.

The pilgrimage and testimony of these Gentile *Megistanes* highlight their awareness that the birth of Israel's King had universal significance, thus foreshadowing a major theme in Matthew's Gospel.[16]

When Herod learned that the *Megistanes* had arrived looking for the real King of the Jews, he was "disturbed, and all Jerusalem with him."[17] The Greek word translated "disturbed" is *etarachtha* and means, "to shake violently."

Now, the counterfeit Christmas would have you think that there were three Wisemen who rode camels into Jerusalem. But, how would that have caused such unprecedented turmoil and fear in Herod the Great and in the people of Jerusalem? That never made any sense to me. What about you?

Ahhh, remember that the Wisemen (the *Megistanes*) were from Parthia and rode horses while being accompanied and protected by cavalry (men on horses). We know that 10,000 cavalrymen protected one Wiseman on a journey so we can conclude that because there were "at least" two *Megistanes*, there would have been a company of 20,000 cavalrymen, approaching the city. The cavalry escorted and protected the powerful and feared *Megistanes* into Jerusalem.

> **Behold!** In modern nativity scenes, we often see the Wisemen ambling along on their camels. But we know from Parthian history that whenever the *Megistanes* made a journey, they were accompanied by thousands of mounted cavalry – soldiers on horses! These *Megistanes* majestically rode into Jerusalem on horses while the entire city, along with ruthless King Herod, cowered in fear.

Wow!

But, there is more!

MURDER ATTEMPT #2

The Parthian *Megistanes* have arrived in Jerusalem!

What happened thirty-six years ago in Herod's life? Do you remember?

Yes, you are correct! The assassination attempt on Herod's life by the Parthians in 40 BC—Rome's greatest enemy!

Taking into account the backdrop of Roman-Parthian hostility that existed back in Israel in 40 BC, Herod's response of "trembling in fear" was quite reasonable. Remember that the Parthian Empire had earlier tried to assassinate Herod in 40 BC and ousted him from Israel.

The ruthless and murderous Herod shook in fear because the Parthian *Megistanes*, the "king-makers," one of the most powerful groups in the world, Rome's biggest enemy, galloped into his city on horses. They were accompanied by "at least" 20,000 cavalry soldiers and "perhaps" intended to make a SECOND assassination attempt!

Think about it? You and I would be "shaking in fear" too!

That makes sense! With the Parthians now back in Jerusalem after a thirty-six year hiatus, Herod and the citizens of Jerusalem were in an uproar—shaking in fear.

But, this time, the Parthian *Megistanes* made no move to assassinate Herod. They were on a more important mission.

HEROD DID NOT KNOW HIS SCRIPTURES

Herod realized that the Parthian *Megistanes* meant him no harm since they were not looking for him, but looking for He who was "born" King of the Jews. You'd better believe that Herod got the message.

Herod's concern over a potential rival led him to consult the experts. So, Herod summoned and assembled all the chief priests, who were the leaders of the twenty-four main divisions of priests,[18] and scribes of the people and "started asking" them where the Christ was to be born.[19]

The chief priests and scribes of the people, together with the lay "elders," made up the Sanhedrin. The Sanhedrin was the central Jewish authority under the Roman-appointed Herod. While relations were not always cordial between the Sanhedrin and Herod, here they worked together.

> **Behold**! Gathering the Jewish legal experts together was a menacing occasion. They were not assembled to find and go to worship this new King of the Jews. This kind of assembling

> was also done in Jesus' ministry when the Jewish religious leaders plotted Jesus' death.[20]

Herod's question to his religious legal experts demonstrated something very interesting. Did you catch it? Herod did NOT know his Jewish Old Testament Scriptures! He had to ask his Jewish specialists where the Messiah was to be born.

With one voice, Herod's legal specialists told him that it had been written through the Prophet that the Christ was to be born in Bethlehem of Judea, the home of King David.[21] The Jewish experts used a combination of scriptures to prove their point—Micah 5:2 with support from 2 Samuel 5:2.[22]

THE JEWISH RELIGIOUS EXPERTS WERE NOT INTERESTED IN JESUS

Herod's legal experts knew their Old Testament. They knew the birthplace of the Messiah, but did you notice that these religious leaders were NOT interested in going to Bethlehem to worship He who was born King of Judea?

Herod's religious specialists quoted Micah 5:2 and 2 Samuel 5:2 to him, highlighting the Judean origin of the Messiah who would be a "ruler" from Judah (from the Micah passage). The ruler would qualify for King David's throne and would be a "leader and shepherd" (from the 2 Samuel passage) just like King David was.[23]

Herod and his religious experts were counterfeit shepherds. Jesus was the true and only shepherd of Israel.[24]

> **Behold!** Matthew wishes to highlight Jesus' ancestor Judah.[25] Bethlehem in Judah is also found in the Bible[26] to distinguish it from another Bethlehem of Zebulon in Galilee.[27]

BETHLEHEM IS NOW A SIGNIFICANT PLACE

Hundreds of years before Jesus was born, the Prophet Micah predicted that the topographical inconsequential village of Bethlehem was not at all least among the rulers of Judah. But, once Jesus, the Messiah, was born in Bethlehem, it made its historic appearance on the stage of world history. The village of Bethlehem would never again be "least" for it would forevermore be famous as the birthplace of the God-man.

Once the sinister Herod had gotten his answer as to where the Messiah was to be born, he made the decision to get rid of his rival, i.e., to murder the Messiah, He who was born King of the Jews.

WHEN DID THE STAR APPEAR

Herod then put his murderous plan into action. "Secretly" calling the *Megistanes,* Herod carefully inquired from them the time when the star appeared.[28] Why did Herod want to know the time when the star appeared? Because if he knew when the star first appeared, he would know that it was the year when He who was born King of the Jews was born. The *Megistanes* told Herod that the star first appeared two years ago![29]

When the *Megistanes* first arrived in Jerusalem they asked WHERE is He who was born King of the Jews.[30] They wanted to know the place of His birth. Herod tried to win the favor of the powerful *Megistanes* by providing what they wanted to know—the place was Bethlehem!

Herod then masqueraded his true objective by sending the *Megistanes* five miles to the south of Jerusalem to Bethlehem, wanting them to make a careful search for the child. Herod said that he wanted them to report to him when they found the child so that he could also come to worship him.[31] It was almost like Herod wanted to use the *Megistanes* as undercover agents. Interestingly, we do know that Herod was known to use undercover agents or spies.[32]

THE KING WAS FOUND IN A HOUSE

After they listened to Herod, the *Megistanes* went to Bethlehem, but the star, which they had previously seen in the east, reappeared and went before them until it stood right over the house and stopped where the child was.[33]

When the *Megistanes* saw the star, they rejoiced with a great exceedingly joy.[34] The *Megistanes* knew that God had been at work in locating this new king. They forgot about Herod and focused their attention on God and the star to direct them to He who was born King of the Jews.

Herod had provided the place, but God had directed and guided the *Megistanes* to the very "house" where Jesus was to be found.

They had found Him!

The *Megistanes* were not at Jesus' birth because they went into a "house" and not into the cold, damp, stinking, urine/feces filled first floor of someone's home where the child was born. By this time, Joseph and Mary had their own two-story home.

The powerful *Megistanes* saw the toddler Jesus with Mary, His mother, and falling down before Jesus, they worshipped Him. This worship was much more than just respect for an earthly king. Opening their protocol treasures fit for a king, they offered Jesus gifts of gold, frankincense and myrrh.[35] Remember that the three gifts had nothing to do with the number of *Megistanes*. Jesus was around two years of age when the *Megistanes* found Him.[36]

After worshipping this unique king, the *Megistanes* were warned by God, in a dream, not to return to Herod so they strategically departed by another route to their country of Parthia.[37] That route back to Parthia would probably have taken them south of the Dead Sea.

HEROD MUST KILL HE WHO WAS BORN KING OF THE JEWS

Herod's religious specialists cited Micah 5:2, pinpointing the town of Bethlehem as the location for the birth of the Messiah King. In order to ensure that this new king would be killed, Herod murdered all male boys from the age of two years old and under. After the *Megistanes* left Herod, the star reappeared and led them to Jesus' home.[38]

> **Behold!** The story of Herod's fear for his throne and his ruthless political massacre could hardly fail to remind us of Pharaoh Thutmoses I at the time of Moses' birth whose infanticide threatened to destroy Israel's future deliverer. Jesus' providential escape to Egypt and subsequent return echoes the story of Moses' escape from slaughter and of his subsequent exile and return when "those who were seeking your life are dead."[39] It was an affirmation of who the true "King of the Jews" actually was and the contrast between Herod's ruthlessly protected political power and Jesus' different way of being a "king."

People of Bethlehem—hide and protect your children.
Herod's soldiers are on their way!

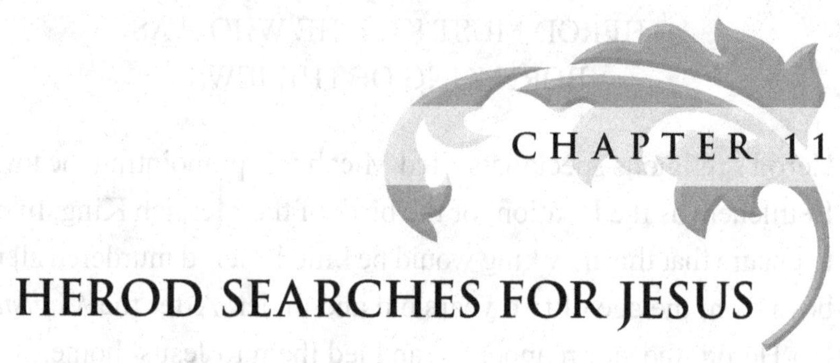

CHAPTER 11

HEROD SEARCHES FOR JESUS

AFTER THE *MEGISTANES* Wisemen left the house of Joseph and Mary, they made a strategic retreat back to Parthia. An angel from God appeared to Joseph in a dream and told him to get up and take the toddler Jesus and His mother Mary and flee into Egypt.[1] Joseph was told to remain in Egypt until he would be told to leave. Why?

HEROD THE MONSTER

Herod the Great was about to seek out the child Jesus in order to destroy Him. In order to accomplish this he ordered that all male children two years of age and under would be killed. Was this a single occurrence of Herod murdering someone? No, not at all!

Herod the Great was a monster, hated by the Jewish people and not accepted as their king. He murdered his forerunners Antigonus[2] and Hyrcanus,[3] his brother-in-law,[4] his mother-in-law,[5] his favorite wife the beautiful Princess Mariamne,[6] and his three oldest sons Alexander and Aristobulus[7] and Antipater.[8]

Have you heard what Herod wanted to be done when he died? You won't believe it!

Now, get this! To ensure that the mourning would be authentic when Herod died, he decreed that, upon his death, all Jewish nobility were to be put to death.[9]

> **Behold!** The writer Macrobius stated that when Emperor Caesar Augustus heard of Herod's murders, he joked that it was better to be Herod's pig (*hus*) than his son (*huios*).

This angelic message was the second time that God had spoken through one of his angelic messengers to Joseph. The first occurrence was when God told Joseph not to be afraid to take Mary home as his wife[10] and to name Mary's son, Jesus, legally adopting Him as his heir and son.[11]

STRATEGIC RETREAT TO EGYPT

There was an extreme urgency in this angelic appearance and message to Joseph. The angel told Joseph to take his family and flee to Egypt because Herod intended to seek out the child born King of the Jews and have him killed.

But—why Egypt? Where in Egypt?

Excellent questions! There are two answers!

WHY EGYPT

First, Joseph knew that Egypt was the ideal place for him to take Jesus and Mary in order to be safe because Egypt was a residence of sanctuary for Jews who faced opposition from powerful foreign governments.[12]

Okay, that makes sense. The King of Judea was going to try to murder the two-year old Jesus—therefore Joseph and his family would find asylum in Egypt.

I got it!

And secondly, Joseph knew that Herod had no legal authority, or jurisdiction in Egypt. This was brilliant!

WHERE IN EGYPT

But, where in Egypt did Joseph, Mary, and Jesus go?

We are not told, but we know that the Egyptian city of Alexandria had a large Jewish population. Indeed, Alexandria's population was one-third Jewish. Joseph knew this fact.

When Alexander the Great founded Alexandria in 331 BC, he allowed the Israelites to live in Alexandria. After Alexander's death, his general Ptolemy I took control of Egypt and continued to allow Jewish people to settle in Alexandria so that it became an important center of Jewish learning.

> **Behold!** Alexandria was a logical place of refuge for Joseph to take Mary and Jesus.[13] Alexandria was divided into five quarters and the Jewish people settled into one of these quarters. If Joseph settled in this Egyptian city, the other Israelites who lived there would have welcomed him and his family.

JOSEPH'S UNQUESTIONABLE OBEDIENCE

After the angelic messenger spoke to Joseph, we are told that Joseph woke up and *immediately* took the toddler Jesus and His mother Mary and departed by night to Egypt.[14]

Did you hear that?

By night!

Joseph did not hesitate or wait for daylight. He immediately took his family and departed. It was nighttime. What is the problem with traveling at night? Well, people did not travel at nighttime because of the threat of bandits and thieves along with the other hazards of traveling in the dark.

But, there was a worse danger than thieves and bandits that threatened the child Jesus—Herod's murderous intent.

So, Joseph with the unquestionable obedience of Joshua of old, gathered his family and covertly left with the speed of light.[15] But, how long would it take Joseph, Mary, and Jesus to get to safety in Egypt?

Well, the closest part of Egypt to Israel was approximately 150 miles away from the city of David, Bethlehem. This journey would have taken a little more than a week to get to Egypt. Joseph and his family were to remain in Egypt, perhaps Alexandria, until Herod was dead.[16]

MONEY FOR THE TRIP

Okay, that all makes sense, but there is one monumental problem. How did Joseph finance this trip to Egypt, his stay there, and his return back to Israel? We know that Joseph and Mary were poor.

Remember, they had to offer the sacrifice of two birds instead of a lamb. How in the world could they afford to take a trip of over 150 miles away?

Wow, that is a great question.

Well, think about it!

God provided the monetary means for the long journey for Joseph, Mary, and Jesus' strategic escape into Egypt by means of the three gifts from the Wisemen! God used the *Megistanes'* expensive gifts to provide the resources needed for the trip.

Of course, little did Joseph know that the gold, frankincense, and myrrh, from the Wisemen (*Megistanes*) would have provided him the monetary means for this trip, stay, and return journey to Israel from Egypt.

ISN'T GOD GOOD—ALL THE TIME

Isn't God good—good all the time! God provided the financial means to get His Son safely into Egypt. But, although the situation called for a swift flight to Egypt to prevent Herod's murderous plot, God had a higher purpose for Jesus being in Egypt and then later His leaving it.

A higher purpose? What purpose?

Thanks for asking!

Mary and Joseph had been told, along with the shepherds, that this little two-year-old Jesus was the promised Messiah, the Son of God, Immanuel, the Savior, the Christ, and the Lord, who would save His people from their sins.

But, Jesus was/is even more! He was/is the new Moses and the new Israel! Please bear with me for a brief history lesson concerning Moses.

THE NEW MOSES

Do you remember when Pharaoh Thutmoses I ordered the murder of all male children one year old and under?[17] The daughter of Pharaoh, Hatshepsut, found a little Jewish baby in a box (ark) in the Nile River. She, along with every other Egyptian, believed that the Nile River was a god named Hapy.

Hatshepsut believed that the Nile god had given her a son. Consequently, she would never have refused this baby who was a gift from the Nile god. So she drew the babe out of the Nile, named him Moses after her powerful father Pharaoh Thutmoses I, and raised Moses as a Prince of Egypt.

Moses was raised as an Egyptian Prince and when he was forty years old he killed an Egyptian taskmaster. Did you know that one of the most sacred laws of Egypt was that the Egyptians could not hurt or kill other Egyptians under penalty of death? Moses was only a Prince and not Pharaoh when he broke that sacred law, so he fled the wrath of his rival Thutmoses III, who later became Pharaoh.[18]

Understand this!

Moses fell from being a potential pharaoh to becoming, in the eyes of the Egyptians, a despised shepherd for forty more years. At the age of eighty years old, God told Moses to go back to Egypt to deliver the Israelites from slavery, for the one who sought the life of Moses was dead.[19]

The one who sought Moses' life but had later died was Pharaoh Thutmoses III. He was the rival of Moses and died in 1450 BC. Moses returned to Egypt in 1447 BC when Thutmoses III's son, Amenhotep II, was the new Pharaoh. With the tenth plague, God broke Pharaoh Amenhotep II and the Israelites were set free. The Exodus from Egypt occurred in 1446 BC.

Jesus was/is the new Moses.

Jesus was/is also the new Israel.

There was a new purpose and significance of Jesus going to Egypt. It was a historical pattern of prophetic prophecy that was the significant thing here.

The Apostle Matthew tells us that Jesus was to remain in Egypt until the death of Herod the Great in order that what was written by the Prophet Hosea might be fulfilled: "Out of Egypt I called my son."[20]

Just as the loving and faithful God called the children of Israel, His firstborn, out of Egypt in the Exodus,[21] God preserved His son Israel from the murderous wrath of Pharaoh Amenhotep II.[22]

> **Behold!** Just after the Exodus, God provided a new people and a new covenant through Moses to the people of Israel. Jesus, God the Son, after coming out of Egypt in the "new exodus" will grow up to bring a new covenant not just for Israel, but for all nations, i.e., Gentiles too.[23] Jesus will build

His church[24] with Twelve Apostles judging the twelve tribes of Israel,[25] i.e., the New Israel, the Church.

Jesus coming out of Egypt after Herod's death was the signpost of a new exodus. He was also seen as God's Son—the "True Israel."

WOW!

Our Jesus, the real historical Jesus of Nazareth, is our new exodus and He is the true Israel, originating an assembly (church) of His people (Jew and Gentile) as part of a new covenant.

Now, back to Herod the Great.

HEROD MURDERS MALE CHILDREN

The *Megistanes* did not return back to Herod with news of the location of where this King Jesus was to be found. Herod believed that the *Megistanes* mocked him and was exceedingly angry. He sent his soldiers to Bethlehem and all of its surrounding districts to murder all male-children two years old and under.[26]

Remember, the incident was reminiscent of another king, Thutmoses I, who ordered that: "every boy that is born must be thrown into the Nile."[27]

Why would Herod murder all male children two years old and under? Because Herod had strictly inquired of the *Megistanes* (Wisemen) as to when the star first appeared. You see, it was very clear to Herod that this new king was born when the star initially appeared to the *Megistanes* two years ago.[28]

We don't know how many innocent male children were murdered. The population of Bethlehem at that time is estimated at around 2,000 people. Around thirty boys may have been murdered.

Herod followed a precedent in killing these toddlers. In 63 BC, the Roman Senate ordered the killing of baby boys to rid their land of a predicted ruler of Rome. Herod followed the precedent set by the Roman Senate. This murder of children fulfilled the Jeremiah 31:15 prophesy.

THE SLAUGHTER OF THE INNOCENTS FULFILLS JEREMIAH 31:15

Do you remember the exile of the Hebrew people into the Babylonian Captivity by the Babylonian King Nebuchadnezzar's conquest of Judah in 586 BC? The children of Israel spent 70 years in captivity until God restored their homeland back to them.[29]

Jeremiah prophesied that "A voice in Rama was heard weeping and bitter lamentation: Rachel from her grave was weeping for her children in being exiled to Babylon, and would not be comforted, because they are no more."[30]

RACHEL MOURNS FOR HER CHILDREN ISRAEL

What does Rama have to do with anything? Well, Rachel's burial place was near Rama in the territory of Benjamin, in the vicinity of Bethlehem.[31] We are told that Rachel died and was buried "on the way to Ephrath (Bethlehem)" and "still some distance from Ephrath."[32]

Plus, it was at Rama where the children of Israel began their march into the Babylonian Captivity.[33]

Just as the Babylonian Captivity ended with the restoration of the children of Israel,[34] the mourning of the mothers of Bethlehem would soon turn to joy when Jesus returned from His Egyptian exile to conduct His three and one half year ministry. He died on a Roman cross, was buried in a rich man's tomb, was physically resurrected from the dead, and physically appeared to His disciples and enemies, proving that He was/is indeed God Almighty.

Jeremiah spoke of Rachel, as the archetypal mother for all Jewish mothers, mourning her children taken to Babylon. Rachel's mourning ended when the children of Israel returned home with a new covenant.

Jeremiah did not go with the exiles to Babylon but stayed in Judah to try to persuade those left behind.[35] Jesus, too, would try to persuade the Jewish religious leaders of their blindness.

HEROD IS DEAD—GO HOME

So, Joseph, Mary, and Jesus waited for a word from God to tell them that the threat to Jesus' life was over. And finally, the word came! Herod the Great was dead![36]

Herod was dead! And, behold, in an unforeseen incident, an angelic messenger of the Lord appeared to Joseph a third time while he was in Egypt.[37]

The angelic messenger commanded Joseph to rise up and take the child and His mother and go into the land of Israel, for those who were seeking the child's life were dead.[38]

Herod's attempt to murder Jesus was the reason for Joseph to flee into Egypt, while Herod's death was the reason for Joseph to return back to Israel. Just as Moses, in Midian, was told to go back to Egypt because those who wanted to kill him were dead,[39] Joseph was told to go back to Israel because those who were seeking to kill Jesus were dead.

> **Behold!** The soldiers of Herod represented Herod himself in "seeking the life" of the child Jesus. Sadly, the Jewish religious leaders who sought to murder Jesus during His public ministry would use the exact same phrase "seeking the life."[40]

Joseph had planned to return back to Bethlehem of Judea since that is where he, Mary, and Jesus had lived for around two years. But, Joseph heard some news that changed his mind.

ARCHELAUS IS NOW REIGNING

Joseph heard that Archelaus was now reigning over Judea instead of his father Herod making it still a dangerous place for Jesus to be.[41] Archelaus was also a brutal murderer. Archelaus seems to have inherited his father's brutal tendencies as evidenced by his slaughter of 3,000 Jewish protestors who brought economic and political grievances before him.[42]

Plus, God warned Joseph in a dream not to go back to Bethlehem of Judea, so instead, Joseph departed into Galilee.

HEROD'S WILL

You see, before Herod died, he made a late change in his will. When Herod died, his kingdom was to be divided up between his three sons:

1. Archelaus, ethnarch, now ruled Judea, Samaria, and Idumea (Archelaus had a reputation for ruthlessness and scandal, and he was banished to Gaul about AD 6).[43]
2. Herod Antipas, tertrarch, now ruled Galilee and Perea, east of the Jordan.[44]
3. Philip, tetrarch, would rule Iturea and Trachonitis.[45]

This is important to us because it gives historical verification for the reason Joseph didn't go back to Bethlehem.

BACK TO NAZARETH

Joseph made the decision to return back to his hometown in the north of Israel, to Nazareth of Galilee, to fulfill what had been spoken by the prophets.

We know through the general teaching of the prophets, Jesus the

Messiah would be called a Nazarene, appearing from an obscure and despised village.[46]

Joseph's decision to move back to the lowly village of Nazareth was ultimately God's decision. Jesus was to be called a Nazarene!

Jesus would grow up, work as a stonemason, conduct a three and one half year ministry, be murdered on a Roman cross, receive an honorable burial, physically rise from the dead, and physically appear to His enemies and followers over a period of forty days.

It's all real!

It's all true!

You can be assured!

SPECIAL STUDIES

SPECIAL STUDY #1

UNWRAPPING THE FOUR GOSPELS

WE HAVE JUST learned the true and real historical account of Jesus' birth from Luke and Matthew. But, there are those who teach that the four Gospels in the New Testament are not historical, but fabricated myths in parable form.

This means that there is no real historical Jesus who was born in Bethlehem, no virgin birth/conception, no miraculous star that guided the *Megistanes* (Wisemen) to the house where the little boy Jesus was living, no substitutionary atonement of Jesus on a Roman cross, no honourable burial in Joseph's tomb, no physical resurrection of Jesus from the dead, and no physical appearances of Jesus to His disciples and enemies.

Do you get my point?

These opponents of Christianity/the Bible believe that God doesn't even exist. Therefore, anything miraculous and supernatural is nothing more than fairy tales.

This chapter is going to provide you with *some* ammunition to use against the negative critics—okay?

WHAT IS A GOSPEL

I believe that most people, whether they are Christians or not, have heard of the word "gospel." They may not know all that the word entails but they have heard of it, nonetheless. I would also venture to say that most Christians believe that the word "gospel" is a Christian word.

Let's talk about what a gospel is—okay?

The Greek word "gospel" (*euangelion*) means "good news." That's easy and straightforward.

THE ROMAN GOSPEL OF CAESAR AUGUSTUS

Did you know the Roman Empire had a gospel before the Christians did? That's right!

The term "gospel" or "evangel" is found in Roman usage where it meant "joyful tidings/good news," and was associated with the divine imperial cult of the Roman Emperor Caesar Augustus.

The historical report of the Roman Emperor's birthday, attainment to majority and victory in His accession to power were celebrated as festival religious occasions for the entire Roman world.

The historical reports of such festivals of Caesar Augustus were called "evangels," i.e., gospels.

For Imperial Rome, you find the plural "gospels" because these Roman historical documents/reports were frequent reenactments that manifested the might and power of Rome.

THE *PRIENE CALENDAR INSCRIPTION*

Amazingly, a calendar inscription from 9 BC, found in Priene in Asia Minor, says of the emperor Octavian (Caesar Augustus):

> "In her display of concern and generosity on our behalf, Providence, who orders all our lives, has ordained our lives with the highest good, namely Augustus . . . And Caesar, [when he was manifest], transcended the expectations of [all

> who had anticipated the good news], not only by surpassing the benefits conferred by his predecessors but by leaving no expectation of surpassing him to those who would come after him, with the result that the *birthday of our god signaled the beginning of good news for the world because of him.*"[1]

Here an "evangel" or "gospel" is a historical event, about a historical person, about what he did and said, that introduces a new situation for the world. Don't forget that definition!

THERE IS ONLY ONE GOSPEL OF JESUS THE CHRIST

Now, when the four writers of the Gospel of Jesus the Christ wrote, they used this word "gospel" not about the Roman Emperor, but of Jesus. Do you remember that Rome used the plural "gospels?" Unlike the Roman "gospels," the Christians only used the singular "gospel," which means that there is only ONE gospel and it never has to be reenacted/repeated over and over again.

This is why from out of the entire New Testament corpus, we find only Luke describing the birth of Jesus in detail. Only Matthew records God speaking to Joseph, the Wisemen (the Parthian *Megistanes*), and the flight into Egypt, while Mark and John do not mention the birth at all.

EXHAUSTIVE ACCOUNTS—NO

The negative critic pompously demands that all of the Gospel writers should each have written every single detail about the birth of Jesus. They say—well, why didn't Matthew, Mark, and John write the very same details as Luke did about Jesus's birth? The answer is simple!

Because Luke already wrote about the details of the virgin conception! It did not need to be repeated over and over again.

The negative critic illogically believes that Matthew, Luke, Mark, and John, should have written exhaustive, chronological accounts of everything Jesus said and did. This is of course ridiculous for 21st negative critics to tell all four Gospel writers 2000 years ago what they should have written. None of the four gospel writers made such a pronouncement (cf. John 21:25).

Just because other Gospel writers did not mention everything (like the Virgin conception) does not mean that someone has erred.

All four Gospel writers each had their own purpose, things that they wanted to include and exclude, and a particular audience to write to. The Gospel writers supplemented (not contradicted) each other's accounts of the events concerning Jesus.

TO EGYPT OR TO NAZARETH

The negative critic also irrationally says that there are two separate contradictory accounts of where Joseph, Mary, and Jesus went after His birth. Matthew has Joseph, Mary, and Jesus going to Egypt in Matthew 2:13-15, but Luke has them going to Nazareth in Luke 2:39. Are these two accounts contradicting each other? Of course not!

Luke simply omitted Joseph, Mary, and Jesus' trip to Egypt, which sequentially is placed between Luke 2:38 and 2:39. NO Gospel writer ever intended to write EVERY detail about every event that took place or to even provide the exact order of the events. Writing in a chronological sequential manner is a modern way of writing—not an ancient one.

It is extremely arrogant and conceited to say what content and what order the four gospel writers (especially Matthew and Luke) should have included in their individual Gospels.

Please remember, there were four men who wrote four portraits of the ONE Gospel of Jesus the Christ. Do not say that there are FOUR Gospels of Jesus. There are four portraits of Jesus that each writer proclaimed to a different audience and for a different purpose.

So, just ONE gospel!

THE APOSTOLIC GUARDIANS OF THE WORD

In Luke 1:1-4, Luke says he received his information from those who were "eyewitnesses and ministers" of what Jesus said and did. The text says:

> "Inasmuch as many have undertaken to compile a narrative of the things that have been accomplished among us, **just as those who from the beginning were eyewitnesses and ministers of THE WORD have delivered them to us**, it seemed good to me also, having followed all things closely for some time past, to write an orderly account for you, most excellent Theophilus, **that you may have certainty** concerning the things you have been taught" (*Emphasis mine*).

The Greek work that Luke used for "ministers" is "*Huperetes*." The Hebrew word for the Greek word "*Huperetes*" is "*Hazzanim*."

Who were the *Huperetes* or *Hazzanim*?

The "*Hazzanim*" were men that were responsible for keeping the Word of God ("the Old Testament scrolls") in the synagogues, i.e., they were THE GUARDIANS. We find the same word used in Luke 4:17, 20 of the attendant ("*Hazzan*") who brought Jesus the scroll of Scripture (Isaiah) that He preached from in the synagogue in Nazareth.

These men were the leaders of the synagogues and conducted the worship in them. The *Huperetes* or *Hazzanim* were preachers and teachers of the Scriptures and served the peoples' needs.[2] They also administered discipline to individuals.[3]

LUKE'S MEANING

What does Luke mean by "*Huperetes* or *Hazzanim*?" Luke states very clearly that the eyewitnesses of Jesus' life and ministry were the "guardians" of THE Word of God.

The Accuracy of Oral Tradition

Jesus and the Apostles lived in a culture rich in oral tradition where persons memorized the entire Old Testament, taught word for word to disciples, and passed down to others with no variation. Education in the ancient world was by rote memorization with Jewish boys memorizing word for word the entire Old Testament by the age of fourteen.[4] We also know that the Greeks memorized the entire *Iliad* or *Odyssey* written by the singer of songs—Homer.

A Controlled Oral Tradition

Jesus and His disciples taught in a controlled oral tradition where the material was memorized and recognized as a preserved tradition. It was not meant to change, but to be permanently preserved. Jesus spent a great deal of time teaching His disciples and fully required them to obey and emulate Him.[5]

The eyewitness tradition about Jesus was not dependent upon a single person. It was a collective group of "eyewitnesses/guardians"

(*Huperetes* or *Hazzanim*), i.e., Apostles working together to preserve the tradition.

As eyewitnesses, the Apostles were the authoritative Christian "*Huperetes/Hazzanim*" or guardians who kept, protected, preserved, taught, and preached the oral tradition about what Jesus said and did intact—without variation. This oral material was taught/preached to entire communities and repeated numerous times for people to memorize. No distortion or intentionally changing details would be permitted in an oral tradition/transmission. Any error would have been corrected immediately by the "Apostolic *Huperetes/Hazzanim*."

The Oral Tradition Was Written Down (Codified)

But, because these apostolic eyewitnesses could not be everywhere at the same time and would soon die out, what was orally spoken was therefore written down (codified) so that a permanent record of their eyewitness testimony would be preserved and available for all future generations in what we call the New Testament.

The New Testament documents originated in multiple places, written by multiple authoritative authors, with books being sent to multiple locations.

This apostolic testimony of "the eyewitnesses and *Huperetes/Hazzanim*" was written down as the sacred Word of God. For example, the Apostles Matthew and John were at ground zero with Jesus and wrote Gospels, with John writing three epistles, and the Revelation. Mark wrote what the Apostle Peter taught and preached and was approved by Peter as God's Word. The Apostle Paul had a traveling companion, Luke (2 Tim. 4:11), who no doubt approved of his Gospel as being God's Word. James, the half-brother of Jesus and Apostle wrote an authoritative book titled "James," along with his brother and half-brother of Jesus—Jude writing a New Testament book that bears his name.

QUALIFICATIONS TO BE AN APOSTLE

Do you remember when the Apostle Judas hung himself (Matt. 27:3-8; Acts 1:16-19) and the eleven Apostles replaced him? In Acts 1:21-22 the Apostles, the guardians (*Huperetes/Hazzanim*) of THE Word, decreed that there were three qualifications to be an Apostle of Christ. Listen to the three qualifications:

> "So one of the men who have accompanied us during all the time that the Lord Jesus went in and out among us, beginning from the baptism of John until the day when he was taken up from us—one of these men must become with us a witness to his resurrection."

Luke very clearly says that the Apostles mandated and required three qualifications. First, this Apostle or Guardian must be a man. Second, he must have accompanied the Apostles (and Jesus) from the beginning of John the Baptist's ministry to Jesus' ascension into heaven. In other words, this person must be an eyewitness of the entire earthly ministry of Jesus. And third, he must be an eyewitness of Jesus' physical bodily resurrection from the dead.

So, the Gospels were written by authorized Apostles (Matthew & John) and associates of the Apostles (Luke and Mark), being approved by the Apostolic Guardians ("*Huperetes/Hazzanim*") of Holy Scripture, i.e., THE Word of God (Luke 1:2). And, remember Luke 1:4 states that Luke's Gospel (and the rest of the New Testament) provides CERTAINTY of what Jesus really did and said.

WHERE DID THE INFORMATION COME FROM

In Luke 2:1-4, Luke tells us that he undertook to write an orderly account/narrative of the historical things concerning Jesus that have been accomplished among us. Luke then says that those people from the beginning who were eyewitnesses and ministers of the Word delivered these things to him. Luke wrote his Gospel for us to have "certainty," i.e., to provide proof that the things, people, and events in his Gospel were true, real, and historical.

Now, if you were a historian like Luke, whom would you have talked to about the facts of Jesus' birth?

MARY

What about Mary?

Since Mary was twelve in about 6-5 BC and Luke completed writing his Gospel in AD 60, Mary would have been around seventy-seven years old. So, this is not an impossibility! Luke most probably talked to Mary at an earlier time before he wrote his Gospel.

We also know that Mary was with the first believers who repented and were baptized on the Day of Pentecost in AD 30 (Acts 1:14; 2:7-38). And, guess who was there with Mary in that upper room? It was the Apostle Matthew, the very author of the Gospel of Matthew (Acts 1:13)! In AD 30 Mary would have been around forty-seven years old and Matthew would have had a great deal of time to chat with her.

THE COLLECTED AND COPIED NEW TESTAMENT

The entire New Testament was written and collected by AD 96 as a corpus with the writing of the last book of the New Testament—the Revelation. Of the Gospels, Matthew was written first in AD 40-50,

Luke is second in AD 60, Mark is third at AD 68, and John is fourth, being written in the late 80s or early AD 90s.

As each New Testament book was written, it was copied and sent to other local autonomous churches so that they too would have the Biblical documents. So, the four Gospels were united in one collection. This fourfold collection was known originally as "The Gospel" in the singular, not "The Gospels" in the plural. There was only one Gospel, narrated in four records, distinguished as "according to Matthew," "according to Luke," and so on.[6]

The Epistles of Paul, the General Epistles of Peter, James, Jude, John, and the book of Hebrews, were also collected and sent to other churches for copying. So, the first century AD Christians knew and circulated the New Testament books throughout the Roman world. For example, Paul had read the Gospel of Luke since he made reference to Luke 10:7 in 1 Timothy 5:18.

The book of Galatians was a circular letter written to the churches of Galatia (Gal. 1:1-2a) and not to just one church in the Roman province of southern Galatia.

Also, 1 & 2 Peter, and Jude were circular letters, meaning that they were copied in local churches and passed on to other churches. 1 Peter 1:1 states, "Peter, an apostle of Jesus Christ, To those who are elect exiles of the Dispersion in Pontus, Galatia, Cappadocia, Asia, and Bithynia."

THE APOSTLE PAUL

Peter recognized Paul's writings as Scripture (2 Pet. 3:15-16). Again, the books of the New Testament were being circulated among the churches (Col. 4:16; 1 Thess. 5:27).[7] Again, Paul considered Luke's Gospel to be as authoritative as the Old Testament.[8]

Think about this! In 1 Timothy 5:18 Paul calls the Gospel of Luke (at Luke 10:7)—Scripture. Paul wrote 1 Timothy in AD 65 with Luke being written in AD 60. In 2 Timothy 3:16, Paul said that ALL Scripture (included Luke's Gospel) is inspired of God. Therefore, Paul had read the Gospel of Luke—including the virgin birth/conception of Jesus.

The critics cry that only Luke and Matthew mention the virgin birth (conception) and no other New Testament writer does. This is absolutely not true. Go to my next footnote and you will see the examples (Rom. 1:3; 8:3; 1 Cor. 15:47; Gal. 4:4; 1 Tim. 3:16) of the Apostle Paul talking about the virgin birth/conception.[9]

Neither Paul nor any other New Testament writer elaborated on the virgin conception like Luke did. Why not? Because Luke already had done it! It's that simple! Paul and the other New Testament writers (with the exception of John) were dealing with other matters and problems. The virgin birth/conception was not one of them.

Paul became a Christian in AD 34—just four years after the Day of Pentecost,[10] when the church began. Paul could have easily talked to the around fifty-one year old Mary about the details of Jesus' birth and passed them on to his traveling companion—Luke.

THE INSPIRATION OF GOD THE HOLY SPIRIT

Plus, 1 Timothy 3:16 states that all of the writers of the Biblical books were inspired (a supernatural guidance) by God the Holy Spirit to write and speak without error or omission what God wanted mankind to know. In God's eternal wisdom, He chose Luke to write the details about the virgin birth/conception.

THE GOSPEL ACCORDING TO MARK

Let's pick on the Gospel of Mark.

Mark wrote his Gospel around the year AD 68 from Rome itself. He is primarily writing to Romans about Jesus.

In the very first verse of Mark, he said: "The beginning of the gospel of Jesus Christ, the Son of God."[11]

Does this sound familiar?

You bet it does! It sounds somewhat like the gospel from the Roman Emperor Caesar Augustus, doesn't it?

In Mark's proclamation of the beginning of the Gospel of Jesus the Christ, he announced Jesus' coming as a historical event that would bring about a radically new state of affairs for mankind.

Don't forget that a "gospel" is a historical document, about a historical person, about what he said and did, that brought a new situation to the world. But, Mark's Gospel is not about Caesar Augustus, but about Jesus of Nazareth. The good news is the announcement about Jesus and His salvation.

For Mark, he was more interested in the Prophet Isaiah than in Caesar Augustus. Mark's Gospel goes back to the Prophet Isaiah.[12] In the book of Isaiah the word "gospel" is found in Isaiah 40:1-11; 41:21-29; 52: 7-12; 60:1-7; and 61:1-11. For Mark, the prophesized good news of Isaiah is about God's arrival to Zion that ends Israel's deportation and the encounter and conquest of sin and death from the world. Mark says all of those things were fulfilled in Jesus of Nazareth. This is the good news (gospel) to the entire world.

Now, what are the Biblical Gospels? Tell me!

The four Biblical Gospels are four historical documents, about a historical person (Jesus), about what He said and did that brought a new situation to the world. The four Bible Gospels are not parables or myths—but historical documents about the real historical Jesus who is God, real places that He visited, real miracles that He performed, real sermons and teaching lessons that He spoke, and real events that He did.

THE GENEALOGIES OF JOSEPH AND MARY

There are two genealogies in the New Testament Gospels. One is in the Gospel of Matthew and the other one is in the Gospel of Luke. Both of them are genealogical lists for Jesus.

The purpose of these Jewish genealogies, as in all ancient ones, was to establish factual succession, not to list every single person/generation.

Ancient genealogies did not always include "every" person/generation and rarely listed women. So, sometimes they skipped and omitted individuals/generations. Plus, there is no Greek word for "grandson" or "great grandson." The word "son" would always be used even if that son was born 1,000 years after his "father." Let me explain!

For example, in Matthew 1:1 Jesus is called the son of David and the son of Abraham. But David lived around 1,000 years before Jesus and Abraham lived around 2,000 years before Jesus. So, Jesus was the son (really great grandson) or descendent of both David and Abraham.

Does this make sense? Good!

JOSEPH'S GENEALOGY

The descent genealogy recorded in Matthew is Joseph's genealogy and traces the royal and legal line of Jesus—thus giving Jesus the legal claim to the throne of David. It begins with Abraham and then goes from King David to King Solomon, which of course is the royal line. Matthew wrote his Gospel around AD 40-50 primarily to the Jewish people, proving that Jesus is the true King of the Jews—the long-awaited Messiah.

Note carefully how Matthew expressed Jesus' genealogy with reference to the birth of Jesus.

When you read Matthew's twenty-six progenitors between David and Jesus you will notice that Matthew changes his formula when Jesus is mentioned. Matthew 1:16 states: "Jacob was the father of Joseph the husband of Mary, by whom Jesus was born, who is called the Messiah." This clearly shows that Joseph was not the father of Jesus. Jesus was born of Mary.

MARY'S GENEALOGY

The ascent genealogy in the Gospel of Luke is Mary's genealogy not Joseph's. Mary, like Joseph, was in the line of David, but her lineage went through Nathan (a son of David) and through Solomon. Mary's ascent genealogy is a departure from other ancient genealogies since it begins with Jesus and goes backwards (ascends) in time all the way to the first man—Adam. Luke does this because he is portraying Jesus' solidarity with humanity as the "Son of Man" who came to save all of humanity.

In Luke 3:23 we are told that Jesus was the son (so it was thought, of Joseph) of Heli. Joseph was "of Heli," which means that Heli was Mary's father. In the Greek, all of the individuals in Mary's genealogy listed have the definite article "the" with their names—all except Joseph. The definite article is missing when Joseph is mentioned, meaning that Joseph is not part of the list. Jesus was only "thought" to be Joseph's son. Jesus was the grandson of Heli, Mary's progenitor.

THE GOSPELS ARE RELIABLE HISTORICAL DOCUMENTS

As we have just learned, there is only one Gospel of Jesus. We have four records of that one Gospel. It is the Gospel of Jesus the Christ! The four canonical Gospels are reliable and therefore provide the correct interpretation of the real historical Jesus. This is so because of their apostolic *imprimatur*: Matthew and John were two of the original Twelve Apostles who passed on "first-hand" eyewitness accounts of the earthly Jesus. They were both at "ground-zero" with Jesus!

The Bible clearly teaches that the Gospel writers were supernaturally supervised and guided by God the Holy Spirit. The Biblical writers possessed, as they wrote, the divine intent along with their own personalities, style, and vocabulary. This is called inspiration. In selecting and arranging their material, they demonstrated a unity in person and theme, although exhibiting their own characteristics in a highly artistic pattern.

> **Behold!** The four Gospel writers tell the historical story of Jesus and his mission from four perspectives. They are "didactic or teaching treatises" of what Jesus said (discourse) and did (narrative) and are, therefore, indispensable as the sources of information relevant to that story.

The four Gospel authors arranged their material according to different thematic and narrative purposes that they developed into portraits of Jesus. Each portrait of Jesus was intended originally for distinct audiences.

MATTHEW

Matthew presented Jesus to the Jewish people as the King of Israel, the promised Messiah. The Apostle Matthew wrote the Gospel of Matthew in AD 40-50. This book was written primarily to the Jewish people, proving through fulfilled Old Testament prophecy that Jesus is the promised Messiah and Almighty God. The major themes are the Kingdom of God, that Jesus is the King of Kings, and that He is the rightful heir to King David's throne.

Behold! Matthew used 129 quotations or allusions to the Old Testament. Twenty miracles and six messages of Jesus were recorded.

LUKE

Luke portrayed Jesus to the Greeks as the Son of Man who came to seek and save the lost. Luke, a Greek medical doctor, wrote the Gospel of Luke in AD 60.[13] Luke received his information from Mary, Jesus' earthly mother, and others in the know about Jesus the Christ.

Luke journeyed and worked with the Apostle Paul in his missionary journeys around the Roman Empire. This Gospel was written to Greeks, emphasizing the compassionate Son of Man (a title emphasizing Jesus' deity and humanity).

MARK

Mark was the Apostle Peter's scribe. Mark addressed his Gospel to the Romans and stressed Jesus as the powerful servant of mankind. The Gospel of Mark was the third Gospel to be written in AD 68 to the Roman people. Mark wrote his Gospel right before the Apostle Peter was executed in AD 68 by the Roman Emperor Nero. This Gospel emphasized Jesus as the "powerful servant" in ministering to and saving humanity.

JOHN

John emphasized Jesus' deity to the world. The Apostle John wrote the last of the four Gospels in the early AD 90s. The Gospel of John emphasized the deity of Jesus to the entire world—Jews and Gentiles. He focused on the meaning of events in Jesus' life and emphasized that the person who personally believes that Jesus is God the Son will have eternal life.[14]

Each Gospel contributed to the entire extant life of Christ. Each Gospel complemented and supplemented the others; none was quite satisfactory by itself. There were four human minds that wrote the Gospels, but one divine mind inspiring them as they wrote.

HARMONIZING THE FOUR GOSPELS "CHIASM"

The three and one half year ministry of Jesus began when Jesus was baptized in the Jordan River in AD 26. There are four historical books called Gospels that record the earthly life and ministry of Jesus. Separately, they record four "portraits" of Jesus to four particular audiences. Together, in a chronological sequence called a harmony, there is only one Gospel of Jesus the Christ.

Harmonizing the separate accounts of the four Gospels into a chronologically meaningful sequence is an indispensable step toward coming to terms with the "so-called" differences between the books. A harmonization serves as an antidote to the prevailing tendency to stress the four Gospels' diversity, providing an important means to study all the Gospels at once and gain an overview of the historical life and mission of Jesus.

A careful composite of the four Gospels using a stylistic feature called "chiasm" is the key to harmonization. I have identified several unifying elements that span all the Gospels and provide an interpretive matrix within which the sequence of the unfolding story of Jesus may be ordered.

These elements appear in a corresponding "obverse" and "reverse" form that has as its main functions to:

1. highlight the center emphasis of a work, which shows the emphasis of the whole;
2. express exact equivalents or startling contrasts;
3. help elucidate a point the author is making; and
4. provide understanding and clarification of the information provided by its parallel statement in the structure. An analysis of this recurring structure provides a key to a proper identification of a hierarchy of events in the story of Jesus.

My Gospel harmony outline has eleven parts.

1. Part One deals with the prologue and arrival of the preexistent Christ into the world. This section begins an analysis of the first half of the overall chiasm, which proceeds in a descending mode.
2. Part Two covers the birth and childhood narrative.
3. Part Three describes the beginning of Jesus' ministry, His teaching with authority and working of miracles, showing that the Kingdom of God had arrived.
4. Part Four chronicles Jesus' presentation of the Kingdom to Israel and its unofficial rejection by the Jewish people.
5. Part Five records Jesus' response to this rejection in His instruction to His Twelve Apostles concerning His identity and mission.
6. Part Six focuses on the center point of the overall chiasm, the opposition to the revelation of Jesus' incarnation and mission.
7. Part Seven begins the ascent of the second half of the chiasm. Jesus again prepares the Twelve Apostles concerning the nature of the Kingdom.
8. Part Eight deals with Israel's official rejection of Jesus and the Kingdom.
9. In Part Nine, Jesus concludes His ministry with the events in the upper room, Gethsemane, the cross and tomb.

10. Part Ten climaxes the narrative with the empty tomb and the physical post-resurrection appearances.
11. Part Eleven concludes the narrative with the ascension and epilogue.

Every event from Jesus' birth in Bethlehem to His ascension back into Heaven fits into this design matrix. A chronological narrative can be constructed in order to allow one to start at the beginning and read a sequential account of the life of Jesus as presented through the eyes of the four Gospel writers. This narrative thus arranges the material of the four Gospels into the ONE Gospel of Jesus the Christ.

You see, one Gospel by itself does not provide the "complete" narrative. We need all four Gospels placed into a coherent whole in order to be given the one and only Gospel of Jesus the Christ.

All four Gospels can be harmonized into a chronological narrative in the following outline. These structural elements may be diagramed as follows:

Prologue

A The Arrival of God-Man
B Birth From the Womb and Childhood
C The Beginning of Jesus' Ministry
D Presentation of the Kingdom of God
E Preparation of the Twelve
F Opposition Against Jesus
E' Preparation of the Twelve
D' Rejection of the Kingdom of God
C' The End of Jesus' Ministry
B' Birth From the Tomb and Appearances
A' The Return of the God-man

Epilogue

In the above chiastic analysis, the complementary pairs of elements are balanced with an exact number of narrative units. The Prologue and Epilogue each contain two units. Parts Two (A) and Ten (A') each contain fourteen units. Parts Three (B) and Nine (B') each contain twenty-seven units. Parts Four (C) and Eight (C') each contain twenty-seven units. Parts Five (D) and Seven (D') each contain twenty-two units. And Part Six contains twenty-five units.

> **Behold!** There are 210 individual unit narratives that comprise the total picture of Christ's life from the four Gospels. Luke includes 130 units for 62% of the whole. Matthew contains 118 units for 56% of the whole. Mark includes 94 units for 45% of the whole, while John has 56 units for 27% of the whole.

THE HISTORICAL ACCURACY OF LUKE

It is now time for us to "briefly" investigate how accurate the four Gospel writers were in writing their Gospels. I will use Luke as my example—okay? We are going to see that Luke was extremely accurate in everything he did. Let's now investigate some of his points of accuracy.

TITLES OF OFFICIALS

Luke's New Testament writings, both his Gospel and the Book of Acts, were once considered by a few individuals to be unreliable because they identified places and people for which there was no other historical evidence.

Guess what? In time, archaeological discoveries confirmed that Luke was an unerringly accurate historian and his two books are reliable historical documents.

For example, Luke gives the correct titles for a variety of government officials, from "politarchs" in Thessalonica, "temple wardens" in Ephesus, "proconsuls" in Cyprus, and even "the chief official of the island" in Malta.[15]

Luke refers to Lysanius, tetrarch of Abilene.[16] The only other reference to a Lysanius was a person by that name who was the ruler of Chalcis in 40-36 BC.

> **Do You Dig It!** Near the city of Damascus, archaeologists discovered an inscription of a temple dedication that referred to a Lysanius who was the tetrarch of Abila. The date of this inscription is from the Emperorship of Tiberius Caesar (AD 14-37). Luke was right all along.

You see, as Christians, we can be very confident that the Gospel of Luke (and the entire Bible) is very accurate. Is it real? Is it true? You better believe it!

GABBATHA

An architectural structure of the Roman Headquarters (the Praetorium) in Jerusalem was called the *Lithostrotos* or Gabbatha. Gabbatha was covered with a tessellated pavement and a *bema* (judgment seat). The *bema* was placed on this pavement outside the hall of the Praetorium where Pontius Pilate sentenced Jesus to die.[17]

> **Do You Dig It!** Critics called Gabbatha a myth until archaeologists discovered it. Jewish archaeologist Shimon Gibson located Pontius Pilate's judgment seat and the scene of Jesus' trial. Tourists frequently visit the Gabbatha court in Jerusalem.

Have you been to see the Gabbatha?

THE PROCONSUL GALLIO

Luke records in the Book of Acts that the Apostle Paul was prosecuted in front of the Proconsul Gallio at the bema in the Greek city of Corinth.[18] Critics claimed there was no bema in Corinth, but archaeologists found that it stood in the forum (*agora*, marketplace). Corinth's bema was built of blue and white marble in 44 BC.

> **Do You Dig It**! An inscription of a letter from Emperor Claudius was discovered near Delphi in the AD 1880s that refers to "Lucius Junios Gallio, my friend, and the proconsul of Achaia." The inscription is dated at AD 52, about the time Paul was in Corinth. Luke was exactly right.

Once again, the science of archaeology substantiates a Biblical claim from Luke.

THE ERASTUS INSCRIPTION

Erastus, a Christian who worked with the Apostle Paul was called the city treasurer of Corinth.[19]

> **Do You Dig It!** In 1928, archaeologists discovered a Corinthian theater with the following inscription: "Erastus in return for his aedilship laid the pavement at his own expense." An *aedilship* designated the office of treasurer. Luke was right again.

THE PUBLIUS INSCRIPTION

The Gospel writer Luke called Publius "the chief official of the island" of Malta.[20]

> **Do You Dig It**! Recently, archaeologists discovered inscriptions that prove that this was Publius' governmental title.

Historians point out that, in total, Luke precisely identified an astounding thirty-two countries, fifty-four cities, and nine islands *without error.*

Now, do you see what I mean when I say that the Bible is accurate and therefore trustworthy?

REAL HISTORY: ONLY ONE JESUS

What do you say when the critics tell you that there was not one Jesus, but TWO? What? How can there be two Jesuses? Anyone who believes in two Jesuses would be crazy, wouldn't they?

Yes, I have to agree with you, but there are the critics who actually do believe in two Jesuses. Permit me to explain.

The critics believe in the person Jesus who lived in Israel around 2000 years ago. They believe this Jesus was not God in the flesh. Rather, they say that he was a Jewish mystic and comedian whom we know virtually nothing about.

The second Jesus is a "theological" or "Christ of Faith" Jesus. This means that this Jesus is what a few people have made up, a fictitious invention. This Jesus is not God and did not physically rise from the dead. Is this Jesus real? No, not at all! He is simply the fabrication of a few people.

For these critics, they believe that the first historical Jesus was just a man who died with his body being eaten by dogs. To the critics, the real miracle-working Jesus is nothing more than a Santa Claus figure that is not real or true. It is this phony Jesus or what I call the counterfeit Jesus that the critics want you to believe in and for

Christians to give up our misguided belief that the historical divine Jesus is real.

It looks like this:

The Historical Jesus	The Christ of Faith
Jesus was "perhaps" a real person in space-time history. He was a Jewish mystic and comedian who died and whose body was eaten by dogs. He was a lunatic.	Jesus was/is a fictitious creation by a few people who made him God, a miracle-worker, and one who physically rose from the dead. This Jesus is just an invention and myth.

The critics believe in these two Jesuses: one who was just a man and the second one who was nothing more than a fictitious parabolic myth. They emphatically want you to get rid of the historical Jesus and put your faith, time, talent, and money in the phony "Christ of Faith," i.e., the counterfeit "souped-up" Santa Claus.

What do you think about that?

Do we Christians have to accept the critics' fictitious counterfeit Jesus who doesn't exist?

No, we don't!

The critics are offering a "false choice."

I absolutely reject their historical Jesus who was the Jewish comedian and was not God. I also reject their "Christ of Faith," who is nothing more than a made-up story—a fabricated souped-up Santa Claus.

There is a third choice! The truth of the matter is that the historical Jesus and Christ of Faith are one in the same person. There are not two Jesuses! The Jesus of History is God-in-the-flesh!

The historical and theological aspects of Jesus' identity and mission exist together; they are not mutually exclusive.

Now, listen to my confession! Tell me if you agree!

I hold that the Christian faith, historically understood, originated in the conviction that the transcendent God entered history personally in the incarnation of Jesus in a virgin conception. This incarnate God conducted a three and one-half-year ministry and performed miracles. He was executed during Pontius Pilate's jurisdiction, was honorably and physically buried in Joseph of Arimathea's tomb, rose physically from the dead, physically appeared to His disciples and enemies (Jesus was seen, talked to, ate with, touched by numerous individuals), and physically ascended into Heaven.

Is this what you believe? I hope so!

That is the real historical Jesus!

SPECIAL STUDY #2

UNWRAPPING THE AUTHORS OF THE GOSPELS

DID JESUS' DISCIPLES WRITE THE GOSPELS

CRITICS TELL US that the four Gospels were written many decades after the time of the events—by literate and educated persons who fabricated the stories into a belief system called Christianity. They say that the disciples of Jesus could NOT have written the Gospels because they were moderately mentally challenged imbeciles who barely financially made ends meet ("living hand-to-mouth") and who spoke in Galilean grunts that were barely understandable.

Wow, is this correct?

The answer is a resounding "NO!"

These critics know better!

Now, listen to a critic in his own words:

> "Most of the apostles were illiterate and could not in fact write. . . . They could not have left an authoritative writing if their souls depended on it."[1]

> "Jesus' own followers...were mainly lower-class peasants—fishermen and artisans, for example—and . . . they spoke Aramaic rather than Greek. If they did have any kind of facility in Greek, it would have been simply for rough

> communication at best (kind of like when I bungle my way through Germany, to the general consternation of native speakers). Even more strikingly, the two leaders among Jesus' followers, Peter and John, are explicitly said in the New Testament to be "illiterate." [Acts 4:13]...In the end, it seems unlikely that the uneducated, lower-class, illiterate disciples of Jesus played the decisive role in the literary compositions that have come down through history under their names."[2]

This critic also states that Peter, an illiterate fisherman could not have written 1 & 2 Peter because he was from "a backwoods Jewish village made up of hand-to-mouth laborers who did not have an education."[3]

Let's do a very BRIEF investigation of this matter to conclusively show that the critics' claim that Jesus' disciples were backward and illiterate persons is totally false.

KOINE GREEK: LANGUAGE OF THE WORLD

From the time of Alexander the Great through the Apostolic Age (AD 30-100) *Koine* Greek was the language of the world. It began with Alexander the Great conquering the world and Hellenizing it through its Greek culture and language. Around 275 BC in Alexandria, Egypt, the Hebrew Old Testament was translated into *Koine* Greek for the world to read and learn from. This translation was called the *Septuagint* (Seventy), abbreviated *LXX* (70).

Jewish people living outside of Israel (in the Diaspora) spoke and wrote *Koine* Greek with those living in Israel being able to speak/write Greek in addition to Aramaic and Hebrew. Many Israelites became Hellenists in that they adopted the Greek language and customs. When Rome conquered Israel, the Latin language was introduced.

This is why Pontus Pilate wrote that Jesus is the "King of the Jews" in the three language of Hebrew, Greek, and Latin.[4] John 19:20 says that many of the Jews READ this sign and John 19:21 says that the Chief Priests of the Jews READ it also—a sign that was written in three different languages.

Therefore, *Koine* Greek was in common use in Israel being understood by the Jewish people in Israel especially under the rule of the second century BC Seleucid King Antiochus IV Epiphanes, and later under particular Jewish Hasmonean and Herodian rulers. *Koine* Greek was the world's universal language (*the lingua franca*).

The Great Commission of Jesus provided the reason why all of the New Testament documents were written in *Koine* Greek.[5] Christians were to take the Christian Gospel into all the world, teach it, make disciples, baptize those learners, and to obey everything else Jesus said to do. But, not everyone in the world knew Hebrew or Aramaic, but they all did know *Koine* Greek. Pure genius! With the writing of the New Testament documents in *Koine* Greek everyone could read or hear the plan of salvation and be saved.

THE APOSTLES WERE NOT ILLITERATE

First, there was an almost universal literacy in New Testament times, and especially as the result of extensive synagogue schools. All Jewish parents were ordered to teach their children the Torah—including the Apostles.[6] The Jewish parents were to "write them (the words of the *Shema*) on the doorposts of your house and on your gates."[7] You see, literacy was of an essential importance in Israel with Jewish children being taught to read and write.

The Jewish historian Josephus said, "Above all we pride ourselves on the education of our children, and regard as the most essential task in life the observance of our laws and of the pious practices, based thereupon, which we have inherited."[8] He says later: "(The Law) orders that (children) shall be taught to read, and shall learn both the laws and the deeds of their forefathers."[9]

So, Jesus and His disciples could read and write. They were not illiterate!

Second, let's look at Acts 4:13.

> "Now when they saw the boldness of Peter and John, and perceived that they were uneducated, common men, they were astonished. And they recognized that they had been with Jesus."

The Greek word for "uneducated" is ἀγράμματοί (*agrammatoi*) and it does NOT mean illiterate, i.e., one who cannot read or write, but as one who is "unlettered," lacking formal rabbinic training.

In other words, the members of the Sanhedrin said that Peter and John didn't go to a rabbinic school and earn a degree.

Third, notice from this passage that the Sanhedrin members, who were officially trained as rabbis, were astonished that Peter and John addressed them in boldness and in what they said to them as if it came from formally trained rabbis. Interestingly, the Jewish council did not say that their interpretation of the Hebrew Scriptures was wrong. They were simply amazed that they could speak (quote and explain Scriptures) as trained rabbis, without attending the rabbinic schools.

And fourth, if the Sanhedrin thought that Peter and John were illiterate they would have had them read and write something for them to make such a statement, but they did not do that–did they?

Fifth, as fishermen, Peter and John would need to be able to read and write with some degree of proficiency in order to conduct business. I will say more on this later.

WHAT ABOUT PETER & ANDREW

We all know the Apostle Simon Peter. Did you know that Simon is a Greek name? It is! What is Simon doing with a Greek name if he could not read/write Greek? The Jewish parents of Simon must have made a huge mistake in naming their little illiterate boy with the Greek name Simon.

We also know of the Apostle Andrew—the brother of Peter. Did you know that Andrew is a Greek name too? Yes it is!

Here we have two brothers with Greek names and the critics still say that Peter and Andrew could not read/write Greek. Nonsense!

John 1:44 tells us that the hometown (place of birth) for the Apostles Peter and Andrew was Bethsaida (modern et-Tell). Bethsaida was a decidedly Hellenized town with a Roman temple in the Gentile tetrarchy of Herod Philip.[10]

What are Simon and Andrew doing living in a town where most of the people spoke Greek? How did they survive and conduct their fishing business with Jews *and* Gentiles? The answer is that both knew Greek.

In this very Greek oriented town of Bethsaida, Peter and Andrew most certainly knew how to read and write Greek in order to do business with both Israelites and Gentiles.[11]

PETER AT CAESARIA PHILIPPI

At a place called Caesarea Philippi, Jesus wanted to know who people thought He was. Listen to what Simon said and what Jesus called Simon.

> "Simon Peter replied, "You are the **Christ**, the Son of the living God." And Jesus answered him, "Blessed are you,

> Simon Bar-Jonah! For flesh and blood has not revealed this to you, but my Father who is in heaven. And I tell you, you are **Peter**, and on this rock I will build my church, and the gates of hell-shall not prevail against it" (Matt. 16:16-18; *emphasis mine*).

First, Peter called Jesus "Christ!" That is a Greek word for "Messiah." If Simon was illiterate and did not know Greek where did he learn about the Greek word "Christ" to call Jesus? Simon would not know the Greek word "Christ"— would he? But, Simon did know Greek!

Second, Jesus blessed Simon for his answer in that He most definitely understood that Simon called Him the Greek word "Christ." How did Jesus understand Peter if He did not know Greek? Jesus then called Simon—"Peter" (*petros*)! Peter is guess what—a Greek name! If Simon was illiterate (along with the other apostles), how did he understand the new name that Jesus gave to him? Jesus gave Simon (a Greek name) another Greek name of "Peter" (*Petros*) meaning a "small pebble."

Do you see how foolish and ridiculous the critics' claim is that the apostles were illiterate, imbecilic fishermen who "could not have left an authoritative writing if their souls depended on it?"

PETER WITH CORNELIUS IN ACTS 10

The Apostle Peter was chosen by God to go to a Roman Centurion, Cornelius, in order to bring to him the plan of salvation, i.e., the good news (Acts 10:1-48). What language did Peter speak to this Roman who knew Latin—Hebrew or Aramaic? No, a Roman would not be proficient in Hebrew or Aramaic. Greek is the answer since the Romans could also speak Greek. Peter spoke Greek to Cornelius.

WHAT ABOUT PHILIP WITH HIS GREEK NAME

Another Apostle, Philip, was from the very same village of Greek speaking people, Bethsaida—which was a place of commerce and international trade, where Greek would have been the normal language of business.

John 1:44 states:

> "Now Philip was from Bethsaida, the city of Andrew and Peter."

Did you know that the name Philip is also a Greek name? Again, what is wrong with Philip's (and Simon & Andrew's) Jewish parents in giving their sons Greek names? The answer is that Simon Peter, Andrew, and Philip could read and write Greek.

Also, even more remarkable was a time when Greek-speaking Jews came to Jerusalem for the Passover and wanted to see/meet Jesus (John 12:20-21). These Greek-speaking Jews went to Philip to get an audience with Jesus. Philip then went to Andrew. Why? These Greek-speaking Jews, no doubt, heard Philip speaking Greek. This incident makes no sense if Philip and Andrew did not know how to speak/write Greek.

WHAT ABOUT MATTHEW THE TAX COLLECTOR

The Apostle Matthew was formerly a tax collector or "publican" in the town of Capernaum (Matt. 9:9; 10:3). Matthew is also called Levi, the son of Alphaeus, by Luke and Mark (Mark 2:14; Luke 5:27).

In order to be a tax collector working for Rome, Matthew would have had to be able to read and write—in multiple languages of

Hebrew, Greek, and Latin. In order to demand taxes from people, Matthew would have kept detailed records of his transactions, write registers and receipts, collect, copy, record information, and report back to his employers—the Romans.

Before Matthew met Jesus, he was a wealthy businessman for he hosted "a great banquet for Jesus" with "a large crowd" in attendance (Luke 5:29).

WHAT ABOUT THE HISTORIAN AND DOCTOR LUKE

Luke, a medical doctor and historian, wrote the Gospel of Luke and the book of Acts. But, the critics believe that Luke was illiterate. This is ridiculous. Again, Luke is a "Greek" name!

As a physician (Colossians 4:14), Luke would have been able to read and write Greek. He would have read medical works and have written reports for law-enforcement officials regarding suspicious injuries and possible causes of death, as well as statements for slave masters certifying the health of slaves.

Also, Luke very clearly states in Luke 1:3 that he would WRITE an orderly account—IN GREEK!

THE DECISION IN JERUSALEM: ACTS 15

The issue of whether a person (specifically Gentiles) had to be circumcised in order to become a Christian was settled by the Apostles in Jerusalem. The answer was "no," people do not have to be circumcised in order to go to Heaven. What is interesting is that the Apostles WROTE letters to all the churches throughout the Greek-speaking world with their decision (Acts 15:19-20, 23).

Here the Apostles could write and they would have written these to primarily Gentile churches in Greek.

WHAT LANGUAGE DID PETER AND THE APOSTLES PREACH IN

Many scholars also believe that Peter preached in Greek in Acts 2, which would have been the most widely understood language by the Jews from many different countries. Peter must have preached in Greek in Acts 2, since that language would have been more widely understood than even Aramaic by the visiting Jews.

GREEK SPEAKING JEWS IN ACTS 6:1

Acts 6 also provides possible evidence that, side by side with Aramaic-speaking (or Hebrew-speaking) widows, there were Greek-speaking widows, all part of the same believing community in Jerusalem. The Apostles had six Greek-speaking Israelites chosen to help these Greek-speaking widows—not because the Apostles did not know Greek, but because they were to devote themselves to preaching the Word (Acts 6:2) and to "prayer and to the ministry of the word" (Acts 6:4).

FISHING—BIG BUSINESS

I have briefly but convincingly shown that the disciples of Jesus (especially Matthew, Luke, Mark, and John) were not illiterate but could speak and write three languages—Hebrew, Aramaic, and Greek.

Now, let's dispel the critics' belief that the Apostles were from "a backwoods Jewish village made up of hand-to-mouth laborers who did not have an education."

A PROFITABLE ENTERPRISE

Did you know that during the days of Jesus and the Apostles, fishing was not only a major business in Israel but it was an international business?[12] That's right! Today, we all know that English is the international language of business and trade, but back in the days of the Apostles, Greek served the same purpose. The fishermen disciples/Apostles of Jesus were businessmen who dealt with Gentiles and had to speak/write Greek in order to sustain a profitable business.

How do we know that they were upper-middle-class businessmen? Well, they worked in partnership (Luke 5:7) with James and John, the sons of Zebedee (Luke 5:10). They owned their own boats and nets (Matt. 4:20-22), and had hired employees (Mark 1:20), which makes no sense if they were nothing but backwoods fishermen living "by hand-to-mouth." They could work when they wanted to (John 21:1-3) and completely walk away from their occupation (Luke 5:11).

The fishing business was a very profitable enterprise.[13]

THIRTEEN ANCIENT HARBORS AROUND THE SEA OF GALILEE

Archaeologists have uncovered *et-Tell* as the site of ancient Bethsaida.[14] Bethsaida was the hometown of Peter, Andrew, and Philip (John 1:44). It was also one of 13 ancient harbors that have been discovered around the coast of the Sea of Galilee.[15]

One of the finds in ancient Bethsaida from the first century AD was what is called "the house of the fisherman"—a spacious 1,750 square-foot house built around three sides of a courtyard. Here was found different kinds of fishing equipment, a long, crooked needle, fishhooks, net lead weights, and 156 broken pieces of Roman fineware pottery as evidence of wealth.[16]

This may be just where Peter and Andrew once lived.

FISH COST HOW MUCH

Did you know that a fish cost more than a cow? That's right!

Plutarch (AD 45-120), a Greek biographer and essayist, reported a complaint about the cost of fish when he said, "a fish sells for more at Rome than a cow, and they sell a cask of smoked fish for a price that a hundred sheep plus one ox in the lead wouldn't bring, cut in pieces."[17]

Fresh fish was expensive and were not eaten by the poor. I always thought everyone who lived around the Sea of Galilee ate fish all the time. Not at all! The poor, slaves, and soldiers could only afford dried and salted fish.[18] What is interesting is that if people saw any poor person buying fish, that poor person was believed to be a thief and even put in prison.[19]

THE APOSTLES

Two business partner teams of fishermen brothers (Mark 1:16-20), Peter and Andrew, James and John (the sons of Zebedee), owned a prosperous commercial fishing business. The Apostle Philip was probably a fisherman being from the same hometown as Peter and Andrew—Bethsaida, on the northern shore of the Sea of Galilee (John 1:44).

Speaking of Peter and his partners, Luke 5:7 states:

> "So they motioned to their *partners* in the other boat to come and help them. And they came and filled both boats, so that they were about to sink."

The word "partners" ("*metachoi*") refers to a collective/cooperative business between the families of Jonah (Peter and Andrew's father) and Zebedee (James and John's father).

Luke 5:10 states:

> "and so were James and John, Zebedee's sons, who were Simon's *business partners*."

Again, the words "business partners" ("*koinônoi*") really means cooperative members who share in the business.

These men were not, as the critics say, backwoods "hand-to-mouth laborers who did not have an education." There is absolutely no evidence for that—just the opposite—and these critics know it—or they should know it as scholars. I am not saying that they were millionaires, but they did make a good living and in order to deal with Gentiles, they most definitely had to be fluent in *Koine* Greek.

The above material was a very brief section that most certainly shows that the disciples/Apostles of Jesus could and did write in *Koine* Greek and did write the New Testament books (especially the four Gospels) that are ascribed to them.

SPECIAL STUDY #3

UNWRAPPING THE ROMAN CENSUS

THE TIMING AND PLACE OF THE BIRTH OF JESUS

DO YOU REMEMBER that God spoke to Joseph in a dream? He used an angelic messenger to tell Joseph not to be afraid to take Mary home as his wife. Joseph was obedient and accepted Mary as his wife by taking her to his home and not providing a private bill of divorce.

We know that Mary was near the end of her pregnancy term when she and Joseph made their journey to Bethlehem. Even today's airlines with plush seats and food service have strict regulations against women flying in their final trimester. Mary was certainly made of stern stuff, making this trek on foot.

We do not know the month and day of Jesus birth, but we can narrow it down to a couple of years. We can date the birth of Jesus at 6-5 BC. Now, it's important to substantiate that date, so let's dig in.

LUKE THE FIRST-RATE HISTORIAN

Now, the historian Luke accurately places the birth of Jesus in space-time-history, during the mighty and ruthless period of the Roman Empire. The lives of Caesar Augustus and Herod the Great, Mary and Joseph's trip from Nazareth to Bethlehem, the birth of Jesus, and Jesus are all historical realities.

These historical persons and events are NOT fictitious parables. Parables do not *define* peoples' names and places precisely, but rather use *comparisons* to describe some aspect of how God acts or interacts with human beings. The four Gospels contain parables, but they are not in and of themselves parables. To say that the Gospels are parables is ridiculous!

CAESAR AUGUSTUS AND HIS ROMAN CENSUS

Mary and Joseph lived at the time of world history when the most powerful man ever to live on planet earth was the first Roman Emperor. He was Caesar Augustus, whose name was Octavian (Gaius Octavius).[1]

Luke, as a first-rate historian, provides us with the standard description of a "world-wide" edict of registration issued by Caesar Augustus that covered most of the Roman Empire.

Of course, this imperial census came by means of a formal decree of the Roman Senate.[2] Luke also grounds this Augustan census as taking place "in those days," i.e., in the days of the birth of John the Baptist.[3]

This Augustan registration was called a Roman census, which happened to be conducted in Israel the same year that Jesus was born of Mary.

THE ROMAN CENSUS

Now, what is a Roman census? In today's reality, a census is done every ten years to determine household size.

A Roman census had three requirements:

1. Return to the Ancestral Place of Birth.
2. Register.
3. Pay Taxes.

ANCESTRAL PLACE OF BIRTH

For Jews, an ancestral registration would be a most natural way to sign up for taxes.[4] The Romans allowed these censuses to be conducted on the basis of local customs. For Israel, the Jewish people had a traditional concern for their permanent ancestral place of birth, and not where they were temporarily living. This means that they were to go back to the town where they were born. Since both Joseph and Mary's place of origin was Bethlehem, they both had to travel there.

Thus, an ancestral registration is what the Jewish people did, including Mary and Joseph.[5]

REGISTRATION TAXES

This tax of Caesar Augustus was a census/head tax, and not a property tax. Each person would pay a Roman silver denarius.[6] A denarius was a day's wage for a common worker and for a Roman soldier. Mary, along with all women, would be accountable to go back to their place of origin.

If Joseph and Mary did not pay it, they would be charged with treason and revolutionary sentiment against Imperial Rome. The charge of treason meant death by crucifixion.

THREE AUGUSTAN CENSUSES

Okay, here we go!

Interestingly, Luke says that Jesus' birth occurred when the Roman Emperor Caesar Augustus decreed:

> "In those days a decree went out from Caesar Augustus that all the world should be registered." (Luke 2:1).

The Greek verb in the above passage is a present tense verb; in other words, Caesar ordered censuses to be regularly taken throughout the whole provincial empire.

We know that Caesar Augustus took three major censuses while he was emperor.[7] Records still exist of censuses taken by Caesar Augustus in 28 BC, 8 BC, and AD 14 the year that Augustus died.[8]

The timing of the only Augustan census that makes any sense in dating the birth of Jesus is 8 BC. It cannot be the 28 BC census because Octavian was not yet Emperor Caesar Augustus, which occurred in 27 BC. And, the AD 14 date certainly cannot be the year since Herod the Great died in 4 BC and he is the one who tried to murder the little boy Jesus. You simply cannot have a dead Herod ordering the deaths of little boys in Bethlehem.

QUIRINIUS WAS "NOT" THE GOVERNOR

Doctor Luke also tells us that this Augustan census was the first one conducted in Israel by Quirinius.

Modern Bible translations say Quirinius was the "Governor" of Syria. They are not correct. All that Luke 2:2 says is that Quirinius was "exercising control over" Syria, not that he was the Governor. Luke knew how to use the word "governor" as he did in Luke 20:20; Acts 23:24; 24:1; 26:30.

> **Behold!** Luke does not say Quirinius was the "Governor" of Syria. According to Luke 2:2, Quirinius was "exercising control over Syria." Luke uses the participle, ἡγεμονεύοντος, which is incorrectly translated as governor." Luke's participle in no way, shape, or form means that Quirinius was a governor.

Luke 2:2 should be translated: "This enrollment was the first census when Quirinius exercised control over Syria."

So, Quirinius was NOT the Governor of Syria at this time, but he did hold some type of a unique administrative position as the representative of Caesar Augustus.[9]

Caesar Augustus would have initiated Luke's census in 8 BC with Quirinius working as the administrator of the census in Israel. A major census takes some time to accomplish and requires special administrative skills and authority to complete.

> **Behold**! We also know from the Jewish historian Josephus that Quirinius took a Roman census in the thirty-seventh year after Octavian defeated the combined forces of Mark Antony and Cleopatra at the battle of Actium in 31 BC.[10] Doing simple arithmetic in subtracting thirty-seven from 31 BC, we come to the year AD 6.

But, the census that Luke 2:1 speaks about is not the one in AD 6 because Luke's census is tied to the period before Herod the Great's death according to Matthew 2:1 and Luke 1:5. Luke and Matthew both agree in tying the birth of Jesus to the reign of Herod the Great.

So, let me tell you about Herod the Great's death. This is important because Jesus was born before Herod died.

HEROD THE GREAT'S DEATH

The Jewish historian Josephus tells us that an eclipse occurred right before Herod's death, which allows one to set the date of his death with some specificity.[11] The only eclipse mentioned by Josephus in this period was in March 4 BC.

Josephus also notes that Passover followed Herod's death, which puts the latest he could have died at April 11, 4 BC.[12] Thus, the birth of Jesus and the census must be dated before April 4 BC.

ABOUT A TWO-YEAR DELAY

In 8 BC, Caesar Augustus ordered the census. However, there was not compliance with that census apparently in Israel until two years later. The Jewish people did not like to pay taxes to Rome and apparently Herod was able to put it off as long as possible. Finally, sometime around 6-5 BC, the Jewish people were forced to comply.

And, with Israel being over 1,500 miles from Rome, it would take the Roman officials some time to get established in every Jewish city, in order to undertake and conduct the registration. Therefore, the Augustan census that Luke mentions took place sometime in 6-5 BC.

Now, because of the imperial order of Caesar Augustus to go back to one's ancestral place of birth, everyone journeyed to register back to his own city.[13]

So Joseph also went up from Galilee out of his city of Nazareth to Judea to the city of David, which is called Bethlehem because he was from the house and family of King David.[14] Joseph went to Bethlehem for the sole purpose of being enrolled/registered along with his pregnant wife Mary, the one having been betrothed to Joseph.

LITTLE DID AUGUSTUS KNOW—THAT GOD . . .

Have you ever wondered why Joseph and Mary made that long journey to Bethlehem with Mary being pregnant? It was because the Roman Emperor said so! It is as simple as that. They were required to make a journey to their ancestral home of Bethlehem to fulfill Caesar Augustus' decree.

Think about it for a minute!

God the Father used the first Roman Emperor, Caesar Augustus, and his census to get Mary and Joseph to Bethlehem in order to fulfill Scripture. Little did Augustus know that God used his secular and political census to fulfill prophecy! Mary's son, Jesus, is of Davidic heritage, hence Luke's note that Bethlehem is the city of David.

So, now you know why Joseph and Mary had to journey to Bethlehem—because Caesar Augustus so ordered it.

They're on their way!

But, more importantly, they were on their way to fulfill prophecy.

SPECIAL STUDY #4

UNWRAPPING THE HISTORY OF THE WISEMEN

DO YOU REMEMBER what Matthew 2:1 says? Let me refresh your memory.

> "After Jesus was born in Bethlehem in Judea, during the time of King Herod, Magi from the east came to Jerusalem and asked, 'Where is the one who has been born King of the Jews? We saw his star in the east and have come to worship him.'"

The Wisemen (the Parthian *Megistanes*) came to worship Jesus *after* He was born, which in reality occurred about two years after His birth. The *Megistanes* came from the East to find He who was born King of the Jews. These Wisemen were the *Megistanes* from Parthia, the most feared and powerful group of Parthian king-makers. These noble Wisemen entered Jerusalem in the later days of the reign of Herod the Great when he was in Jerusalem.[1]

When Matthew tells us about the Wisemen, he does not explain who they were and what their history entailed. The people that Matthew addressed in his Gospel already knew those facts. You and I have to study in order to really understand the identity of who the *Megistanes* Wisemen were, where they came from, and what their history was.

If you permit me, I will now provide you with the answers.

THE HISTORY OF THE WISEMEN

The Wisemen have a long and illustrious history. They served the kings of the greatest empires of the ancient world. But to identify these unnamed, unnumbered travelers from the East, we have to journey back through time into the centuries before Jesus' birth.

Are you ready to go back in time? Hang on—here we go!

History tells us that four great world empires successively ruled the ancient world. These were, in order: the Babylonian Empire; the Medo-Persian Empire; the Greek Empire ruled by Alexander the Great; and, at the time of Jesus' birth, the Roman Empire ruled first by the Emperor Octavian (Caesar Augustus).

WISEMEN IN BABYLON

Are you familiar with King Nebuchadnezzar of the Babylonian Empire? You probably remember him when he threw Shadrach, Meshach and Abednego into the fiery furnace.[2]

In 606 BC and again in 586 BC, the Babylonian Empire, under King Nebuchadnezzar, besieged the city of Jerusalem. Eventually, all of Israel was under his domination and many Jews, including the prophet-statesman Daniel, were taken as captives to Babylon.

Now, here is where we first meet the Wisemen.

In King Nebuchadnezzar's royal court, there was a group of natural philosophers (scientists) known as the Magi (Wisemen). The Magi were scientists who were experts in the sciences, especially in astronomy. The Magi were part of the great Babylonian kings' administrations as advisors and consultants.

> **Behold!** In Jeremiah 39:3 and 39:13, we read of a Wiseman named Nergal-Sharezer, the head of the Magi in King Nebuchadnezzar's court. Nebuchadnezzar elevated the Magi

> to exalted positions within his court. He named Daniel, a Jewish prophet, the *Rab-mag* or "Chief Magus" because Daniel interpreted a dream that the other Magi could not.[3]

How amazing is that? The Biblical Daniel was chief Wisemen in the court of King Nebuchadnezzar.

Amazing!

WISEMEN WITH CYRUS THE GREAT

Now, we move in time to the Medo-Persian Empire.

Did you know that Cyrus the Great, King of the Medo-Persian Empire, is mentioned in the Bible? You will be surprised that you already know a number of things about Cyrus the Great.

THE WISEMEN: TEACHERS AND PRIESTS

The Greek historian Herodotus tells us that the Wisemen were the teachers and illuminators of the Persians, especially of the Persian kings, and that they specialized in the interpretation of dreams.[4]

The Wisemen also served as priests in controlling all religious functions in Persia. In 401 BC, the Athenian author Xenophon (c. 430-355 BC) called the Wisemen professional specialists "in everything religious."[5]

CYRUS THE GREAT INCORPORATES THE BABYLONIAN WISEMEN

Herodotus tells us that the King of Media (Astyages) had Wisemen in his royal administration. Cyrus the Great (580-529 BC) defeated the Median Empire and founded the Achaemenid Empire and ruled as its first emperor.

After Cyrus the Great defeated the Median Dynasty and its Wisemen, he united the Medes and the Persians by incorporating nobles from both countries as civilian officials. Some of the Median noblemen were Babylonian Wisemen whom Cyrus the Great had completely conquered when Babylon fell.

When Cyrus the Great subjugated the Babylonian Empire, he laid claim to the powerful Babylonian Empire. Cyrus the Great became "King of Babylon-King of the Land."

> **Behold!** Cyrus the Great allowed more than 40,000 Jews to leave Babylon and return to Israel after 70 years of captivity in the Babylonian Empire.[6]

Cyrus dreamed of establishing a *Pax Achaemenica* where peoples and cultures would be fused into "one world," thus bringing peace to mankind. Cyrus the Great dreamed of this "one-world peace" centuries before the *Pax Romana* (27 BC – AD 180) of the Roman Emperor Caesar Augustus.

When Cyrus the Great subjugated the Babylonian Empire and its Wisemen in the sixth century BC, the Medo-Persian Magi came into contact with the teachings of the Babylonian Wisemen, astronomers and natural philosophers who were also known as the Chaldeans. The Medo-Persian Wisemen and the Babylonian Wisemen became one group designated as the Persian Magi or Wisemen.

WISEMEN WITH DARIUS THE GREAT

THE KILLING OF THE MAGI: A NATIONAL HOLIDAY

When Cyrus the Great's son, Cambyses, came to power as the next Persian king, he subjugated the Magians (Wisemen). But the Magians revolted and crowned head Magi, Gaumata, the King of Persia. Gaumata took the name of Smerdis. In spite of this takeover, a Persian nobleman, Darius, killed Gaumata on September 29, 522 BC. Darius became the new King of Persia.

> **Behold!** Herodotus tells us that the downfall of the Magi (Wisemen) was celebrated by a national Persian holiday called *Magophonia* or the "Killing of the Magian." On that anniversary, a red-letter day in the Persian calendar, no Magian was allowed to appear in public.[7]

THE *PERSEPOLIS FORTIFICATION TABLETS*

Darius the Great established the authority of the Magi over the state religion of Persia. A sizeable collection of governmental texts called the *Persepolis Fortification Tablets* was found in Persepolis, the capital of the Achaemenid Empire. These *Tablets* date to the reign of King Darius I the Great (522-486 BC).

> **Do You Dig It!** In the *Persepolis Fortification Tablets*, archaeologists learned that the Magians (Wisemen) accompanied the Persian kings on their campaigns, serving as accountants and controllers involved in administrative details.[8]

The *Persepolis Fortification Tablets* also mention the Magians' (Wisemen's) religious authority and priestly responsibilities. They were responsible for the most important sacrifices in the Persian state religion.

THE MAGI: "THE KING-MAKERS"

The authority of the Persian Wisemen was so entrenched in the Medo-Persian Empire that *no one* became king without being personally instructed in the academic disciplines by the Wisemen. The Wisemen sanctioned and crowned each new Persian king. With this kind of power, the Wisemen controlled the known Middle-Eastern world as the king-makers!

WISEMEN WITH XERXES

Have you heard of the Persian Wars? These wars were decisive moments in history. The Persian king, Darius the Great, lost the Battle of Marathon against the Athenian Greeks, under the leadership of Miltiades in 490 BC. Later, Darius planned for an all-out campaign against Greece. But, Darius the Great died before carrying out his plan and his son, Xerxes, became the new king of Persia.

The Persian King Xerxes launched an attack against Greece with a massive naval armada of 1,000 warships and with an army of 300,000 men. It was King Xerxes who fought the Spartan war machine of three hundred Spartans under the leadership of the Spartan King Leonidas, along with 7,000 Thespian Greeks who joined Leonidas and his 300 Spartans, at the Battle of Thermopylae in 479 BC.

Now, get this!

According to Pliny, Osthanes, the "Prince of the Magi (Wisemen)," accompanied the Persian King Xerxes as "Chief Magus (Wiseman)" on the campaign against Greece.[9]

How cool is that?

So, when King Xerxes came to burn Athens to the ground and destroy Greece, he brought his Chief Wiseman, Osthanes, with him as an advisor.

> **Behold!** Osthanes also taught Democritus (ca. 460 BC) who is credited as the father of the theory of atomic structure. After visiting Babylon, Democritus wrote two works, *Chaldean Treatise* and *On the Sacred Writings of Those in Babylon.* After visiting Persia, he wrote *Mageia.*

It may be that the atomic theory came not from the Greek Democritus, but from the Wiseman Osthanes who taught Democritus. Time to change all science books—don't you think?

WISEMEN WITH ALEXANDER THE GREAT

I believe that we all have heard of Alexander the Great and how he defeated the great Persian Empire.

The Medo-Persian Empire eventually fell to the military genius and might of Alexander the Great, bringing an end to the powerful Achaemenid Dynasty. Greek sources mention Magians (Wisemen) at Alexander's court performing the usual political and religious duties while others, wearing the garments of the Magian (Wisemen), were killed. This seems to indicate that *some* of the Medo-Persian Wisemen collaborated with Alexander the Great; the Wisemen who refused to join Alexander were murdered.

In time, Alexander's divided empire was systematically crushed by the juggernaut of the ancient world, the Roman war machine. The old Medo-Persian Empire evolved into the Parthian Empire. The

Persian Wisemen, now known as the Parthian *Megistanes*, wielded immense power in the ancient world.

THE PARTHIAN *MEGISTANES*: THE WISEMEN

THE PARTHIAN EMPIRE

The Parthian Empire ruled over the Middle East and Southwest Asia from 247 BC to 228 AD in ancient Persia. In about 150 BC, the Parthian king Mithradates I (ca. 195-138 BC) conquered Media, i.e., the Medo-Persian Empire (Justin xli. 6). The Persian Magians were incorporated into the Parthian Empire and became known as the Parthian *Megistanes.*

THE ROMANS & THE PARTHIANS

The world now had two adversarial superpowers—Rome in the West and Parthia in the East. The borderline was the Euphrates River. Neither one dared cross the boundary.

MARCUS LISINIUS CRASSUS VS THE PARTHIANS

The Roman general, Marcus Lisinius Crassus, attacked Jerusalem. Later, his army lost 30,000 soldiers and was decisively defeated by the Parthians at the Battle of Carrhae in June, 53 BC. Crassus was killed in the battle and the Parthians took Rome's eagle standards.

MARK ANTONY VS THE PARTHIANS

Julius Caesar spoke pointedly of the need to suppress the Parthian danger on the frontiers. He was preparing an expedition to destroy the Parthians when he was assassinated on March 15, 44 BC.

In 40 BC, an assassination attempt on the life of Herod the Great, King of Judea, was made. Herod was deposed and with Parthian collaboration, Jewish sovereignty was restored to Israel with the installation of Antigonus II, the last of the Maccabees, as a Parthian puppet king in Israel.

> **Behold!** In midsummer of 36 BC, Mark Antony led the greatest army that had ever been assembled against the Parthians. With him were sixteen legions, 100,000 men, 10,000 cavalry from Spain and France, and some 30,000 troops from the Roman allies bordering on Persia. Antony had entered into a secret treaty with King Artavasdes of Armenia. Since Orodes, the King of Parthia, had just been murdered by his son, Phraates, everything seemed to be in Antony's favor.
>
> In the course of twenty-seven weary days, the Romans fought eighteen battles and lost 20,000-foot soldiers and 4,000 horsemen. More than half of these perished from hunger and disease. In the following year, Antony determined to avenge his honor and entered Parthia again. But he did not succeed in defeating the powerful Parthian enemy.

OCTAVIAN AND THE PARTHIANS

When Octavian (Caesar Augustus) became the first Roman emperor, many Romans believed the time had come for one last punitive expedition against Parthia. Instead, Augustus feared the Parthians and took pains to keep the peace with them. The captured eagle standards that were confiscated during the Battle of Carrhae were returned to Rome, a sign that peace had been established. But then the Parthian Wisemen arrived looking for He who was born King of the Jews! They crossed the boundary of no return to find Jesus.

NAMES WERE MADE UP FOR THE WISEMEN

As we move through time, we come to a period when names were made up for the Wisemen. Have you heard of the names of Caspar, Melchior, and Balthazar? If you haven't, then your children have. They are the names that have been given to the Wisemen who came to worship the little boy Jesus.

Remember that we have already learned that the *Megistanes* (Wisemen) were not Kings and there were not three of them. AND, their names were not Caspar, Melchior, and Balthazar.

How then did the counterfeit Christmas come up with Wisemen with the names of Caspar, Melchior, and Balthazar?

Here's how!

Our twenty-first century world mistakenly believes that the Wisemen had the names of Caspar, Melchior, and Balthazar. During the second half of the sixth century AD, the identities of the Wisemen were not known so names were fabricated for them in a Greek chronicle from Alexandria, Egypt. That Greek chronicle was translated into the Latin *Excerpta Latina Barbari.*

Gathaspa, Melichior, and Bithisarea were those fabricated names for the Wisemen. It was even claimed that the bones (relics) of the three Wisemen were once kept in Constantinople, then taken to Milan in the fifth century AD, and then to Cologne in AD 1162.

A sixth century AD informant wrongly gave the three kings the Persian names of Hormizdah (King of Persia), Yazdegerd (King of Saba), and Perozadh (King of Sheba). Their Persian names then became orientalized to Caspar, Melchior, and Balthazar. But there is no truth to these names.

In the ninth century AD, an Irish pseudo-Bedan text (Bede the Venerable) titled *Collectanea* or *Excerpta et Collectanea,*[10] added to the lore by saying that Melchior, the oldest Wiseman and the King of Arabia, presented Jesus with gold. Balthazar, the King of Ethiopia, presented Jesus with frankincense. And Caspar, the youngest and King of Tarsus, gave Jesus myrrh.

> **Behold!** In the fourteenth century AD, Caspar was said to be the King of India, Melchior the King of Persia, and Balthasar the King of Arabia.[11]

Other individuals in the fourteenth century AD claimed that there were two, three, four, eight, and as many as a dozen Wisemen.

None of the above points are true!

THE THREE WISEMEN (KINGS) IN MODERNITY

Now let's deal with the modern-day origin of the counterfeit Christmas' three kings. What could be so powerful and influential that the world would listen to instead of what the Bible and history teaches? The answer is a song and a story!

The popular Christmas carol, *We Three Kings*, written by John Henry Hopkins, Jr. in AD 1857, perpetuated the "three Wisemen" myth. The familiar names of Caspar, Melchior, and Balthazar were used in clergyman Henry Van Dyke's story, *The Other Wise Man*, written in AD 1896.

> **Behold!** You may be more familiar with Henry Van Dyke as the author of the hymn "Joyful, Joyful, We Adore Thee," set to the tune of Beethoven's "Ode to Joy" from his Ninth Symphony.

It is truly amazing that virtually the entire world has followed Hopkins and Van Dyke on the number and names of the Wisemen. Just astounding!

Remember, there is no historical evidence that there were exactly three Wisemen, that they were kings, or that their names were Caspar, Melchior, and Balthasar. These descriptors *do not* come from authoritative works, but are the fabrications of imaginative individuals (including the heretic Origen).

The Bible uses the plural construction of Wisemen (*Magoi*) so we know that more than one Wiseman brought gifts and worshipped Jesus. Remember that 80,000 Wisemen lived in Parthia. It's highly unlikely that all 80,000 made the journey.

The most we can say is that the historical evidence indicates that at least two of the powerful Parthian *Megistanes* traveled from the East to worship Jesus. For such an important journey to find the new King, there were probably more than two Wisemen.

I hope that you enjoyed learning a bit more about the history of the Wisemen.

SPECIAL STUDY #5

UNWRAPPING A FEW ADDITIONAL GIFTS

THIS CHAPTER WILL accomplish two purposes. First, it will provide Christians the evidence that they can, without a shadow of a doubt, know that Christianity is true and real. And, secondly, it will abolish barriers established by critics who do not accept Christianity as true and real. We are going to learn a number of *basic* principles that you as a Christian need to know when confronted by the critics' bogus claims.

IS THE BIBLE A MYTH

There are many critics, skeptics, atheists, agnostics, who will tell you to your face that the Bible is nothing but a myth, i.e., just made-up fabricated parables and stories. Well, are they right? If not, how do you answer them?

It's very important to consider whether the Bible is history or myth (Greek, *muthos*).

WHAT IS A MYTH

C.F. Nosgen defines a myth as: "Any unhistorical tale, however it may have arisen, in which a religious society finds a constituent part of its sacred foundations, because an absolute expression of its institutions, experiences, and ideas, is a myth."[1]

According to Nosgen, a myth has no historicity to it. The people and events of a myth (if named at all) cannot be confirmed by other historical documents or by the science of archaeology.

THE NEW TESTAMENT CONDEMNS MYTHS

The critics act like the Biblical writers knew nothing of myths in their times. Not true! The Biblical writers knew of cultural myths and warned Christians against believing them. The following passages explicitly condemn myths.

> "For we did not follow cleverly devised **myths** [*muthos*] when we made known to you the power and coming of our Lord Jesus Christ, but we were eyewitnesses of his majesty" (2 Pet. 1:16; *emphasis added*).

> "As I urged you when I was going to Macedonia, remain at Ephesus so that you may charge certain persons not to teach any different doctrine, nor to devote themselves to **myths** and endless genealogies, which promote speculations rather than the stewardship from God that is by faith" (1 Tim. 1:3-4; *emphasis added*).

> "For the time is coming when people will not endure sound teaching, but having itching ears they will accumulate for themselves teachers to suit their own passions, and will turn away from listening to the truth and wander off into **myths**." (2 Tim. 4:3-4; *emphasis added*).

> "Have nothing to do with irreverent, silly **myths**. Rather train yourself for godliness" (1 Tim. 4:7; *emphasis added*).

"Not devoting themselves to Jewish **myths** and the commands of people who turn away from the truth" (Titus 1:14; *emphasis added*).

Myth is a genre of literature and, like any genre, has its own style. For example, let's briefly look at the book of Genesis. The opening pages of Genesis are not written in the literary style of the myth genre, but in historical prose. For example, Abraham, Isaac, Jacob, Joseph, Noah, and Adam are disclosed as real human beings.

> **Behold!** The Genesis text does not switch literary styles after talking about the Garden of Eden when is discusses places like Ur, Babel, Hebron, Shechem, Haran, Beersheba, Bethel, Egypt, the Mountains of Ararat, and the Tigris and Euphrates Rivers. Archaeologists have found all of the places just mentioned.

The literary scheme doesn't alter as the narrative moves forward. Genesis' literary style doesn't bear *any* resemblance to the myths of antiquity. Whether one agrees or disagrees with what Genesis teaches is irrelevant. What is true is that Genesis (or any other Biblical document) is not classified in the myth genre.

Are the Biblical documents myths, made-up stories, or even parables? Of course not! Any historian worth his/her salt can tell you that. When the Bible books are laid side-by-side with documents from the ancient world that are myths, there is a distinct and dramatic difference between them—like night and day.

When we examine the Biblical books, Genesis through the Revelation, we find that these documents contain the names of hundreds of people, places and events. The Biblical books provide details of events and other cultural information, such as the titles for officials in numerous cultures. These names and details demonstrate that the sixty-six Biblical books belong in the genre of historical prose and not myth.

WHAT IS SAVING FAITH

Yes, it is true that in order to go to Heaven you must accept God's free gift of grace. Your parents, your family, your friends, or any group cannot make that choice for you. The gift of grace is the *only* basis of salvation, but how do we receive this gracious and wonderful gift? The answer is through faith in Jesus.[2]

Let me give you an example. If you were to give me a gift, I have the freedom to accept it or reject it. It is my choice.

By the way, if you want to give me a gift—I will accept it—okay?

Faith is the means that takes the gift of grace salvation—with God alone being the object of that faith.[3]

What is this saving faith that accepts the gift of grace salvation? It's time to look at what God says about the *faith that saves* which *prepares* you for the moment of salvation, i.e., the moment when you become a Christian.

Belief in Jesus as God and what the Bible teaches is absolutely essential to the faith that saves. Listen to a few scriptures. "Without faith, it is impossible to please God."[4] The Apostle Paul tells us that faith comes by "hearing God's Word."[5] God cleanses a person's heart (justifies us) through faith[6] apart from works,[7] so that he can become a Christian.[8] Belief in Jesus' physical resurrection from the dead is absolutely essential for salvation.[9]

It is quite clear that faith is *absolutely* necessary in order to go to Heaven. But, what is this faith that saves?

TWO ESSENTIAL ELEMENTS OF FAITH

But the question is, "what kind of faith are we talking about in order to get to Heaven?" There are two essential and necessary elements, which comprise a saving faith: belief and trust. Remember that grace is a gift and faith is the means and proper response in order to receive God's promise of grace. The Apostle Paul says, "That is why it depends on faith, in order that the promise may rest on grace and be guaranteed to all his offspring—not only to the adherent of the law but also to the one who shares the faith of Abraham, who is the father of us all"[10] Let's look at the two elements of a saving faith.

INTELLECTUAL BELIEF IS "BELIEVING THAT"

What about intellectual faith? This is also called *assent*, which is an intellectual judgment of whether things are true, based on the authoritative testimony of others. In Christianity, you assent to or believe the testimony of Jesus concerning Himself, and what the prophets and apostles wrote in the Bible about Jesus because it is reasonable and logical to do so.[11]

And, never let the critics tell you that the opposite of faith is knowledge. This is not true. The opposite of faith is unbelief.

Faith is Evidentiary

Saving faith is *always* based on the sufficiency of objective evidence. A person "believes that" something is true because the evidence warrants no other conclusion. Look at the following examples. In John 8:24, Jesus said, "I told you that you would die in your sins, for unless you believe that I am He, you will die in your sins." Philip was told by Jesus to "believe that" He is in the Father, and the Father is in Him.[12]

The Apostle John wrote his Gospel so that mankind may "believe that" Jesus is the Christ, the Son of God.[13] Paul said that those who "believe that" God raised Jesus from the dead will be saved.[14] The writer to the Hebrews said that we must "believe that" God exists and that He rewards those who seek Him.[15]

Faith is Always Based on Evidence

Many people believe as the famous skeptic Mark Twain believed when he said, "*Faith* is believing what you know ain't so."[16] This quote demonstrates that famous people can be willfully ignorant and make uneducated and ridiculous statements. Evidently, Mark Twain did not know (or did not take the time to know) what the Greek word "faith" means. Twain's statement is not the meaning of the Greek word "faith" that is used in the Bible. Anyone who believes as Twain did is naïve, gullible, and to be pitied.

Faith is Based on Forensic Proof

The Greek word "faith" in the New Testament is *pistis*. As a noun, *pistis* is a word that was used as a technical rhetorical term for *forensic proof.* Examples of this usage are found in the works of the Greek natural philosopher Aristotle,[17] the Roman Rhetorician Quintilian,[18] and in the Bible.

A form of *pistis* is used over 240 times in the New Testament. In Matthew 9:1-8, the paralytic man, Jairus,[19] the blind man,[20] and the Syrophoenician woman,[21] all came to Jesus to be healed because *they knew* of Jesus' ability to heal, i.e., their actions were based on *evidence and proof.*

Acts 17:31 also uses this word "*pistis*." Peter in Acts 17:31 states, "because he has fixed a day on which he will judge the world in righteousness by a man whom he has appointed; and of this he has given assurance (proof) to all by raising him from the dead" (*emphasis mine*). Peter states that Jesus' physical resurrection is *proof* that God will judge the world.

In Act 2:22-36, the Apostle Peter appealed to the *evidence of the wonders and signs* performed by Jesus; Peter appealed to the *empty tomb*, and appealed to *fulfillment of Old Testament prophecy.* In short, Peter's appeals were *evidentiary.* The point is that Peter grounded faith in Christianity on *evidence* or, as the definition of *pistis* in Acts 17:31 puts it—*proofs*.

INTELLECTUAL BELIEF BY ITSELF WILL NOT SAVE YOU

While intellectual belief is a part of the faith that saves, intellectual belief, by itself, *is not* enough for you to be saved. James says that even the demons (fallen angels) believe that Jesus is God and they tremble and are definitely not saved.[22]

Ironically, we often hear that America is a "Christian nation" because it believes in God. This is a false statement. What God does America believe in? Is it Jesus, Allah, or one of the seventy billion Hindu gods and goddesses? Even if America believes only in Jesus as God, many people do not trust Him and submit to His Lordship in obedience. These people have not surrendered their lives to Jesus. Therefore, they have nothing more than a "demonic faith," which is only an intellectual faith—which *does not* save in and of itself.[23]

Jesus Did Not Believe
in Their Believing

John 2:23. In John 2:23, Jesus was in Jerusalem at the Passover during the feast. Many people believed in Jesus' name, i.e., they believed in who He was. They believed but their believing was not adequate, it was not genuine. Jesus would not entrust Himself to them for they only had an intellectual acknowledgment of who He was and nothing more. Jesus had no faith in their faith. He didn't believe in their believing. Why not? Because though these people believed that Jesus was the Messiah and God, they were unwilling to accept His Lordship and turn from their sins. These people wanted nothing to do with personal sacrifice, repentance, daily obedience to Jesus, and dying daily to self.

John 6:14. After Jesus fed five thousand men plus women and children, the people believed He was the Messiah and wanted to make Him king. But, Jesus withdrew from them to a mountain. He wanted nothing to do with their kind of faith. Yes, they had intellectual assent–but nothing more! Were they willing to give (trust) their lives to Jesus in obedience? No!

John 6:66-69. On another occasion, Jesus told a crowd of people that they had to be willing to accept Him and His teachings into their lives. The sad thing about this occasion was that many of Jesus' disciples withdrew and were not walking with Him anymore.[24] When these disciples left Jesus, He asked His Twelve Apostles: "So Jesus said to the Twelve, 'Do you want to go away as well?' Simon Peter answered him, 'Lord, to whom shall we go? You have the words of eternal life, and we have believed, and have come to know, that you are the Holy One of God.'"[25]

John 8:30-32. On another occasion, Jesus dialogued with some Jewish leaders. The Apostle John said, "As he was saying these things, many believed in him."[26] "So Jesus said to the Jews who had believed him, 'If you abide in my word, you are truly my disciples, and you will know the truth, and the truth will set you free.'"[27] You see, intellectual belief is not saving faith. Yes, saving faith includes intellectual belief, but it *also* includes trusting Jesus in obedience, which includes living the kind of life that He wants you to live.

John 12:42. Also, John 12:42 states, "Nevertheless, many even of the authorities believed in him, but for fear of the Pharisees they did not confess it, so that they would not be put out of the synagogue." You see, these Jewish religious leaders believed in Jesus, but they would not publicly acknowledge Him. They only wanted the approval of men. These religious leaders were going to believe up to a point, but when a total commitment came—they left! Yes, intellectual belief is essential as part of the faith that saves, but it is *not* enough to save you. In order to go to Heaven, the faith that saves must include a second element–trust!

Even in the midst of those disciples who followed Jesus, there were many who momentarily believed and wanted to make Him a king. But, they were not willing to trust Jesus with their lives in total submission to His Lordship. In order to be saved and go to Heaven, you too, must be willing to trust your entire life to Jesus and have Him save you.

TRUST

Many erroneously believe that they can come to Jesus simply by just believing in Him and then walk away to continue living their lives anyway they please. These people only have an intellectual belief in Jesus but no desire to be freed particularly from sin's bondage.

They certainly have no overwhelming desire to obey Jesus and live the way He commands them to live. The faith they are receiving and the faith they are relying on is only an intellectual acquiesce.

A saving faith includes an intellectual belief but it also includes the second element of trust. Trust is a decision of your will to personally submit and surrender your entire life to Jesus, His Lordship, and to the truth about Him that you just believed or assented to. By embracing this kind of trust, you no longer rely on *yourself.* Instead, confidence and reliance in oneself are exclusively to be placed in Jesus and His power to save you.

Listen to the Apostle Paul's trust: "But I am not ashamed, for I know whom I have believed, and I am convinced that he is able to guard until that Day what has been entrusted to me."[28] John 3:16 states, "whosoever believes shall not perish." The word "believe" here is the same word in John 2:24 translated "commit." A saving faith is something deeper than just believing facts; it's committing one's life and submitting to and trusting in Christ.

TRUST IS "BELIEVING IN"

In Scripture, the element of trust is seen in the phrase "believing in" Jesus. For example, the familiar John 3:16 states, "For God so loved the world, that he gave his only Son, that whoever *believes in* him should not perish but have eternal life (*emphasis mine*)."[29] Paul said, "To him all the prophets bear witness that everyone who *believes in* him receives forgiveness of sins through his name (*emphasis mine*)."[30]

Paul told the Philippian jailer to "*Believe in* the Lord Jesus, and you will be saved" (Acts 16:31; *emphasis mine*). Paul also said, "We "*believe in* Him for eternal life" (1 Tim. 1:16; *emphasis mine*).

THE OBJECT OF FATIH

Many individuals claim to have no faith whatsoever. But, this is not true. Every human being believes and trusts in something or someone in their lives—even the atheist and agnostic. The object of that faith is where the difference lies. Every person has faith in something or someone. Some place their faith in themselves or in some false god. The object of the Christian's faith (belief and trust) is Jesus.

The Christian's faith is powerful and effective because it is in the Lord, God, and Savior, Jesus the Christ. If you want to go to Heaven, then you must "believe that" Jesus is Almighty God and that He has physically risen from the dead. And, you must "believe in" Jesus to save you, i.e., you must trust Him and commit your life in obedience to His Lordship.

THE BEST ILLUSTRATION OF FAITH

We now have a great definition! Faith is belief and trust in some person or thing – based upon the evidence. For Christians, we believe and trust in Jesus as our Lord, God, and Savior.

Permit me to give you a true story that will really clarify what faith is.

On June 30, 1859, a 1,100-foot tightrope was stretched across the famous Niagara Falls. This rope was suspended 160 feet above Niagara Falls with no net. It was a crowd of over twenty-five thousand people who witnessed a Frenchman, the great Charles Blondin, become the first man in history to walk across Niagara Falls on a tightrope, without any kind of safety harness.

The Great Blondin made it! Actually he did it several times, seventeen times in all, even pushing a wheelbarrow of cement over the Falls. A remarkable achievement!

Now, after one of his crossings, the Great Blondin asked his cheering audience: "Do you believe I can carry a person across in this wheelbarrow?"

The crowd devotedly shouted, "Yes! You are the greatest tightrope walker in the world. We believe!"

"Okay," said Blondin, "Who wants to get into the wheelbarrow?"

NO ONE ACCEPTED!

You see the people believed Blondin could push a person in a wheelbarrow across the Falls, but they did not "trust" him enough to get into that wheelbarrow. That is what Biblical saving faith is. Faith is "believing that" the facts of the Bible, like Jesus' physical resurrection from the dead, are true and real. Then "believing in" Jesus means trusting Him by giving your life to Him as He pushes you in His wheelbarrow across the journey of life to Heaven.

FAITH IS NOT SUBJECTIVE FEELINGS

God's Word, the Bible, is the only objective and trustworthy account of God's plan of salvation. Faith comes from scholarly, objective, and evidentiary inquiry, not as some sanctified denial of reality, guesswork, or subjective feelings. What a person *feels* is totally irrelevant in light of God's objective truth.

Listen to the following scriptures: "For what can be known about God is plain to them, because God has shown it to them. For His invisible attributes, namely, His eternal power and divine nature, have been clearly perceived, ever since the creation of the world, *in the things that have been made*. So they are without excuse (*emphasis mine*)."[31] "Now faith is the assurance of things hoped for, the conviction of things not seen."[32]

A person has faith in God and the Bible because one can *know* the *plain* and *clearly seen* objective facts. Faith is "being sure" and "being certain" of the objective facts about Jesus and what the Bible teaches. Christians believe in what the Bible says about God and salvation through Jesus Christ, because it is shown to be *accurate* and *factual* through historical, literary, and the science of archaeological *proofs*.

KIERKEGAARD'S FALSE VIEW OF FAITH "A LEAP OF FAITH"

Genuine salvation requires true saving faith, i.e., faith based on evidence! But, it has to be the right kind of faith. You see, there is more than one kind of faith. There is a false and heretical view of faith that says that faith is "a leap of faith," i.e., believing in what is illogical, or what has been called "blind faith," or what I call "Mark Twain faith!" This "blind ignorance" view of faith is in itself illogical and willfully made by fools who live on emotion and not by reason.

A leap of faith is the act of believing in something without, or in spite of, available empirical evidence. But, remember, the Greek word "*pistis*" that is used in the Bible means "forensic proof." The phrase "a leap of faith" originated with the philosopher Søren Kierkegaard (AD 1813-1855), who stated that the only way to accept genuine Christianity is through a leap of faith, a faith that is totally independent of reason or evidence. Kierkegaard's view of faith is totally false and to be completely rejected. Only a fool would give his life, finances, and time to anything or anyone that could not be verified as true!

MIRACLES

What are miracles? Many Christians today call all kinds of things miracles when they are not. You always hear—the birth of a baby is miraculous. NO, not really. The birth of a child is wondrous but not a miracle. If a child's birth is a miracle, then we have around seven billion birth miracles on planet earth today.

Many people recognize events as miracles when they are not miracles at all but rather they are God's supernatural providence. Have you heard of the Biblical teaching of God's providence?

SUPERNATURAL PROVIDENCE

Let's make a distinction between miracles and providence—okay?

Providence is anytime that God intervenes in our lives as Christians. These interventions are of course supernatural, but not miraculous. Why not? Because acts of providence happen within the boundaries of natural law that God has ordered in this universe. They do not violate the laws of nature, but are from God alone. For example, when a person is healed through prayer, that is God directly, and yes, supernaturally, intervening in one's life.

Does God supernaturally and providentially work in our lives as Christians? Of course, every day!

DO MIRACLES VIOLATE NATURAL LAW

Now, do I personally believe in miracles? Absolutely!

Let's talk about miracles. Do miracles violate the laws of nature?

First, I have to tell you that critics say the laws of nature are unchallengeable, unchangeable patterns in a closed universe. The critic says that the laws of nature are fixed in our space-time universe.

They say that there is a uniformity in our universe that remains the same day-by-day. What they are saying is that everything that has happened or will happen is an instance of some law of nature to which there are no exceptions. This is not correct.

Then, just what are the laws of nature?

The laws of nature are only descriptions of what we humans have observed in the ordinary course of time. Over mankind's history on planet Earth, men have made revisions to these laws in accordance with more observations. Who is to say that there are no other laws?

So, what does a miracle do to the laws of nature? Does it violate the laws of nature? No! Miracles simply *transcend* nature. The cause-effect pattern that operates in our physical universe is not violated.

A miracle is a divine introduction of a supernatural effect coming outside of nature into the day-by-day course of nature. Nature is not violated by a miracle; it only exists outside the ordinary course of nature.

Let me explain.

When Jesus, the divine source, did the miracle of feeding 5000 men plus women and children, the bread and fish were real bread and fish. The bread and fish were created from nothing but once they were present in Jesus' hands, they were part of nature. If not eaten, the bread would have gotten old, the fish would have stunk and rotted — things that are part of the ordinary course of nature. Therefore, miracles presuppose and require natural law.

Think about this!

Because of sin, we all live in a universe that has been cursed and affected by sin. Miracles, rare as they have been, are the promise of healing this sin-affected universe. Because miracles did not happen every day, when they did occur in Bible times, it was very plain that God was behind them. Miracles are evidence of the divine authority of the one who is doing the miracle.

Miracles are a higher pattern or law that intervenes in the ordinary course of nature.

Look at this:

In the Bible when God brought about redemptive works, there was always revelation from a Prophet or Apostle to explain those redemptive works. How do miracles fit into this equation? Miracles authenticate the revelation from the Prophet or Apostle to verify that it was God alone who brought about this redemptive act and it confirms the message (the revelation) as God's alone.

Now, every effect must have a sufficient cause but there are some effects that cannot be explained unless we allow for a miraculous cause. Just because we do not presently see physical resurrections from the dead today that in no way states that they never happened in the past. There are testimonies of people who have experienced miracles—the people from the Bible. These testimonies cannot be excluded; they must be investigated.

Once a miracle occurred in nature, it was now in the domain of the historian to investigate.

UNWRAPPING THE TRUTH ABOUT MITHRA

Did the four Gospel writers in the New Testament copy a pagan Roman myth and turn it into the birth of Jesus, the miraculous ministry of Jesus, and His death and physical resurrection?

The answer is a resounding "no!"

In this section, I will provide you with one of the answers to this error-ridden claim that Christians copied the life of a pagan Roman deity named Mithra and recreated it into the birth of Jesus in the New Testament.

These critics guard and cherish twelve claims that *supposedly* prove that the four Gospel writers copied the story of the Roman Mithra to create the life of Jesus.

You can see the twelve points from the book of one of these critics, D. Murdock. Her book is titled, *The Christ Conspiracy.*[33] Murdock prefers to be called Acharya S. Acharya, meaning teacher or guru. I will address her by Ms. Murdock.

For our purposes in this book, I will only refute the first claim that the virgin birth of Jesus was copied from the pagan Roman god Mithra. For the other eleven claims see Mike Liona's refutation of Ms. Murdock's entire book.[34]

The historical evidence clearly demonstrates that Roman Mithraism did not come before Christianity. As we investigate this first claim, you will learn how ridiculous this claim is.

These critics try to dupe and lure you into believing one of the most unscholarly viewpoints ever told. Again, I will only refute the first claim.

But first—please allow me to provide you with some background material on Roman Mithraism. It will help you understand what I will be telling you.

BACKGROUND OF MITHRAISM

THE PERSIAN MITHRA

As early as 1400 BC, Mithra was part of a Hindu deity called Mitra and was later included in the Persian pantheon (550-330 BC). Because Mithra was mentioned in a few hymns in the Vedic and Persian versions, scholars know very little about this secretive deity.[35] The worshippers of the Persian Mithra held their ceremonies in cave-like structures.

> **BEHOLD!** Called Lord of the Contract, the Persian Mithra spied on people from the portals of the heavens. Mithra and his sidekick, Victory, descended in a boar's head chariot and

punished people who didn't fulfill their contracts. Nothing else is known about this deity.

THE ROMAN MITHRA

In the third century AD, a different version of Mithra was created. The historical documentation for this new Roman Mithra doesn't come from its worshippers, but from Christians who were intent on exposing this false deity. The Roman Mithra wore a Phrygian hat and a cape. Though he had animal friends, his two torch-bearing assistants helped him slay a bull. The Roman Emperor Aurelian was the one who fabricated the Roman Mithra.

AURELIAN: THE ROMAN EMPEROR WHO DELIBERATELY COPIED THE CHRISTIANS' DECEMBER 25 DATE

Aurelian only reigned as a Roman Emperor for about five years, from AD 270 to 275. He was besieged by barbarian incursions that had taken control of former Roman territories. Queen Zenobia, from the city of Palmyra, controlled the domains of Israel, Syria, Egypt, and Asia Minor. Her Palmyrene Empire posed a great threat to Aurelian and his Roman Empire.

Aurelian defeated Queen Zenobia and regained former Roman lands. Desperate to reinvigorate the collapsing Roman Empire, Aurelian did what no Roman had ever done in the illustrious annals of Roman history. He tried to create a monotheistic religion for the entire Roman Empire—"one god, one empire."

Aurelian reestablished the sun god, *Sol Invictus*, in AD 274 who was the deity of a previous Roman Emperor, Elagabalus (AD 204-222).

He gave *Sol Invictus* a new name and identity, Mithra, and built a new temple. He hoped to reunite his people around the worship of his Roman Mithra.

By the time of Aurelian's reign, Christians were already celebrating Jesus' birth on December 25. To curtail Christianity's popularity and to give his new god Mithra a boost, Aurelian created a competing alternative to the rapidly spreading movement of Christianity.

The Roman Emperor Aurelian appropriated (copied/stole) the Christian's December 25 date for the birth of Jesus and instituted a pagan festival, to be held each December 25, that he called the *Sol Invictus* ("Birth of the Unconquered Sun").

> **BEHOLD!** Aurelian planned to replace Christianity with his Roman Mithra by using the Christian December 25 date to give new life to his dying empire. His new "one god-one empire" collapsed when he failed to gain the trust and respect of the people of Rome. Aurelian did breathe life back into a dying Empire, but it was short lived. His own soldiers murdered him.

A BRIEF HISTORY OF DECEMBER 25

Ancient literature in the second century AD supports December 25 as the date of Jesus' birth. But, the Bible does NOT say Jesus was born on December 25. This date has no bearing on whether Jesus' birth is a historical event. The only relevance that it does have is that Christians in the second century AD were celebrating December 25 as the day Jesus was born. And, that it was the Romans who copied the Christians' date of December 25—not the other way around. Please keep this in mind—okay?

Telesphorus

Telesphorus of Rome during AD 129-137 instituted the tradition of celebrating midnight Mass, which means Christmas already was being celebrated. He stated: "in the holy night of the Nativity of our Lord and Savior, they do celebrate public church services, and in them solemnly sing the *Angels' Hymn*, because also the same night he was declared unto the shepherds by an angel, as the truth itself doth witness."

Without mentioning the date, Telesphorus does tell us that Christians were celebrating Jesus' birth in the 120s-130's AD. This celebration most certainly implies that a celebration of the birth of Jesus had earlier been practiced before the authorized tradition.

Theophilus

Theophilus (AD 115-181), Bishop of Caesarea and a contemporary of Telesphorus, insisted on "the observance or celebration of the birthday of our Lord [be held] on what day soever the 25 of December shall happen."[36]

> **BEHOLD!** Theophilus (c. AD 181) specifically records Christians celebrating the December 25 date for Jesus' birthday 93 years *before* the Emperor Aurelian copied the Christian date in order compete with Christianity and to resuscitate his dying Empire.

Hippolytus

Several manuscripts of the *Commentary on Daniel*, written by Hippolytus (AD 170-236), state: "For the first appearance of our Lord in the flesh took place in Bethlehem eight days before the Kalends of January [25 December], on the fourth day [Wednesday], under Emperor Augustus, in the year 5500 from Adam."[37]

Hippolytus specifically records the December 25 date as Jesus' birthdate almost 200 years before the first Roman celebration of Mithra's birthdate as December 25.

Justin Martyr

Justin Martyr (AD 100-165) wrote a comprehensive letter to Emperor Marcus Aurelius concerning the birth of Jesus taking place in Bethlehem "as you can ascertain also from the registers of the taxing."[38]

In other words, Justin Martyr told the emperor that the December 25 date could be confirmed by researching the Roman tax registries from the census decreed by Caesar Augustus.

Interestingly, there are no documents stating that "the registers of the taxing" did not include the date of Jesus' birth.

Tertullian

Tertullian (AD 160-250) writes of "the census of Augustus – that most faithful witness of the Lord's nativity, kept in the archives of Rome."[39] Here again, an early Christian writer provided a governmental resource that confirmed Jesus' date of birth.

Again, there are no documents stating that the archives of Rome did not include "the census of Augustus" and the date of Jesus' birth.

Sextus Julius Africanus

In AD 211, the Syrian Sextus Julius Africanus (AD 180-250) was the regional ambassador to Rome. He then became a protégé of the

Roman Emperor Severus Alexander. Africanus assumed that Jesus' conception occurred on March 25 and that he was born nine months later on December 25.

> **BEHOLD!** Africanus' intent was to provide additional support to the widely held tradition, passed down from the earliest days of the Church of Christ that Jesus was born on December 25. We know that, as early as AD 181, Christians celebrated Jesus' birth on December 25 as recorded as Jesus' birthdate.

Cyril

Over a hundred years later, Cyril of Jerusalem (AD 348-386) inquired of Julius, the Bishop of Rome, to learn the date Jesus' birth "from the census documents brought by Titus to Rome" after he had annihilated the city and people of Jerusalem in AD 70. Julius claimed he had access to the original Roman birth census that documented Jesus' birth on December 25.

Once again, there are no documents stating that Jesus' birth on December 25, as found in the census documents of Titus, were wrong.

John Chrysostom

In a sermon preached by John Chrysostom (AD 345-407) of Antioch, he stated that Christians were celebrating Jesus' birth on December 25.[40] Chrysostom claimed that Julius, at the request of Cyril of Jerusalem, had the official records of the Roman census examined and determined December 25 was the correct birthdate.

There are no documents stating that Jesus' birth on December 25, as the official records of the Roman census, were wrong.

THE PAGANS COPIED THE CHRISTIANS

In AD 274, the winter solstice occurred on December 25. To celebrate the event, the Roman Emperor Aurelian (AD 214-275) declared the pagan cult of *Sol Invictus* (now identified with Mithra) as the official religion of Rome. Aurelian proclaimed December 25 as *Natalis Solis Invicti*, a civic holiday celebrating the birth of the invincible sun god Mithra. This new cult played no role in Rome (or anywhere else) until Aurelian instituted the festival.

> **BEHOLD!** According to the literary evidence of Theophilus and Hippolytus, December 25 had been established as Jesus' birthdate long before Aurelian's first winter solstice celebration. The emperor appropriated the Christian date as a pagan alternative and to make a political statement – that his god Mithra was an important deity in competition with the Christian God—Jesus.

DECEMBER 25 MADE OFFICIAL

Other Roman emperors attempted to renew the Christian celebrations. Constantine the Great (AD 274-337), the first Roman emperor to become a Christian, introduced Christmas as a day of feasting in AD 336 to celebrate Jesus' birth on December 25. Julius I (d. AD 352) established December 25 as the "official" date of the birth of Jesus in AD 350.

Historical records provide evidence that efforts were made to celebrate Jesus' birth on December 25. In AD 336, the Philoclian Calendar had Jesus' birth on December 25. Bishop Liberius of Rome officially ordered the celebration of Christmas on December 25 in

AD 354. Chrysostom (AD 345-407), one of the most important Church Fathers, officially reconfirmed December 25 as the date of Jesus' birth in AD 386.

The notion that Christianity copied Mithra's December 25 birthday is an absolute myth with no historical verification. The *earliest* record of a *Sol Invictus* festival being celebrated on December 25 was in AD 274 by the Emperor Aurelian who copied the Christians' December 25 date in order to compete with Christianity. This was done 93 years AFTER the first recorded celebration of Christmas on December 25 as recorded by Theophilus (c. AD 181).

> **BEHOLD!** The very first notion that Christianity copied the pagan celebration of December 25 comes from Protestant preacher Paul Ernst Jablonski (AD 1693-1757) who said December 25 was nothing more than one of the many "paganizations" of a pagan Roman feast created by the medieval Roman Catholic Church.[41]
>
> A Catholic Benedictine monk named Dom Jean Hardouin (AD 1646-1729), responded to Jablonski affirming his theory that the Roman Catholic Church did adopt the pagan celebration of December 25 for Christian purposes, but without compromising the integrity of the gospel.
>
> Both Jablonski and Hardouin were wrong! Without any corroborating evidence, these men asserted that Christianity's December 25 date for Jesus' birth was a "paganization" from a Roman belief. However, the evidence supports the exact opposite: that the pagan Romans copied Christianity's December 25 date.

WHAT ABOUT SATURNALIA

The Romans celebrated a festival of Saturnalia each December 17. The Romans enjoyed the festival so much it became a multi-day event, lasting until December 23. But the Saturnalia festival had nothing to do with Christianity. Remember that the first occurrence of the Romans celebrating December 25 as the birthdate of Mithra did not occur until AD 274!

There is no evidence of a major sun cult at the time of the Northern Hemisphere's winter solstice, nor was there a religious significance for any Roman festival until AD 274. Rome had two sun temples – the festival day for one was August 9 and the festival day for the other was August 28. Neither of these dates correlates to solstices or equinoxes.

NOW WE ARE READY!

What I have just shown you is there were Christians celebrating Jesus birth on December 25 many years before the pagan Romans used that date for their pagan god Mithra. It was the pagan Roman Emperor Aurelian who stole the December 25 day from Christians and not the other way around.

AGAIN, please let me say that the Bible does not say December 25 is the day Jesus was born. The date of December 25 is not relevant in the Bible, but ONLY that it was used by Christians in the second century AD onward—many years before the pagan Romans made use of it—okay?

Now that you know a little bit about the Roman Mithra, it's time to show you that the Gospel of Luke did NOT copy the "so-called" virgin birth of the Roman Mithra.

Again, you decide! Here we go!

CLAIM #1 – THE ROMAN MITHRA WAS BORN OF A VIRGIN ON DECEMBER 25 IN A CAVE AND SHEPHERDS ATTENDED HIS BIRTH

My position is that the actual date of Jesus' birth is not mentioned in Scripture and has nothing to do with the legitimacy of New Testament Christianity. That's the bottom line—the end of the matter!

But, church leaders in the second century AD report that Christians celebrated Jesus' birth on December 25. These early leaders had the date of December 25 long before the writings of Roman Mithraism.

Okay, listen to this first point of Mithraism. According to the Roman mythology, the Roman Mithra's virgin birth was when he came out of a rock, a fully-grown man. Wearing a Phrygian cap, he clutched torches that exploded red flames all around him.

You have just heard the account of the virgin birth of the pagan Roman god Mithra. Now, I am thinking the very same thing as you are.

Where is the virgin birth of the Roman Mithra? Roman mythology doesn't mention a virgin mom or a first-floor stable of a two-story home. The Roman Mithra myth does not speak of a virgin conception.

In the Roman Mithra mythology, shepherds helped the Roman Mithra emerge from a rock "fully grown" and gave him the first fruits of their flock.

Please answer me a very simple question!

Where in the New Testament does it say that Jesus' virgin birth/conception has Him coming out of a rock as a fully-grown man with the aid of shepherds, wearing a Phrygian cap from Asia Minor, clutching torches that exploded red flames all around him?

Now, I cannot see where this is found. And remember, the critics are telling us that the Biblical document of Luke's birth of Jesus directly copied the pagan Roman Mithra birth story!

Where is it?

This Roman Mithra incident has *no* parallel in the New Testament accounts of Jesus' birth. It is beyond reason and common sense to believe that Christians copied a story about a fully-grown man coming out of a rock with firecrackers ablazing in each hand. How does one go from that bizarre story to a virgin conception of God becoming a human male being born in a cold, damp, stinking, urine/feces filled first floor stable of a two-story home?

> **Behold!** Finally, the pagan Roman deity Mithra was supposedly "born" before humans were created. But, remember that the Roman Mithra was helped to come out of a rock—by shepherds! If Mithra was born before any other human beings **then where did the shepherds come from?** Do you get my point? Clearly, the Gospel accounts of Jesus' birth have absolutely nothing in common with the idiotic mythology of Roman Mithraism.

What do you think? I can hear you loud and clear. Claim #1 goes down in flames as a ridiculous assertion.

The Gospel writers did not copy any pagan sources to create Jesus' birth narrative.

This refutation of a laughable and absurd claim is a fitting way to end this book!

Christianity and the Bible are inseparable and both are true.

Both are real!

Both are true!

How do we know? Read the book again!

May you be blessed in your life of service to our great God and Savior, Jesus the Christ.

CLOSING REMARKS

I FELT THAT I could not end this book without offering you a few more words of encouragement.

In preparing this book, my prayer has been that you would come to know the truth about the birth of Jesus. I hope that you got to know Mary and Joseph in a new and fresh way, not as made–up stories, but as real people. I took the historical and Biblical facts and tried to present how Mary and Joseph were feeling, thinking, and what they might possibly have said.

Belief in the virgin conception is an essential teaching of the Christian worldview. Without it there is no Jesus and His earthly ministry, no physical death on a Roman cross, no physical burial in Joseph of Arimathea's tomb, no physical resurrection from the dead, no physical appearances to His enemies and disciples, no substitutionary atonement, and no Heaven. So, do not be dismayed, all of these things are real and true.

You and I have a race to run. I began this book by telling you the beginning of my race, from Vacation Bible School to the present. Throughout all of these years, I have not found even one credible piece of evidence that disproves the historical claims that the Bible makes—not one!

Never let any person—would s/he be a family member, friend, teacher, preacher, or writer sway and persuade you to believe that the Gospels are made-up stories. Don't let anyone lead you to believe in a Jewish man who was nothing more than a Jewish comedian, who died, and whose body was eaten by dogs, i.e., a "souped-up" Santa Claus Jesus. Your eternity in Heaven depends upon it!

Do not allow anyone to tell you that the virgin conception is a myth, a made up story, to cover the adulterous activity of Mary. This is a counterfeit Christmas.

Now you know that our modern day nativity scenes are incorrect. This, too, is a counterfeit Christmas. Am I telling you to discard your nativity scenes? No, not at all! Here is what you can do inside your home. You can move the Wisemen to another room and put up a sign that says "We're on our way, see you in about two years." Then go to a local toy store and buy 20,000 little men on horseback and put them around "at least two" Wisemen.

What do you think of my suggestion?

So many Christians feel frustrated, discouraged, unappreciated, and undervalued. Do not be discouraged because life is hard. Just keep remembering the hardships that Mary and Joseph went through. They remained faithful and obedient—and the Lord provided. That is what you and I must do too.

And, take this with you—My prayers go with you as you continue on your race to Heaven. Just as God gave and is still providing me grace for my race, He will most certainly do the same for you.

Let me say this—the virgin conception is a fact. It happened during the days of the first Roman Emperor, Caesar Augustus. The historical Jesus is the God-man, unlimited God and perfect sinless man. His blood that was shed in death on a Roman cross can cleanse anyone from his/her sins. His substitutionary atonement pays the debt of an eternity in hell for those who will accept it. Jesus physically rose from the dead! Yes, dead men do miraculously come back to life—at least Jesus did. He physically appeared to His enemies and disciples and then ascended back into Heaven. One day Jesus will return again in His second coming—what a glorious day that will be!

None of this would be possible if Jesus had not been born of the

Virgin Mary in a cold, damp, stinking, urine/feces filled first floor of someone's home in the little town of Bethlehem!

It is real!

It is true!

How do we know? Because of the overwhelming evidence!

The message in this book is a simple but profound one. I just took it from the Bible and have passed it on to you.

Now, you do likewise.

Pass it on to others—okay?

Blessings!

ENDNOTES

INTRODUCTION

[1] The print itself is created by cutting into the exterior of a level block of wood, removing regions that will stay white. The elevated areas will take the ink and create the image.

[2] This self-professed group is called the Jesus Seminar.

Two members of the Jesus Seminar, Dominic Crossan and Marcus J. Borg, have written a book titled, *The First Christmas: What the Gospels Really Teach About Jesus's Birth.* HarperOne: 2009. This work is diametrically different than my book *The Counterfeit Christmas: What the Gospels Really Teach About Jesus' Birth.*

The view of Crossan and Borg is that the Gospels are parables, i.e., made-up, fabricated, bogus stories of Jesus. These men do not believe in the supernatural and miraculous. Jesus is not God. The virgin birth did not happen. Jesus did not physically rise from the dead. And, God does not even exist. And, it goes on.

I, on the other hand, believe that Jesus is God. The Gospels are historical documents about a historical person(s). This means that there is a supernatural—and miracles did take place. The virgin birth (conception) happened in space-time history. Jesus was murdered on a Roman cross, buried in a rich man's tomb, physically rose from the dead, and physically appeared to his enemies and disciples.

Do you see the contrast? My book and their book are at polar extremes—like night and day. The viewpoints of both books cannot be right. You, the reader, must decide who is right.

Marcus Borg does not believe that Jesus physically rose from the dead when he said: "Easter need not involve the claim that God supernaturally intervened to raise the corpse of Jesus from the tomb. Rather, the core meaning of Easter is that Jesus continued to be experienced after his death, but in a radically new way: as a spiritual and divine reality" (*The God We Never Knew: Beyond dogmatic Religion to a More Authentic Contemporary Faith.* HarperOne [August 29, 1998]), p. 93.

Borg is wrong!

Borg suggests that "to speak of one God and three persons is to say that God is known to us wearing three different 'masks'—in other words, in three different roles" (*The God We Never Knew*, p. 98).

Borg is wrong!

In regards to Scripture, Borg says, "the stories of Jesus' birth are myths in this sense . . . I do not think these stories report what happened. The virginal conception, the star, the wise men, the birth in Bethlehem where there was no room in the inn, and so forth are not facts of history" (*The God We Never Knew*, p. 102).

Borg is wrong!

Concerning whether Jesus is God, Borg rejects it saying, "Jesus did not speak of himself (and apparently did not think of himself) as divine. So was the pre-Easter Jesus God? Was he divine? Apparently not in any sense of which he and his followers were aware" (*The God We Never Knew*, p. 88).

Borg is wrong!

Robert Funk, the Seminar's founder, says, "It is time for us [scholars] to quit the library and study and speak up....The Jesus Seminar is a clarion call to enlightenment. It is for those who prefer facts to fancies, history to histrionics, science to superstition" (Robert Funk, *The Gospel of Mark, Red Letter Edition* [Sonoma, CA: Polebridge Press, 1991]), pp. xvi- xvii.

Funk is wrong!

Robert Funk calls Jesus a "secular sage who satirized the pious and championed the poor." He then adds, "Jesus was perhaps the first stand-up Jewish comic. Starting a new religion would have been the farthest thing from his mind."

Funk is wrong!

Robert Funk admits: "The Gospels are now assumed to be narratives in which the memory of Jesus is *embellished by mythic elements* that express the church's faith in him, and by *plausible fictions* that enhance the telling of the gospel *story* for first-century listeners. . ." (Robert Funk, Roy Hoover, and the Jesus Seminar, *The Five Gospels: What Did Jesus Really Say?* [New York: Macmillan, 1993]), p. 5.

Funk is wrong!

Dominic Crossan, the Jesus Seminar's co-founder, has stated, "When I look a Buddhist friend in the face, I cannot say with integrity, 'Our story about Jesus' virginal birth is true and factual. Your story that when the Buddha came out of his mother's womb, he was walking, talking, teaching and preaching (which I must admit is even better than our story)---that's a myth. We have the truth; you have a lie." I don't think that can be said any longer, for our insistence that our faith is a fact and that others' faith is a lie is, I think, a cancer that eats at the heart of Christianity (*Will the Real Jesus Stand Up? A Debate Between William Lane Craig and John Dominic Crossan*: Grand Rapids: Baker Book House, 1998, p. 39.

Crossan is wrong!

Hank Hanegraaff has correctly quoted what some of these Jesus Seminar members have stated. These views that you are about to read are contrary to what the Biblical and historical evidence clearly shows.

"According to the Jesus Seminar, Jesus is said to be the illegitimate son of a Roman soldier, while the story of His Virgin Birth was a cover-up; He wasn't born in Bethlehem; the betrayal of Jesus was a fabrication concocted by Christians as an anti-Semitic slur; His dead body was not buried but left on the cross and then eaten by birds and prowling dogs; and His resurrection is a story borrowed from the literature of Eastern pagan cults called mystery religions" (*The Search for Jesus Hoax*. *Christian Research Journal*, volume 23, number 2 (2000).

Hanegraaff quotes Jesus Seminar cofounder John Dominic Crossan's claims that there were dozens of virgin birth stories circulating in Greek and Roman mythology during the first century. Says Crossan, "They're all over Greek and Roman mythology, so what do I do? Do I believe all of those stories, or do I say all of those stories are lies except for our Christian story" (*The Search for Jesus Hoax*).

Yes, they are all lies…except our Christian story!

Hanegraaff quotes Jesus Seminar fellow Marcus Borg who gave one of the more curious suggestions in *The Search For Jesus* with his claim that Jesus was not born in Bethlehem. First, the assertion is made that only two Gospels deal with the place of Christ's birth, and they tell it differently. Luke says Jesus was born in a manger while Matthew says Jesus is born at home. Further, it is argued that there is no record outside the Gospels that Caesar Augustus ordered a worldwide taxation. Moreover, a man was taxed where he worked and women were not even counted. Therefore, Mary and Joseph would not have had to travel to Bethlehem. Finally, it is suggested that people were known by the place where they were born. Since Jesus is known as Jesus of Nazareth, He must have been born there — not Bethlehem.

Hanegraaff quotes Jesus Seminar co-founder Crossan who contends that the story of Jesus' burial is based on hope not history: "Was Jesus buried at all?...The purpose of crucifixion was state terrorism and the function was to leave the body on the cross for the carrion, crows, and the prowling dogs. It was not simply that it made you suffer a lot. It meant that you didn't get buried. That's what made it one of the supreme Roman penalties. Lack of burial. As I read those stories, I feel terribly sympathetic for the followers of Jesus because I hear hope there, not history."

Now, here is what some scholars have said about the members of the Jesus Seminar.

Dr. Richard Hays, New Testament professor at Duke Divinity School, writes that the seminar was "sponsored by not one of the major scholarly societies such as the *Studiorum Novi Testamenti Societas* or the *Society of Biblical Literature*." Also, he observes that: "This self-selected group, though it includes several fine scholars, does not represent a balanced cross section of scholarly opinion. Furthermore, the criteria for judgment that are employed are highly questionable" (*First Things*, May 1994, p. 44).

Dr. D.A. Carson, New Testament professor at Trinity Evangelical Divinity School, writes, "for all its scholarly pretension, the Jesus Seminar is not addressing scholars. It is open grab for the popular mind, for the mass media" (*Christianity Today*, 25 April 1994, p. 33).

Concerning the Jesus Seminar, Joel Belz, editor of *World* magazine, writes about how "loaded the project was' with 'social engineers' with a doctrinal, not theological social agenda" (*World*, 25 December 1993, p. 3).

Dr. Jacob Neusner, professor of religion studies at the University of South Florida "refers to the Jesus Seminar as 'the greatest scholarly hoax since the Piltdown Man'" (*The Lutheran Witness*, April 1994, p. 5).

Oxford University scholar, N.T. Wright, deems the seminar's findings a "freshman mistake" and notes that recent books denying the Biblical accounts of Christ as well as the Jesus Seminar have no credible explanation as to the willingness of obviously sane, reasonable, and extremely ethical disciples and followers of Christ to be willing to die for the cause based on the resurrection of Jesus (*Christianity Today*, 13 September 1993, pp. 22-26).

[3] R.W. Funk, R. W. Hoover (eds.). *The Five Gospels: The Search for the Authentic Words of Jesus*. (Sonoma: Polebridge Press; New York: Macmillan, 1993), p. 32.

[4] The negative critics have two illicit presuppositions.

First, they believe that there is no supernatural realm of any kind. Therefore, this means that God does not exist. And, miracles are not possible. Do you see what the critic throws out the door even before looking at any evidence? There is no virgin conception, no healing miracles, no deliverances from demons, and no physical resurrection from the dead.

Let me share something here. When the critic says that there is no God anywhere, that statement is a broad, universal statement, isn't it? In order to legitimately say that, that critic would have to have a universal experience, i.e., he would have to be in all places in our universe and beyond. Therefore, it is illegitimate to say that there is no God and miracles never happened since we humans are all finite creatures and cannot have access to the entire universe. Do you see my point?

And, the second illicit presupposition from the critics is that there has been absolutely no supernatural intervention in the history of our space-time universe. Here they reject the second person of the Godhead, God the Son, becoming a human being, i.e., the miraculous conception of Jesus.

It is unwarranted to presuppose the non-existence of God. But, we, as Christians, cannot just presuppose the existence of God. As historians, or better yet as human beings, we all must be open to the possibility of God's existence and the intervention of that God into our space-time universe. The evidence must tell us—and it does in the Bible, history, and archeology.

[5] Be looking for my upcoming book titled: *The Counterfeit Easter: What the Bible Really Teaches About Jesus' Death, His Honorable Burial, His Physical Resurrection, and His Physical Appearances.*

CHAPTER 1

[1] Euripides, Meda.

[2] *Apollodorus against Neaera* III.122.

[3] Aristotle, *Politics.*

[4] Josephus, *Antiquities* 4.8.15.

[5] *Talmud, Rosh Hashannah* 1.8.

[6] *Talmud, Sotah* 19a.

[7] *Talmud, Kiddushin* 82b.

[8] See Matt. 1:23; Luke 1:34; Acts 21:9; 1 Cor. 7:25.

[9] Philip King and Lawrence Stager. *Life in Biblical Israel* (Westminster John Knox Press, Louisville, 2001), p. 37; Merrill C. Tenney, editor. *The Zondervan Pictorial Encyclopedia of the Bible* (Regency Reference Library, Grand Rapids, MI, 1976), Vol. 4, "Marriage," p. 96; Alma White. *Jerusalem, Egypt, Palestine, Syria* (Pillar of Fire, Zarephath, New Jersey, 1936), pp. 83, 173; W. M. Thompson. *The Land and the Book* (Baker Book House, Grand Rapids, MI, 1880, reprinted 1973), p. 293; and James Neil. *Everyday Life in the Holy Land* (Society for Promoting Christian Knowledge, London, 1913), p. 223.

[10] Dio Cassius, *Roman History* lvi, 1-10.

[11] Num. 4:1-4.

[12] 2 Sam. 5:4.

[13] Luke 3:23.

[14] See Gen. 2:10-12.

[15] *m. Ketub.* 4.4-5.

[16] *m. Ketub.* 4.4-5.

[17] See Deut. 22:23-28.

CHAPTER 2

[1] See Matt. 26:49; 28:9; Rom. 1:7; 1 Cor. 1:3 for the grace greeting.

[2] Mary would have recognized this expressed Hebrew idiom because she had read and heard this expression before (Gen. 6:8; 18:3; 39:21; 43:14; Judg. 6:17; 1 Sam. 1:18; and 2 Sam. 15:25).

[3] See Luke 1:29.

[4] Luke 1:30.

[5] Luke 1:31.

[6] In Numbers 13:1-16, Moses sent twelve spies to explore the land of Canaan. Joshua was one of the twelve. After Moses died, Joshua became the new leader of the Israelites who led them into the Promised Land.

[7] Luke 1:32.

[8] Also to Moses (Exod. 11:3) and Mordecai (Esther 10:3).

[9] Luke 1:35, 76; 6:35; 8:28; Acts 7:48; 16:17.

[10] The title "Son of God" appears in Gen. 14:18-20, 22; Num. 24:16; Ps. 7:17; 2 Sam. 22:14; Dan. 4:24; Luke 1:35, 76; 6:35; 8:28; Acts 7:48; 16:17; Mark 5:7; Heb. 7:1.

[11] See 2 Sam. 7:9, 13-14, 16 and 1 Chron. 17:11-14.

[12] See Luke 1:27, 69; 2:4, 11; see also Rom. 1:3-4.

[13] See Luke 3:31. To Mary, the word "Son" is also connected to the Messiah who will be the Davidic King (2 Sam. 7:14; 1 Chron. 22:9-10; Pss. 2:7; 89:26).

[14] Luke 1:33.

[15] See Luke 1:33.

[16] See 2 Sam. 7:8-16; 1 Kings 1:48; 2:24.

[17] See Exod. 19:3; Isa. 2:5-6; 8:17; 48:1.

[18] See 2 Sam. 7:12-16; 1 Kings 8:25; Isa. 9:6; Pss. 110:4; 132:12. For God's eternal rule see Isa. 9:6-7; Mic. 4:7; 5:1-4; Dan. 7:14.

[19] See Luke 1:34.

[20] See Gen. 4:1; 19:8; Judg. 11:39; 21:11; Num. 31:17-18; Matt. 1:25.

[21] See Exod. 40:34-35; Num. 9:18: 10:34.

[22] See Pss. 91:4; 140:7.

[23] See Luke 9:34 for the transfiguration cloud overshadowing the apostles.

[24] When the pre-incarnate (the pre-existent) God the Son was conceived in Mary, He became a human being in addition to being God (see John 1:1, 14). Jesus is both God and man—the God-man. Jesus has always been God, but He did not become a human being until He was conceived in the womb of Mary.

This first-born son of Mary has two inseparable natures—divine and human. This is called the *hypostatic union.* Once God the Son was conceived in Mary, Jesus will forever be the God-man, fully God and fully human—two distinct natures in one Person.

Now, do not think of Jesus' humanity and divinity as blended, they are not! But, they are united without loss of separate identity. The divine nature of Jesus is not lessened by His human nature, and His human nature does not lose identity because of His divine nature. Jesus has one personality, but that personality comprises two natures.

[25] Luke 1:69, 76.

[26] Luke 1:36.

[27] Luke 1:37.

[28] Luke 1:31, 35.

[29] Luke 1:36, 39.

[30] The term leaping occurs in Genesis 25:22 for "leaping" baby movements and in Psalm 114:4 for mountains leaping like rams.

[31] Luke 1:44.

[32] Luke 1:42.

[33] Deut. 7:13; 28:4.

[34] Gen. 30:2.

[35] Luke 1:43.

[36] Luke 1:45.

[37] Luke 1:45.

[38] Luke 1:46.

[39] Luke 1:26, 36.

CHAPTER 3

[1] Matt. 1:1-17.

[2] Luke 1:27; 2:5.

[3] *m. Ketub.* 5.2; *m. Ned.* 10.5.

[4] *m. Ketub.* 4:2.

[5] See Deut. 22:23-28.

[6] Matt. 1:19; cf. Luke 1:16.

[7] Deut. 22:23-28.

[8] Matt. 1:19; cf. Deut. 22:23-24.

[9] Also see *m. Git.* 9,10; m. *Sotah* 1:1. Witnesses are a must for a divorce (m. *Git.* 9:3- 8).

[10] See m. *Yebam.* 2:8; *Sotah* 5:1.

[11] Matt. 1:20.

[12] Matt. 1:20.

[13] Matt. 1:1-17.

[14] Cf. Gen. 16:11; 17:19; 1 Kings 13:2; Luke 1:31.

[15] Gen. 1:2; Ps. 33:6.

[16] Gen. 6:3; Job 27:3; 33:4; Pss. 33:6; 104:30; Isa. 32:15; Ezek. 37:1-14.

[17] Matt. 1:21.

[18] Cf. Isa. 43:1, which states: "I have called you by name, you are mine."

[19] Ps. 130:8.

[20] Matt. 3:2, 6; 4:17.

[21] Ps.130:8; Matt. 9:6.

[22] Matt. 26:28.

[23] Matt. 20:28.

[24] Rom. 9:27-28.

[25] Matt. 7:13-14.

[26] Matt. 1:22.

[27] Gen. 24:43; Exod. 2:8; Ps. 68:26; Song of Sol. 1:3; 6:8.

[28] Isa. 9:6-7.

[29] Isa. 11:1-5.

[30] Matt. 1:24.

[31] Matt. 1:25; cf. Gen. 4:1, 17, 25; 38:26; Judg. 11:39; 19:25; 1 Sam. 1:19; 1 Kings 1:4; Luke 1:34.

[32] Matt. 12:46; 13:55-56; Mark 3:31-32; 6:3; Luke 8:19-20; John 2:12; 7:3, 5, 10.

[33] Luke 2:41-52.

CHAPTER 4

[1] Matt. 22:19.

[2] Luke 2:4.

[3] Gen. 48:7; 35:20.

[4] Gen. 35:24; 46:15–18.

[5] Ruth 2:1.

[6] John 8:48.

[7] 2 Kings 17:24; Ezra 4:2-11.

[8] 2 Kings 17:26-28.

[9] Josh. 20:6-7; 21:21.

[10] John 4:9.

[11] John 4:6-26.

[12] Acts 8:25.

[13] The heretical apocryphal *Protoevangelium of James* 17, states the Mary rode a donkey to Bethlehem. This work is false and is not to be believed.

[14] Lev. 12:2-4, 6.

CHAPTER 5

[1] There are two false and heretical apocryphal documents called the *Gospel of Pseudo-Matthew* 13 and the *Protevangelium of James* 17.3-18.1. Both have Mary giving birth somewhere mid-way to Bethlehem. These are heretical documents that are false and are to be totally rejected.

[2] Luke 2:7.

[3] Mark 14:14; 1 Sam. 1:18; 9:22.

[4] Luke 22:11-12.

[5] Luke 19:7.

[6] Deut. 10:19; Lev. 9:13.

CHAPTER 6

[1] Luke 2:7.

[2] See Keith Hopkins, *Death and Renewal* (Cambridge: Cambridge University Press, 1983), p. 225, who approximates that 28% of Roman babies who were born alive died by their first birthday.

[3] Soranus Of Ephesus (AD 98-138) was a Greek gynecologist, obstetrician, and pediatrician. Soranus, and his techniques, was the premier health specialist pertaining to women's diseases, pregnancy, and infant care for over the next 1,500 years. See Johannes Ilberg as volume four of the *Corpus Medicorum Graecorum* (Leipzig and

Berlin: Teubner, 1927) and Soranus' *Gynecology*. Translated by O. Temkin. (Baltimore: The John Hopkins Press, 1956).

[4] What things/equipment were used in childbirth? Soranus, in his *Gynecology*, says that the midwife would use olive oil, warm water, warm fomentations (ointments applied to the body), soft sea sponges, pieces of wool, bandages (to swaddle the infant), a pillow (on which to which to place the infant), things to smell (pennyroral, dirt, barley groats, apples, quinces, lemons, melons, cucumbers; these were used as we use spirits of ammonia to revive someone who has fainted), a midwife's stool or chair. We do not know what Mary used, if anything, in her delivery.

[5] See Aidan Marfarlane. *The Psychology of Childbirth* (Cambridge, Mass.: Harvard, 1978), pp. 29-31; Joyce Prince and Margaret E. Adams. *Minds, Mothers, and Midwives* (New York: Churchill Livingstone, 1978), pp. 116f.; and Barbara Blum, ed., *Psychological Aspects of Pregnancy, Birth, and Bonding* (New York: Human Sciences Press, 1981), pp. 144-45.

[6] For sitting up to give birth see *Helios* entitled "Rescuing Creusa: New Methodological Approaches to Women in Antiquity," (*Helios*, New Series 13[2], 1986, pp. 69-84); Hugo Blummer, *Die romischen Privataltertumer* (Munich: Oskar Beck, 1911), pp. 299-306; Theodore Cianfrani, *A Short History of Obstetrics and Gynecology* (Springfield, Ill.: Charles C. Thomas, 1960), pp. 70-83; Martial Dumont, "*L'Obsterique et la gynecologie dans la Rome antique*," *Cahiers Medicaux Lyonnais*, 41 (1965), pp. 83-91; Palmer Findley, *Priests of Lucina* (Boston: Little, Brown, 1939), pp. 38-65; Harvey Graham, *Eternal Eve* (Garden City, N.Y.: Doubleday, 1951), pp. 56--70; Harold Speert, *Iconographica Gyniatrica* (Philadelphia: l: A. Davis, 1973), pp. 83-84.

Soranus believed that a woman's delivery was more comfortable and not as strenuous if the woman sat up. He has an excellent description of the birthing stool/chair used in delivery.

See Susan McKay and Charles S. Mahart, "Laboring Patients Need More Freedom to Move," *Contemporary OB/GYN*, July 1984, 90-119, for recent research on the upright position reducing the time of labor and delivery for women.

Soranus recommends sitting on the lap of another woman if a birthing chair was not available. But, he says that the woman must be very strong to support the mother's weight and to hold her.

[7] The German journal *Der Spiegel* (1986, Number 43, 278-288) states that women lying on their backs to deliver is: "...the second stupidest position after standing on your head."

[8] *Gynecology.*

CHAPTER 7

[1] Luke 2:22-24.

[2] Heb. 4:15.

[3] Jer. 11:19; Isa. 53:7.

CHAPTER 8

[1] Luke 2:8.

[2] Luke 2:11.

[3] m. *Seqal.* 7.4 and *m. B. Qam.* 7.7.

[4] *Bezah*, 40a.

[5] H. Epstein, *The Awassi sheep with special reference to the improved dairy type*. FAO Animal Production and Health Paper (Food and Agriculture Organization of the United Nations, Rome, 1985), pp. 43-56.

[6] Luke 2:8.

[7] Exod. 9:1, 13; 10:3.

[8] *Kiddushin* 4:14.

[9] Luke 1:38; 4:16-18.

[10] John 10:11; 1 Pet. 5:4; cf. Gen. 49:24; Ezek. 34:23; 37:24; Mic. 5:4; Heb. 13:20.

The leaders called Elders, in each autonomous Church, are also called Shepherds or Pastors (Acts 20:28-31; Eph. 4:11; 1 Pet. 2:24). Even the Apostle Peter was an Elder or Shepherd (1 Pet. 5:1).

[11] Luke 2:9. It is also used to describe an angelic/supernatural appearance (Luke 21:34; 24:4; Acts 12:7; 23:11; 1 Thess. 5:3; 2 Tim. 4:2, 6).

[12] Exod. 16:10; Ps. 63:2; Isa. 40:5; Ezek. 1.

[13] Luke 2:10.

[14] Luke 1:68, 72-74; 2:32. See Matt. 11:5 and Luke 1:19; 2:10; 3:18; 4:18, 43; 7:22; 8:1; 9:6; 16:16; and 20:1, for “proclaiming the good news.”

[15] Luke 2:11.

[16] Luke 2:10.

[17] Luke 1:31-35, 69. See Lam. 4:20.

[18] Luke 20:41-44; Acts 2:33-36.

[19] Exod. 3:12; 1 Sam. 2:34; 14:10; Isa. 37:30; 38:7.

[20] Luke 2:7.

[21] 1 Pet. 2:2.

[22] Luke 1:41, 44.

[23] Luke 18:15; Acts 7:19; 2 Tim. 3:15.

[24] Luke 1:50-53.

[25] Luke 2:13.

[26] Dan. 7:10; 1 Kings 22:19; 2 Chron. 18:18.

[27] Luke 2:14.

[28] Rom. 5:1. See Luke 1:79; 10:5-6; 19:38, 42; Acts 9:31; 10:36.

[29] Luke 2:15.

[30] Luke 2:16.

[31] Luke 2:13-14.

[32] Luke 2:17.

[33] Luke 2:18.

[34] Luke 2:11.

[35] Luke 2:19. Do you know how many times Mary's name is mentioned in the New Testament? The answer is twenty-seven times. Fourteen of these times are used in Luke—Acts, with eleven out of those fourteen times referring to the birth of Jesus. Luke just might have talked to Mary herself! Luke seems to have known Mary.

[36] See Josephus, *Antiquities* 2.5.3 &72.

[37] Luke 2:20. See Josh. 7:19; 1 Chron. 16:35; Pss. 66:2; 106:47; Isa. 42:8, 12; Jer. 13:11; Hab. 3:3; and Dan. 4:34, 37, for the combination of glory and praise.

CHAPTER 9

[1] Lev. 12:2-4, 6; Luke 2:22a, 24.

[2] Luke 2:25-38.

[3] Luke 2:52.

[4] Justin xli. 6.

[5] George Rawlinson. *Parthia* (Cosimo, Inc. New York), p. 78; Strabo, XI, ix, 3. Rawlinson is the world's leading authority on the Parthian Empire.

[6] In AD 554, at the Fifth Ecumenical Council, the Roman Church declared Origen a heretic for his fusion of Greek thought with Biblical exposition and his bizarre and unbiblical teachings. The Fifth Ecumenical Council took place in Constantinople and was also known as the Second Council of Constantinople.

[7] Rawlinson, *Parthia*, p. 80.

[8] Philo, *Every Good Man is Free, 74; On Special Laws* 100.

[9] Acts 8:9. In Acts 13:6, 8, we find the false prophet Bar-Jesus.

[10] E.g., Sophocles, *Oed. Tyr.* 387; Plato, *Republic* 572E. For a Jewish parallel see Josephus, *Ant.* 20.142.

[11] *Adv. Marcion*, III, xiii.

[12] *Antiquities*, XVIII, IX, 1.

[13] Josephus, *War* 1.181. The Idumaeans were the successors to the Edomites who were the offspring of Esau. When the Hasmonean Jewish ruler, John Hyrcanus I, subjugated Idumea in 130-140 BC, he obliged all Idumaeans to observe Jewish law or to get out of Israel. Subsequently, most Idumaeans converted to Judaism.

[14] Josephus, *Ant.* 14.403.

[15] The name "Maccabee" means, "hammer," and was an honorific title bestowed to a man named Judas. He was the son of Mattathias who was the leader of the rebellion against the Seluecid Empire. The rebellion took back control of Judea in the Jewish wars of independence in 168–164 BC. The name "Maccabee" became the names of Judas' father, Mattathias, his four brothers, John, Simon, Eleazar, Jonathan, and to Simon's son, John Hycanus. The line of rulers that descended from Mattathias and his sons was called the Hasmoneans. The Hasmonean Dynasty was founded in Israel from 164 to 63 BC.

[16] Matt. 2:1-7.

CHAPTER 10

[1] Mic. 5:1-2.

[2] Matt. 2:1.

[3] Matt. 2:3.

[4] Matt. 2:1.

[5] Matt. 2:1.

[6] Matt. 1:6.

[7] Matt. 2:2.

[8] Matt. 5:35; Ps. 48:2.

[9] Josephus, *War* 1.181.

[10] Josephus, *Ant*. 16.311.

[11] Matt. 2:2.

[12] Matt. 2:9-11.

[13] Exod. 13:21.

[14] Matt. 17:5; Acts 1:9.

[15] An Animated Peanuts Made-For-Television Special. *I Want a Dog For Christmas, Charlie Brown.* Written by Charles Schulz. Directed by Bill Melenez, Larry Leichliter. First Aired 8-9 pm. ABC. 9 December 2003.

[16] Cf. Isa. 2:1-4; Matt. 8:5-13; 15:21-28; 28:18-20.

[17] Matt. 2:3.

[18] Luke 1:5, 8.

[19] Matt. 2:4.

[20] See Matt. 26:3, 57; 27:17, 27, 62; 28:12.

[21] 1 Sam. 16:1; 17:12, 15.

[22] Matt. 2:5.

[23] Matt. 2:6.

[24] Matt. 9:36; John 10:11-16.

[25] Matt. 1:2-3; cf. Gen. 49:10.

[26] Judg. 17:7-9; 19:1-2, 18; Ruth 1:1-2; 1 Sam. 17:12.

[27] Josh. 19:15.

[28] Matt. 2:7.

[29] Matt. 2:16.

[30] Matt. 2:2.

[31] Matt. 2:8.

[32] Josephus, *Ant*. 15.366-67; 16.236.

[33] Matt. 2:9, 11.

[34] Matt. 2:10.

[35] Matt. 2:11.

[36] Matt. 2:16.

[37] Matt. 2:12.

[38] Matt. 2:9-11.

[39] Exod. 4:19, echoed here in Matt. 2:20.

CHAPTER 11

[1] Matt. 2:13.

[2] *Ant*. 15.8-10.

[3] *Ant*. 15.173-78.

[4] *Ant*. 15.53-55.

[5] *Ant*. 15.247-51.

[6] *Ant*. 15.222-36.

[7] *Ant*. 16.392-94.

[8] *Ant*. 17.182-87.

[9] *Ant*. 17.174-78.

[10] Matt. 1:20.

[11] Matt. 1:21.

[12] 1 Kings 11:40; 2 Kings 25:26; Jer. 41:16-21; 43:1-7.

[13] 1 Kings 11:17, 40; 2 Kings 25:26; Jer. 26:21; 42:13-22; Josephus, *Ant.* 12.387-88; 14.21; 15.45-46; *War* 7.409-10, 416; 2 Macc. 5:8.

[14] Matt. 1:14.

[15] Matt. 2:14; 1:24.

[16] Matt. 2:19.

[17] Exod. 1:22.

[18] Exod. 2:11-15.

[19] Exod. 4:19.

[20] Matt. 2:15.

[21] Hosea 1:6-7; 2:1, 23; 11:1, 8.

[22] The nation of Israel is called the son of God (Exod. 4:22-23; Jer. 31:9, 20; Hosea 1:10). The Davidic kings were also called sons of God (2 Sam. 7:14-15; Pss. 2:6-7, 12; 72:1; 89:26-37).

[23] Matt. 26:27-29; 28:19-20.

[24] Matt. 16:18.

[25] Matt. 19:28.

[26] Matt. 2:16.

[27] Exod. 1:22.

[28] Matt. 2:16.

[29] Jer. 29:4-14; 30:8-9; 33:14-15, 17.

[30] Matt. 2:18.

[31] See 1 Sam. 10:2. Rachel was the younger daughter of Laban. In exchange to marry Rachel, Jacob agreed to work for Laban seven years (Gen. 29:16-20). Jacob ended up working another seven years for Laban in order to marry Rachel (Gen. 29:30). Rachel gave birth to two sons: Joseph and Benjamin (Gen. 35:24). Rachel died giving birth to her second child, Benjamin (Gen. 35:18).

[32] Gen. 35:16-20; 48:7.

[33] Cf. Gen. 35:19; Jer. 40:1-2.

[34] Jer. 31:16-22.

[35] Jer. 40:1-6.

[36] The death of Herod the Great is explained in horrific detail in Josephus, *Ant.* 17.168-81.

[37] Matt. 2:19.

[38] Matt. 2:20.

[39] Exod. 4:19.

[40] Matt. 26:3-4.

[41] Matt. 2:22.

[42] Josephus, *Ant.* 17.213-218.

[43] Suetonius, *Tiberius* 8; Josephus *Ant.* 17.311-17, 342-44.

[44] Matt. 14:1-12.

[45] Cf. Luke 3:1; Matt. 14:3.

[46] John 1:46-47; 7:41-42, 52. In the Gospel of Matthew, the Messiah's anonymity and humility will be reviled and rejected (Pss. 22:6-8, 13; 69:8, 20-21; Isa. 11:1; 49:7; 53:2-3, 8; Dan. 9:26). The disciples of Jesus were called "Nazarene," a word of scorn (Acts 24:5). Jesus was a different and unique Messiah that the Jewish leaders and people did not accept. They wanted a political Messiah to overthrow Rome.

SPECIAL STUDY #1

[1] Frederick W. Danker. *Benefactor: Epigraphic Study of a Graeco-Roman and New Testament Semantic Field:* (St. Louis, MO: Clayton Publishing House, 1982, pp. 216-217; *Inscr. Priene*, 105, 40).

[2] *Y Yevamot* 12, 6, 13a and Y *Shevi'it* 6 1, 36d.

[3] Mish. Nazir iv. 3.

[4] David Carr in *Writing on the Tablet of the Heart: Origins of Scripture and Literature*. Oxford University Press, 2005, said, "Josephus recorded Jews could recite their laws easier than their own names" (see pp. 247-249).

[5] Matt 10:38; 11:28-30; 16:24; 20:28; 23:11.

[6] See F.F. Bruce, Chapter 3 in *The New Testament Documents: Are They Reliable?* (5th edition; Leicester: Intervarsity Press, 1959).

[7] See Robert W. Wall. *Colossians & Philemon. The IVP New Testament Commentary Series* (Downers Grove, Ill.: InterVarsity Press, 1993).

[8] 1 Tim. 5:18; see also Deut. 25:4 and Luke 10:7.

[9] In Romans 1:3 Paul said of the virgin conception:

> "Concerning his Son Jesus Christ our Lord, which was made of the seed of David according to the flesh" (Rom. 1:3).

Here, Paul very clearly states that Jesus was a physical descendent of King David by parentage. But, Jesus' sonship began at conception in the womb of Mary and not at birth.

> "For God has done what the law, weakened by the flesh, could not do. By sending his own Son in the likeness of sinful flesh and for sin, he condemned sin in the flesh," (Rom. 8:3).

> "The first man was from the earth, a man of dust; the second man is from heaven" (1 Cor. 15:47).

The only person that came from heaven to become a man was Jesus. The expression "came from heaven" speaks of Jesus' origin—His heavenly origin in contradistinction from Adam who had an earthly origin being formed from the earth. This again attests to the virgin conception of Jesus.

> "But when the fullness of time had come, God sent forth his Son, born of woman, born under the law" (Gal. 4:4).

Did you notice that Paul said Jesus, the Son, was sent from heaven by God? This absolutely presupposes that He existed before being sent? Paul does not say Jesus was created or born by man, but "made" of a woman. The word "of" designates the place of origin that Jesus humanity was made.

The Greek word that Paul deliberately uses here is "made" (*ginomai*). The word that is used for "born" is the Greek word "*gennao*," which refers to male procreation and also to the process of birthing a child. Paul most certainly has in mind the virgin conception and what Moses predicted back in Genesis 3:15 that the Seed of the woman (Jesus), as promised by God in the very beginning (Gen. 3:15), was not made from a male seed.

Clearly, the concept of "seed" in Genesis (Gen. 22:18; cf. Gal. 3:8, 16) would be fulfilled in the Savior, the seed promise, in the fullness of time, being "made of a woman" (Gal. 4:4). The virgin conception is here in Galatians 4:4.

In fact, the Hebrew writer tells us that Jesus' human body was specially "prepared" by God (Heb. 10:5). This is most certainly the virgin incarnation.

Paul in Philippians 2 speaks of the virgin conception when he says that Jesus was made in the form of a man and did not think it something to hold on to His pre-incarnate state of equality with God, but willingly took on a human form and became a human being.

Paul again speaks of the virgin conception in his first letter to Timothy. Paul states:

> "Great indeed, we confess, is the mystery of godliness: He was manifested in the flesh, vindicated by the Spirit, seen by angels, proclaimed among the nations, believed on in the world, taken up in glory" (1 Tim. 3:16).

Did you see that Paul says: "He (Jesus) who was revealed in the flesh," not created, but rather manifested, made visible, *phaneroo.* It does not mean to bring into existence. Paul is clearly saying that Jesus is God made visible. Jesus Christ in His pre-existent reality was not visible, but in the virgin conception He took on visible human form/ flesh. The invisible transcendent God became visible in the male human being Jesus Christ. In no uncertain terms this is the virgin conception.

So, the critics who state that no one but Matthew and Luke speak of the virgin birth are wrong! I have just given you other examples from the Apostles John and Paul who DID talk about the virgin conception.

Now, ask yourself these questions.

How many times does God the Holy Spirit (who inspired the Biblical writers) have to tell us about anything?

The answer is just once!

[10] Acts 2:1-41.

[11] Mark 1:1.

[12] Mark 1:2-3.

[13] Col. 4:14.

[14] John 20:31.

[15] Acts 28:7.

[16] Luke 3:1.

[17] John 18:28; 19:13.

[18] Acts 18:12-17.

[19] Acts 19:22 and Rom. 16:23.

[20] Acts 28:7.

SPECIAL STUDY #2

[1] Bart Ehrman. *Forged: Writing in the Name of God—Why the Bible's Authors Are not Who We Think They Are* (New York: HarperCollins, 2011), p.8.

[2] As quoted by Timothy Luke Jones in *Misquoting Truth*, IVP Books; PRINT-ON-DEMAND edition (June 23, 2007), p. 113.

[3] *Ibid.*, p. 75.

[4] Matt. 27:37; Luke 23:38; Mark 15:25-26; John 19:19-22.

[5] Matt. 28:19-20; Mark 16:15-16.

[6] Deut. 4:9; 6:7; 11:19; 31:12-13; 2 Chron. 17:7-9; Eccle. 12:9.

[7] Deut. 6:4-9; 11:20; cf. Mark 12:28-33 and James 2:19.

[8] Ag. Ap. 1.12 §60.

[9] Ag. Ap. 2.25 §204.

[10] Pig and nonkosher fish bones were discovered by archaeologists in Bethsaida (Rami Arav, "New Testament Archaeology and the Case of Bethsaida," in *Das Ende der Tage und die Gegenwart des*

Heils: Begegnungen mit dem Neuen Testament und seiner Umwelt, ed. M. Becker and W. Fenske (Leiden, Netherlands: Brill, 1999), 84. For the excavation of a Roman temple at Bethsaida see Rami Arav, "Bethsaida Excavations: Preliminary Report, 1994–1996," in *Bethsaida: A City by the North Shore of the Sea of Galilee*, volume 2, ed. Rami Arav and Richard A. Freund (Kirksville, MO: Truman State University, 1999), pp. 18–24, 32–44.

[11] See Mark Appold, "Peter in Profile: From Bethsaida to Rome," in *Bethsaida: A City by the North Shore of the Sea of Galilee: Volume 3*, ed. Rami Arav and Richard A. Freund (Kirksville, MO: Truman State University, 2004), pp. 133–45; Markus Bockmuehl, "Simon Peter and Bethsaida," *The Missions of James, Peter, and Paul: Tensions in Early Christianity*, ed. Bruce Chilton and Craig Evans (Leiden, Netherlands: Brill, 2005), pp. 53–90, 165–176.

[12] See Jerome Murphy-O'Connor, "Fishers of Fish, Fishers of Men: What We Know of the First Disciples from their Profession," *Bible Review* 15, no. 3 (June 1999): pp. 22–27, 48–49.

[13] F.M. Heichelheim, "Roman Syria," in Tenney Frank, ed., *An Economic Survey of Ancient Rome* (Baltimore: Johns Hopkins Univ. Press, 1938), vol. 4, p. 154.

[14] Rami Arav and Richard A. Freund, eds., *Bethsaida: A City by the North Shore of the Sea of Galilee,* Bethsaida Excavations Project 1 (Kirksville, MO: Thomas Jefferson Univ. Press, 1995), pp. xv, 6.

[15] See the map in Mendel Nun, *Sea of Galilee: Newly Discovered Harbours from New Testament Days* (Kibbutz Ein Gev: Kinnereth Sailing Co., 1989), p. 4. And Mendel Nun, "Ports of Galilee," *Biblical Archaeology Review* 25, no. 4 (July/August 1999): pp. 18–31, 64.

[16] Arav and Freund, *Bethsaida*, p. 27.

[17] Plutarch, *Moralia* 668b. See also Athenaeus, *Deipnosophistai* 6.274f (all quotations from Athenaeus in this special study are from the *Loeb Classical Library* translation by Charles Burton Gulick).

[18] See "Salsamentum" in Charles Daremberg and Edmond Saglio, eds., *Dictionnaire des antiquités grecques et romaines* (Paris, n.d.), vol. 4, pt. 2, pp. 1022-1025.

[19] Athenaeus, *Deipnosophistai* 6.227e.

SPECIAL STUDY #3

[1] Octavian was born in September of 63 BC and was the great nephew of Julius Caesar, who adopted him. It was Octavian and his Roman forces that defeated the combined forces of the Roman general Mark Antony and the Queen Pharaoh of Egypt, Cleopatra VII at the battle of Actium in 31 BC. Octavian became Rome's first emperor. Octavian took his adopted father's name "Caesar" and in 27 BC the Roman Senate granted him the honorific Greek name of *Sebastos*, which in Latin is Augustus (meaning "revered one"). Octavian died in AD 14 with Tiberius Caesar becoming the new emperor. Jesus will conduct His three-and-a-half-year ministry during the reign of Tiberius Caesar.

[2] Josephus, *Jewish War* 1.20.3 393.

[3] Luke 1:80.

[4] 2 Sam. 24.

[5] We know that the Romans allowed the Jews to have a tax exemption every seventh year (Josephus, *Antiquities* 14.10.6 201-10) and freedom for Sabbath observance (*Antiquities* 14.10.20 241-43).

[6] Matt. 22:19.

[7] Tacitus, *Annals* 1.11; Dio Cassius 53.30.2.

[8] *Res Gestae Divi Augusti* 8.

[9] Josephus 18.4.2 88. Such censuses in vassal kingdoms were not unusual in Roman history (examples are found in Syria, Cappadocia, and Nabatea). Tacitus, *Annals* 2.42 and 6.41, discusses Cappadocia, where taxes were reduced by about half. Roman tax rolls existed before Samaria became part of a Roman province in an area that had been under Herod's rule (Josephus, *Antiquities* 17.11.4 319 and *Jewish War* 2.6.3 96).

[10] *Antiquities.* XVIII, 26–28.

[11] *Antiquities* 17.6.4 &167.

[12] *Antiquities* 17.9.3 &213; *Jewish War* 2.1.3 &10.

[13] Luke 2:3.

[14] Matt. 2:4.

SPECIAL STUDY #4

[1] Matt. 2:1-7.

[2] Dan. 3:8-30.

[3] Dan. 2:48.

[4] *Histories* I, ci 101, 132.

[5] *Cyropaedia* of Xenophon, *The Life of Cyrus the Great*, 8.3.11.

[6] *Cyropaedia* of Xenophon, *The Life of Cyrus the Great*, Book 7, section 5, vs. 7-36; *Histories of Herodotus*, Book 1, Clio, pt. II, vs. 191; 2 Chron. 36:22-23; Isa. 45:1, 4; 41:2-25; 42:6; 44:28; Ezra 1:4-11; 6:4-5; and Dan. 6:28; 10:1.

[7] Herodotus, *Histories* 3.79.

[8] Richard T. Hallock. *Persepolis Fortification Tablets*. Oriental Institute Publications (Book 92). Oriental Institute of the University of Chicago (December 1, 1969).

[9] *Natural History*, XXX:8.

[10] *PL* 94,539-560; cf. *PL* 94,541C-D.

[11] Bruce M. Metzger, "Names for the Nameless in the New Testament: A Study in the Growth of Christian Tradition," in: *Kyriakon. Festschrift Johannes Quasten*, ed. Patrick Granfield & Josef A. Jungmann, vol. I, (Munster: Aschendorff, 1970), p. 79-99.

SPECIAL STUDY #5

[1] C. F. Nosgen, cited in *Theological Dictionary of the New Testament*, ed. Gerhard Kittel, vol. 4, (Grand Rapids: Eerdmans), 1967, p. 765.

[2] Rom. 3:22; Phil. 3:9.

[3] Num. 14:11; 20:12; 2 Kings 17:14; Ps. 78:22; Jon. 3.

[4] Heb. 11:6.

[5] Rom. 10:17.

[6] Acts 15:9.

[7] Rom. 3:28; 5:1-2; Gal. 2:16.

[8] Gal. 3:26.

[9] Rom. 4:24.

[10] Rom. 4:16.

[11] Eph. 2:20; 2 Cor. 5:7; Heb. 11:11.

[12] John 14:10-11.

[13] John 20:31.

[14] Rom. 10:9.

[15] Heb. 11:6.

[16] Following the Equator / 1897.

[17] *On Rhetoric* 3.17.15.

[18] *De Institutio Oratoria* 5.10.8 states: "To all these forms of argument the Greeks give the name of *pistis*, a term which, though the literal translation is *fides*, 'a warrant of credibility,' is best translated by *probation*, 'proof.'"

[19] Matt. 9:18-26.

[20] Matt. 9:27-31.

[21] Matt. 15:21-28.

[22] James 2:19; Mark 1:24 and 5:7.

[23] James 2:19.

[24] John 6:66.

[25] John 6:68-69.

[26] John 8:30.

[27] John 8:31-32.

[28] 2 Tim. 1:12.

[29] *Emphasis mine.*

[30] Acts 10:43; *emphasis mine.*

[31] Rom. 1:19-20; *emphasis mine.*

[32] Heb. 11:1; *emphasis mine.*

[33] D. Murdock. *The Christ Conspiracy.* (Adventures Unlimited Press, 1999), pp. 118-120.

[34] See The Risen Jesus: The Ministry of Mike Licona. His article titled "A Refutation of Acharya S' book *The Christ Conspiracy* thoroughly refutes Ms. Murdock and all who join her in her imaginative theories.

[35] *Rigveda*, III, 59.

[36] *Magdeburgenses*, Cent. 2. c. 6. Hospinian, *De origine Festorum Chirstianorum.*

[37] Hippolytus, *Commentary on Daniel* 2.4.

[38] *Apology*, I, 34.

[39] *Contra Marcion*, Book 4, 7.

[40] *Homil. Diem Natal.*, 2; PL, 49, 552ff.

[41] Thomas Talley. *The Origins of the Liturgical Year* (Collegeville, MN: Liturgical Press, 1991), p. 88.

STUDY GUIDE

CHAPTER 1

JOSEPH SPEAKS TO MARY'S FATHER

1. *What do you think about how women were thought of and treated in the ancient world?*

   A. When Jeffery quoted one of the most famous Greek philosophers, Aristotle, stating that he believed women were "defective" men, what were your thoughts? How have women progressed from the days of Aristotle to our present time? Do women have equal rights today?

   B. How do you think Mary thought of herself as a person? Ladies, as Christian women, how do you see yourself in our present modern day world?

2. *We know that Mary was a virgin. Read Matthew 1:23 and Luke 1:27, 34. What was your reaction when you learned about Jewish girls getting engaged at the age of twelve?*

   A. A Jewish father would never allow his daughter to marry a young person who had no home, no career/business, or no means of supporting his daughter. Could you live back in the days that Mary and Joseph lived? Why or why not?

   B. Hollywood Bible movies always have Mary played by an actress that is much older than a twelve-year-old. Why do you think that is so?

3. *How did you respond to Jeffery's depiction of Mary and Joseph's courtship and two-part marriage ceremony?*

A. Jeffery created a visual image of Mary describing the two-part marriage of Jewish couples. Was this effective for you?

B. Why do you think the Jewish culture used a two-part marriage?

4. *Joseph is always portrayed as a worker of wood, i.e., a carpenter. But, did Jeffery's description of Joseph being a stonemason surprise you?*

A. Why do you think God chose Joseph to serve as Jesus' earthly father?

B. The Shroud of Turin is a burial garment that has the image of a man who was crucified—Roman style! Many Christians believe that the man in the shroud is Jesus at the moment of His physical resurrection from the dead. The right arm of the man in the shroud is larger, more developed, than his left. Since Jesus was a carpenter (stonemason), His right arm would have been more developed than His left. What do think about this?

5. *Do you believe that the relationship that Mary and Joseph had was unique? Why or why not?*

A. Is Mary and Joseph's relationship and marriage a good model for married couples today? Why or why not?

B. Would a year-long engagement like Mary and Joseph's be something that might work today?

CHAPTER 2

GOD SPEAKS TO MARY

1. *If the mighty angel Gabriel appeared to you as he did to Mary, what do you think your reaction would be?*

    A. In describing God's angelic messengers like Gabriel, Jeffery said that Biblical angels always appeared as Jewish men who had short hair—and not as men with long blond hair or as little babies. Is this new information for you?

    B. Why do many Christians believe that angels are in the form of women, or men with long blond hair, or even little babies?

2. *Have you ever thought why God chose Mary to give birth to Jesus?*

    A. What was it about Mary's character that prompted God to choose her? Read Genesis 6:8; 18:3; 39:21; 43:14; Judges 6:17; 1 Samuel 1:18; and 2 Samuel 15:25. Mary would have known these passages where individuals "found favor" with God. Would this well-known phrase have comforted Mary?

    B. Why did God choose Mary from out of all the maidens in Israel?

3. *Why did Mary hurry off so quickly to see Elizabeth?*

    A. Mary was so very happy that God had chosen her to give birth to the Messiah, but why was she happy when she learned about her relative Elizabeth being with child? Read Deuteronomy 7:13; 28:4 and Genesis 30:2.

B. Why did Mary take off in a flash to visit her relative Elizabeth? Read Luke 1:31, 35.

4. *Why did Mary leave Elizabeth in the ninth month of her pregnancy to return back to Nazareth? Why did Mary sing? Read Luke 1:46-55. Did you know that Mary was a singer? What do you think about that fact?*

A. In Elizabeth's ninth month of pregnancy, Mary is three months pregnant. Read Luke 1:26, 36. Why do you believe that Mary did not wait to return back to Nazareth at least until Elizabeth gave birth to her son—John the Baptist?

B. If you were Mary, three months pregnant, and going back to your hometown in your condition, what would your thoughts be on how you would tell Joseph and how he would respond?

CHAPTER 3

GOD SPEAKS TO JOSEPH

1. *How do you think Joseph took the news that Mary was pregnant?*

   A. We know that Joseph didn't believe Mary's virgin conception by the power of God the Holy Spirit because he was firmly set on giving Mary a private written divorce document. Read Matthew 1:19, Luke 1:16, and Deuteronomy 24:1-4. Why do you think Joseph didn't believe Mary about her virgin conception?

   B. Do you think Jeffery created an accurate visual picture of Joseph when he was thinking about Mary? Why or why not? Did you feel Joseph's sadness?

2. *With what Joseph was thinking was his decision to divorce Mary privately the right thing to do?*

   A. We learned that Joseph had two options for what he believed was a wife that had committed adultery—public trial and stoning or a private divorce document presented to Mary in the presence of witnesses. Read Deuteronomy 22:23-28; 24:1-4.

   B. Did Joseph, given what he understood, make the right decision instead of having Mary stoned to death as the Old Testament Law prescribed? Why?

3. *Once God spoke to Joseph in a dream, Joseph demonstrated unquestionable obedience. Read Matthew 1:20, 24. Is Joseph's obedience a model for Christians today?*

A. Ladies, what do you think of Joseph's unquestionable obedience to God once He told him that Mary's child was of God the Holy Spirit? How did Joseph's obedience differ from Mary's?

B. Mary and Joseph did not begin normal sexual relations until AFTER Jesus was born. Read Matthew 1:25. We therefore know that Mary and Joseph had other children. Did you know this? Read Matthew 12:46; 13:55-56; Mark 3:31-32; 6:3; Luke 8:19-20; and John 2:12; 7:3, 5, 10. Did you know that two half-brothers of Jesus wrote the two New Testament books of James and Jude?

CHAPTER 4

THE TRIP TO BETHLEHEM "NO DONKEY"

1. *What did you think of Joseph's obedience to God when he came to fetch Mary to take her to his home? If others also knew she was pregnant, do you think that fact would have made it more difficult for him?*

   A. Discuss the visual image that Jeffery portrayed of Mary's thoughts/words in waiting and waiting for Joseph to come to take her home with him.

   B. How did this scenario that Jeffery painted differ from what you may have envisioned or been taught?

2. *Did you know that Joseph and Mary went to Bethlehem on the orders of the first Roman Emperor Caesar Augustus? Read Luke 2:1, 4-5.*

   A. If Caesar Augustus knew of Mary's pregnant condition, would he have given her an exemption not to travel to Bethlehem and register?

   B. Is there a difference in how women did daily chores in Mary's time as compared to our present time?

3. *Why would the Jewish people bypass Samaria and not go through it when they traveled?*

   A. If Samaria was off limits to Jewish people, why did Jesus talk to a Samaritan woman? Read John 4:1-42.

B. Why did the Apostles take the Gospel of salvation to the Samaritans? Read Acts 8:4-25.

4. *Have you always thought that Mary rode a donkey to Bethlehem?*

   A. All Christmas plays, Hollywood and television Christmas specials and movies, and all nativity scenes have Mary on a donkey. Why do you think that is so when there is no evidence to support it?

   B. Imagine how difficult it would have been for Mary to walk about 100 miles while pregnant. Why do you think she was determined to get to Bethlehem?

5. *What mental image did Jeffery create when Joseph and Mary traveled to Bethlehem?*

   A. Jeffery gave us the story of the arduous journey to Bethlehem from Joseph's perspective. Is this how you envisioned it?

   B. Did you ever wonder at the extreme difficulty Mary had in walking from Nazareth to Bethlehem while with child? How does it make you feel to realize the hardships that she went through?

CHAPTER 5

THE ARRIVAL IN BETHLEHEM "NO UPPER GUEST ROOM"

1. *Before you read this book, what was your concept of "no room in the inn?" Read Luke 2:7.*

   A. Jeffery explained the differences between an "upper guest room" and a commercial inn. What were the differences between the two? Compare and contrast them. Read Mark 14:14; 1 Samuel 1:18; 9:22; and Luke 22:11-12; 19:7.

   B. Discuss the possible reasons why no one in Bethlehem would provide Mary an upper guest room where she could give birth to her child. Read Deuteronomy 10:19 and Leviticus 9:13; 15:19-27.

2. *The modern nativity scene has Mary, Joseph, and baby Jesus in a nice manger with fresh straw and a warm fire. Were you shocked at the cold, damp, stinking, urine/feces filled room of someone's first floor home that Mary gave birth in?*

   A. How have your feelings changed about traditional nativity scenes and Jesus' actual birth now that you know how harsh the conditions were for Mary in that cold, damp, stinking, urine/feces filled room of someone's first floor home?

   B. Ladies, could you have given birth in the very same conditions as Mary? Why or why not?

3. *When Jeffery created the visual image from Joseph's perspective of Mary going into that cold, damp, stinking, urine/feces filled room of someone's first floor home, what was your reaction?*

   A. When Mary saw where she would give birth was she taken back, but yet made the best of what was given to her and Joseph? Or, do you believe that Mary would have shouted, cried, hit, and put up a wail of a fuss in having to give birth in a cold, damp, stinking, urine/feces filled room of someone's first floor home?

   B. Describe Mary's character traits.

CHAPTER 6

THE BIRTH OF JESUS "NO MIDWIFE"

1. *Did the birthing process in the ancient world surprise you in any way? Read Luke 2:7; Cf. Genesis 30:1-3; 50:23; Exodus 1:16. Your Bible translations do not correctly translate the first passage of Luke 2:7. Look for supplemental notes explaining these passages for what the original Greek and Hebrew really say.*

   A. Ladies, were you shocked at how women in the ancient world gave birth sitting on a midwife's lap—who was sitting on a birthing chair/stool?

   B. Describe the two possible scenarios of Mary giving birth—one in Nazareth and the other in Bethlehem. Compare and contrast them.

2. *How do you assess Joseph as a person and husband when he became a chair for Mary?*

   A. Husbands, would you have done for your wives what Joseph did for Mary?

   B. Husbands, how would you have reacted if you were in Joseph's situation?

CHAPTER 7

WRAPPED IN A WHAT "NO BLUE OR WHITE BLANKET"

1. *With what did Mary and Joseph swaddle baby Jesus? What do modern nativity scenes use to cover baby Jesus?*
   - A. Why would a baby be swaddled? What are the benefits?
   - B. Were you surprised that baby Jesus wasn't covered with a blue or white blanket? Could Mary and Joseph have afforded these color blankets? Read Luke 2:22-24; Leviticus 12:2-4, 6.
2. *How was swaddling baby Jesus similar to the swaddling of perfect newborn lambs?*
   - A. For what Jewish festival were the shepherds swaddling their perfect newborn lambs?
   - B. What conclusions can you reach about Jesus, the perfect Lamb of God, being swaddled? Read Hebrews 4:15. Is there symbolism that related to later events for Jesus? Read Jeremiah 11:19 and Isaiah 53:7.
3. *What was baby Jesus placed into after He was swaddled?*
   - A. Where were the shepherds told they would find He who was the Savior, Christ, and Lord? Why did this provide a frame of reference for the shepherds?
   - B. Why do you think God chose to have Jesus born in a cold, damp, stinking, urine/feces filled first floor home of someone's home?

CHAPTER 8

SHEPHERDS SEARCH FOR JESUS

1. *Why would Jesus have been born sometime in December/January?*

   A. What evidence did Jeffery present for a winter birth of Jesus? Read Luke 2:8.

   B. What did the Jewish *Mishnah* tell us about grazing sheep in Israel?

2. *Shepherds were viewed differently by God and by mankind. Describe the two pictures of shepherds that Jeffery painted for us. Compare and contrast them.*

3. *Describe the appearance of a singing angelic army to the shepherds. Read Luke 2:9-10; Exodus 16:10; Psalm 63:2; Isaiah 40:5; and Ezekiel 1.*

   A. What did the angelic army tell the shepherds? Read Luke 1:68, 72-74; 2:32.

   B. Would you have gone about sharing the good news that the Savior was born—at nighttime—just as the shepherds did?

4. *What kind of peace did Jesus bring? Read Romans 5:1; Luke 1:79; 10:5-6; 19:38, 42; Acts 9:31; 10:36.*

   A. What kind of Messiah/Deliverer was the Jewish people looking for?

   B. How would Jesus be a different Messiah?

CHAPTER 9

THE WISEMEN SEARCH FOR JESUS PART 1

1. *Did you believe that the Wisemen were at the birth of Jesus like all of the nativity scenes present? Read Matthew 2:1-7.*

   A. Now that you know the Wisemen (*Megistanes*) were not at the birth of Jesus, will you do anything differently this Christmas with your own nativity scene?

   B. What will you do?

2. *What do you think about learning that the Wisemen were actually the powerful Parthian Megistanes?*

   A. Jeffery has shown us that the Wisemen were not three kings who rode camels, but one of the most powerful groups in the ancient world. What did they ride?

   B. How has your personal view of the Wisemen changed?

3. *Who were the Parthian Megistanes?*

   A. Describe why it was so significant that the *Megistanes* (Wisemen) were from Parthia.

   B. Who and what accompanied the *Megistanes* on their journey to worship He who was born King of the Jews?

4. *Discuss what you learned about Herod the Great.*

   A. Why was/is Herod called the "great?"

   B. How did Herod treat his family members? Discuss the moral character of Herod the Great.

CHAPTER 10

THE WISEMEN SEARCH FOR JESUS PART 2

1. *What was the troubling new event that happened in the city of Jerusalem?*

   A. Why would the monster Herod the Great and the inhabitants of the city of Jerusalem be so shaken and troubled when the *Megistanes* (Wisemen) came to Jerusalem? Read Matthew 2:1, 3.

   B. Who accompanied the *Megistanes* into Jerusalem? Where did the *Megistanes* find He who was born King of the Jews? Read Matthew 2:9, 11. Define "protocol gifts" for a new king.

2. *What was the Star of Bethlehem? Read Exodus 13:21; Matthew 17:5; and Acts 1:9.*

   A. Jeffery gave us some convincing information that the star was not a literal star, but a supernatural phenomenon from God. Read Matthew 2:2, 9-11.

   B. What peculiar things did the "Star of Bethlehem" do that made it unique?

3. *What was Herod the Great thinking about when the Megistanes arrived in his city of Jerusalem?*

   A. Who previously made an assassination attempt on Herod's life? Why?

B. If someone or a foreign power had made an attempt on your life, would you have reacted like Herod did when the powerful *Megistanes* (Wisemen) came riding into Jerusalem on horses?

4. *Did Herod the Great know the Jewish Scriptures?*

   A. Why would you think that Herod, the King of Israel, was so ignorant of what the Bible predicted over 400 years ago about the birthplace of the Messiah? Read Micah 5:2-3. Who was Herod paralleled with in his act of killing the innocent male children of Bethlehem? Read Exodus 4:19. Compare and contrast them.

   B. Do we as Christians know our Bibles well enough? Would it be fair for non-Christians to expect us as Christians to know "what the Bible says?"

CHAPTER 11

HEROD SEARCHES FOR JESUS

1. *Why do we believe that Joseph took Mary and Jesus to Alexandria, Egypt? Read Matthew 1:14; 2:19.*

   A. Can you believe it! Joseph and especially Mary have done considerable walking. She first went on a 200-mile round trip journey to visit her relative Elizabeth. Then she made the trip to Bethlehem—another 100 miles or so. And, finally she made the 150-mile trip to Egypt and another 250-mile trip from Egypt to Nazareth. Are you impressed? Why?

   B. Read 1 Kings 11:17, 40; 2 Kings 25:26; Jeremiah 41:16-21; 42:13-22; and 43:1-7.

2. *Where did Joseph and Mary get the funds for the trip to Egypt, while they were there, and the return trip home?*

   A. What do you believe Joseph did with the three protocol gifts given to Jesus by the *Megistanes* (Wisemen)?

   B. Do you believe that Joseph bought a donkey for Mary and Jesus to ride on since they now had the financial means to secure it? Or, did Mary and Jesus walk?

3. *Discuss the murder of children by Herod the Great. Read Matthew 2:16-17 and Jeremiah 29:4-14; 30:8-9; 31:15; 33:14-15, 17.*

   A. Discuss the horror of Herod murdering baby boys in Bethlehem. Again, what was the historical parallel killing of innocents? Read Exodus 1:22.

   B. Discuss the many "family" murders that Herod accomplished.

4. *Why did Joseph take his family to Nazareth instead of returning back to Bethlehem?*

SPECIAL STUDY #1

UNWRAPPING THE FOUR GOSEPLS

1. *Did you know that the Romans had a "gospel" before the Christians? What is a "gospel?"*

    A. Look at the beginning of Mark's Gospel and discuss the implications of what Mark said about the Gospel. What is the *Priene Calendar Inscription* and why is it important?

    B. What are the different themes and audiences of the Gospels according to Matthew, Luke, Mark, and John?

2. *Before this book, did you believe that there were "four" Gospels of Jesus the Christ?*

    A. Discuss how there is only one Gospel of Jesus the Christ through the eyes of four divinely inspired writers.

    B. What did Jeffery describe as the key to harmonizing the four Gospels into a coherent chronological narrative?

3. *List the archaeological pieces of evidence that show the remarkable historical accuracy in the Gospel of Luke.*

4. *God has allowed mankind to discover thousands of archeological artifacts that substantiate the Biblical claims. Just right now, say a prayer to our great God and Savior—Jesus the Christ for providing so much evidence to believe. Be thankful and grateful to our good God.*

5. *What Jesus do you believe in—the Jesus who was a Jewish comic whose dead body was eaten by dogs, the Jesus who is the fabrication that a few people invented, i.e., a souped-up Santa Claus, or the real historical and divine Jesus—God who become a human being in the virgin conception?*
6. *Who were the Christian Hazzanim? What was their purpose concerning THE Word of God? How did oral tradition factor into preserving God's Word until it was written down?*

SPECIAL STUDY #2

UNWRAPPING THE AUTHORS OF THE GOSPELS

1. *Who do the critics say wrote the Gospels?*

   A. Were the disciples/Apostles of Jesus poor, dumb, illiterate, and imbecilic fisherman who could not read or write?

   B. What evidence did Jeffery provide you about Acts 4:13? What does this Scripture really say about John and Peter?

2. *Discuss what was your impression of Jesus' disciples/Apostles as far as their intelligence goes?*

   A. Discuss the Greek names Simon, Peter, Andrew, and Philip. Why would their Jewish parents give them Greek names if they could not read or write Greek?

   B. What language did Jeffery teach that Peter spoke to Cornelius, a Roman Centurion, who only knew Latin and not Aramaic or Hebrew?

3. *Discuss the fishing business in the days of the Apostles. Did Jeffery convince you that Peter, Andrew, James, John, and Philip (perhaps more) were successful businessmen as fishermen?*

4. *What archaeological evidence was discovered around the Sea of Galilee that most definitely shows that fishing was a "big business" in Israel?*

5. *What does it show that the Apostles owned their own boats and nets, hired other employees, and started and stopped fishing when they wanted to?*

6. *Do you agree that the critics look very foolish and even dishonest when Peter calls Jesus a Greek name ("Christ") when they say that he did not know Greek? And, how did Simon understand Jesus when He called him the Greek name of "Peter"?*

SPECIAL STUDY #3

UNWRAPPING THE ROMAN CENSUS

1. *Describe and discuss a Roman census.*

   A. How is a Roman census different than an American census?

   B. Where did Joseph and Mary have to return to in the Augustan census of Luke 2:1? Read Luke 2:3.

2. *What were the three major Augustan censuses?*

   A. Why is the Augustan census of 8 BC the correct one pertaining to Jesus' birth?

   B. Why did it take around two years to finally get the census done in Israel?

3. *What does Luke 2:2 really say about Quirinius?*

   A. Jeffery has shown us that Luke does not say Quirinius was the Governor of Syria, but only that he was "exercising control over Syria." What do you think?

   B. Why then do our Bible translations incorrectly say Quirinius was the Governor of Syria when Luke does not?

4. *The Augustan census was the thing that made Joseph and Mary travel to Bethlehem. But, who was the real force behind the Roman Emperor?*

   A. As Christians, we know that God is with us and that we pray to always be in His will. But, the road is not always easy. Take

Mary and Joseph for example. They were both in God's will for Mary to be the virgin of Isaiah 7:14 and for her to give birth to the Messiah in Bethlehem. But, did you notice how difficult and even dangerous that journey was for the both of them? Share with someone a difficulty that you have faced knowing that God was always with you.

B. Who was in control throughout—from the Augustan census to Joseph and Mary's arrival in Bethlehem?

SPECIAL STUDY #4

UNWRAPPING THE HISTORY OF THE WISEMEN

1. *Discuss the Babylonian and Persian Wisemen.*

   A. Did you know that the Wisemen had such a rich history?

   B. Did you know that Daniel was a Chief Wiseman in the Babylonian Empire? Read Daniel 2:48.

2. *Discuss the history of interactions that the Romans had with the Parthians.*

   A. The Roman army faced off against the Parthian army a number of times. Discuss the significance of those confrontations.

   B. Why did the Roman Emperor, Caesar Augustus, try to make peace with the Parthians instead of trying to destroy them as a number of previous powerful Roman generals wanted to do?

3. *Where did the false names of Caspar, Melchior, and Balthazar, originate?*

   A. We have all heard of the false names of the Wisemen as Caspar, Melchior, and Balthazar that are taught from Hollywood movies, kids' television shows, and even from the pulpit. Why are we believing these sources?

   B. Why is modern day culture more influential than the Bible?

4. *What two modern things (a song and a story) about the Wisemen have our modern twenty-first century mindset accepted?*

A. Play the song "We Three Kings" so that you and everyone can hear it. Now, discuss it!

B. Why have Christians allowed so much false tradition into our Christian belief system? As Christians, what can or should we do about it?

SPECIAL STUDY #5

UNWRAPPING A FEW ADDITIONAL GIFTS

1. *What is a myth? Is the Bible a myth? Read 1 Timothy 1:3-4; 4:7; Titus 1:14; 2 Timothy 4:3-4; and 2 Peter 1:16.*

   A. Have you ever been confronted by a relative, friend, teacher, preacher, or college professor, telling you that the Bible is nothing more than a myth?

   B. How would you now respond to such people after reading this book?

2. *What comprises "saving faith"?*

   A. How many of us believed faith was nothing more that a "leap of faith"—believing in what cannot be proven? After reading this book how do you define "faith?"

   B. What illustration did Jeffery teach us about the two component parts of faith? Does this illustration help you to understand what "faith" means?

3. *What did you learn about miracles?*

   A. When someone tells you that miracles never happened, how do you respond?

   B. What is the difference between God's providence and miracles? Compare and contrast them.

4. *Discuss how Jesus' birth differed from the birth of the pagan Roman god Mithra.*

A. Have some fun with this one! Have a debate. Have some people on one side arguing that Christians copied the birthdate of December 25 from the pagan Roman god Mithra and created the birth of Jesus as found in the Gospel of Luke. And, others will be on the other side that will claim that the Roman Emperor Aurelian copied second century AD Christians' December 25 date for the birth of Mithra.

B. Were you shocked to learn that it was the pagan Romans who copied the second century AD Christians' date of December 25 for the birth of Jesus? Thank God in prayer that Christianity, the Bible, and Jesus are true, real, and historical!

ABOUT THE AUTHOR

Jeffery Donley is a husband, dad, grandfather, teacher, preacher, college professor, theologian, New Testament scholar, historian, and can dunk a basketball!

For a number of years, Jeffery volunteered at the *Coalition for the Homeless* in Orlando, Florida and at *Give Kids the World*, Kissimmee, Florida. *Give Kids the World* Village is a 70-acre, non-profit resort in Central Florida that creates magical memories for children with life-threatening illnesses and their families. Jeffery was in the entertainment division where he dressed up as Kailey the Penguin and Mayor Clayton (a giant rabbit) to make the children happy.

He was appointed by two Florida Governors to serve two terms on the state's Commission for *Volunteer Florida* and is presently an Emeritus Commissioner—with the title of "The Honorable Dr. Jeffery Donley."

Being a national award winning college professor and writer, Jeffery likes college football (Nebraska Cornhuskers), track and field, and his musical tastes are: Sissel, Marilyn McCoo, Ella Fitzgerald, Andrea Bocelli, Andy Williams, and Pavarotti.

As a master story-teller, Jeffery has the gift of being able to bring his audience into any given situation and not only see what transpires but feel the emotions as if they were there themselves. He has spoken on numerous Biblical and other historical topics in many churches across the United States.

Jeffery has also spoken at state, national, and international conferences in Singapore, Canada, and the United States.

The Carnegie Foundation for the Advancement of Teaching and the Council for Advancement and Support of Education in Washington, DC, selected Jeffery as Professor of the Year for the State of Florida. And, he was selected to receive a *National Endowment for the Humanities* Award (NEH) to work in a summer session with Dr. Hans Hildebrand and other scholars at Duke University.

Jeffery translated one of the more famous of the Dead Sea Scrolls, *The Copper Scroll*, at the University of Manchester, United Kingdom.

Jeffery's academic credentials are:

PHD	The University of Wales, United Kingdom
MLitt	The University of Birmingham, United Kingdom
ThM	Princeton Theological Seminary
MDiv	Cincinnati Christian University
MA	Cincinnati Christian University
BA	Central Christian College

Additionally, Jeffery completed one year of doctorate work (THD) in history at The University of South Africa.

He is married to another Doctor, Dr. Kathy Donley.

For speaking engagements, the author may be contacted at:
Jdonley879@aol.com

Printed in the United States
By Bookmasters